French Historical Method
The *Annales* Paradigm

Also by Traian Stoianovich

A Study in Balkan Civilization

French Historical Method

⋙ The *Annales* Paradigm

by Traian Stoianovich

WITH A FOREWORD BY
Fernand Braudel

Cornell University Press

ITHACA AND LONDON

First published 1976 by Cornell University Press.
Published in the United Kingdom by Cornell University Press Ltd.,
2-4 Brook Street, London W1Y 1AA.

International Standard Book Number 0-8014-0861-X
Library of Congress Catalog Card Number 75-36996
Printed in the United States of America by York Composition Co., Inc.
*Librarians: Library of Congress cataloging information
appears on the last page of the book.*

To

Fernand Braudel

⩺ Contents

	Foreword by Fernand Braudel	9
	Preface	19
1	The Three Paradigms	25
2	Third Generation	40
3	Hermes and Hidden Hestia	62
4	An Impossible *Histoire Globale*	102
5	Culture Areas and Modes of Production	134
6	Historyless and Nonconsensual	154
7	Series and Functions	183
8	Mass and Event: *"Une Histoire Autre"*	204
9	The *Annales* Paradigm	232
	Subject and Reference Index	241

⚞ Foreword

As I read the work of Traian Stoianovich, which is of such great interest to me, I was tempted to renege on my promise to write a brief presentation. This enthusiastic book centers so much on me, my interpretations, and my responsibility for guiding the *Annales* and building the Sixième Section of the Ecole Pratique des Hautes Etudes that I cannot help feeling a bit awkward in the role of commentator. I lay no claim to militant modesty, despite modesty's real merits. I am afraid, however, that Traian Stoianovich, who was a student in Paris during my last youth and when he was in the éclat of his own early youth, may have been so carried away by his experience of my teaching, actions, and work that he may have slighted the part played by others. Abetted by such sympathy, he may have magnified my role. It is this bias that rather distorts this well-informed focus, this objective account of the *Annales* model, including its internal and external contradictions.

A concern for historical truth finally convinced me to write this short foreword. Given the Anglo-American public's current interest in French historiography of the last half-century, this book deservedly will draw many readers. They will find in it a history told with precision by a person who was for some time a witness to the movement. They also will find an exact analysis of the various attitudes and interpretations of the *Annales* group (which has never been monolithic and, indeed, has ever less chance of becoming so), along with a chronological delineation of succes-

sive phases, to which I subscribe entirely. Nevertheless, for some-
one who has lived through the movement from the inside and has
known the underside of the cards, some corrections and suggestions demand attention. These are nuances, to be sure, but
nuances are valuable.

In brief, I do not believe that "the period during which a
full-blown Annales paradigm emerged" was that between 1946/
1949 and 1968/1972, that this was the great period of theoretical
construction of the model. I would set this decisive stage between
1929 and 1940.

The moment at which Traian Stoianovich came into contact
with the Parisian historical milieus, on the morrow of the Second
World War and during the first forward thrust of the Sixième
Section, may explain the divergence of view between the author
and myself. It is logical that he should magnify the significance
of that which played a role in his own intellectual experience. It
is likewise logical that he should be more attentive to *current*
divergences and contradictions among historians who are his
contemporaries than to what happened some fifty years ago in
Strasbourg. For me, however, the great date remains that of the
birth of the *Annales*, in 1929. I repeat that the period of creation
of the "paradigm" is that of 1929–1940.

What exactly is the formation of a paradigm? If, for example,
one refers to Thomas S. Kuhn, *The Structure of Scientific Revolutions*, the first sign of a new paradigm is the building up of
doubt over many years. What once was regarded as true or
tolerably true "no longer stacks up" with reality. Thus, a
physicist or chemist may be persuaded that a host of problems
will remain unsolved if he continues to hold fast to the theoretical
framework of his received instruction. The same thing may
happen to the historian who comes to grips with obstacles in his
own craft. Traian Stoianovich rightly situates this preliminary
period, marked by doubt and criticism, before the actual founding of the review. The preliminary period corresponds to the
agony of positivism in France at the close of the nineteenth cen-

tury. It was affirmed through the pre-*Annales* review *Annales de Géographie*, founded in 1891 by P. Vidal de la Blache, whose student Lucien Gallois (made an editor in 1894) was to be Lucien Febvre's prestigious mentor at the Ecole Normale; through *L'Année Sociologique*, founded by Emile Durkheim in 1896–1898; and through Henri Berr's *Revue de Synthèse* (1900), in which Lucien Febvre and Marc Bloch waged their first campaigns. These last two participated and collaborated in a struggle that was led above all by philosophers, sociologists, and geographers. For them, as historians, the slow work of destruction tore down what the great German historiography of the nineteenth century had founded, what Traian Stoianovich calls "the developmental type of history." It should be noted, nevertheless, that neither Lucien Febvre nor Marc Bloch, both of whom were thoroughly familiar with the German historical literature of their time, reacted against this historiography in the name of an obtuse nationalism that was never theirs. The German review *Vierteljahrschrift für Sozial- und Wirtschaftsgeschichte*, which they justly admired, even provided them with a title for their *Annales d'histoire économique et sociale*. What they mainly turned against was the purely political history and the narrative history (the *récit événementiel*, a word not yet in current use) of the Sorbonne, while their attack against the German school was at best indirect. It sheds no light on their action.

Did they have the impression at the start, in 1929, that they had created a new paradigm, or did they entertain any such desire? The answer is no, if one understands a paradigm as a strictly articulated and closed system of thought, a description that has never applied to the *Annales*. The word "paradigm" would have surprised them without giving them pleasure, while the words "model" and "school"—this last employed so frequently in their regard—would have annoyed them. But it is certain that they were conscious of laboring toward an absolutely new and even revolutionary history. Their means were relatively simple. History was for them one human science among others.

Without even standing on tiptoe, the historian could glimpse the fields and gardens of the neighboring disciplines. Was it so complicated, then, so extraordinary, to set out to see what was happening there, to plead in favor of a community of the human sciences, despite the walls that separated them from one another, and to regard them as necessary auxiliaries of history? To think that the historian might be able to render service for service? An exchange of services: such was and such is still, I believe, the last and profoundest motto of the *Annales*, its only rallying cry. But in 1929 the cry was new, and the program it called for seemed aberrant or ludicrous to traditional historians, perhaps too ambitious even for the partisans of the new current of thought. Henri Berr, for example, had dreamed only of joining history to sociology. The goal of uniting history and economics, a discipline of which he knew nothing, in fact, seemed to him too perilous an operation. For in those distant times, Marx savored of heresy.

The task of the two Strasbourg professors was crystal clear: to go out among the other disciplines, return with the booty, and set forth again on the quest of discovery, demolishing obstructing walls at each occasion. To pounce on their opponents, moreover, seemed the best defense. In addition, polemics was the mark of their good temper, of their intellectual pleasure, the continuation, pen in hand, of their recurrent personal discussions, which were facilitated by the contiguity of their offices at the University and by the nearness of their homes in the city. In retrospect, nothing would be easier than to show how they spoke, then, of the other sciences of man, how they mastered their language and concepts. By doing this they gave history its new dimensions, still its dimensions today. They unveiled a world of wonders in which travel became a delight. The two *Annales* directors possessed a sensational literary talent. And in France literature reigns. Who, indeed, can write better than Lucien Febvre, who can be more ferocious in disputation, more joyous, and more Rabelaisian?

Lucien Febvre imagined, felt, understood, and puzzled out everything. Compare him to Diderot or (closer to himself) to one of his dearest friends, Paul Langevin, the great physicist who was the physicists' "paymaster," in a time sorely in need of ideas. Lucien Febvre was the historians' paymaster, an unstinting distributor of ideas. His talent lay in helping others surpass themselves. Thus did he form or "make" Marc Bloch, who was six years his junior; later he helped me to rise above myself. Without him, Marc Bloch might not have become a second Fustel de Coulanges, and without him the *Méditerranée* would doubtless not have seen the light of day. Moreover, Lucien Febvre had a feeling for teamwork, for collective endeavor. Marc Bloch, rather late in his career, developed an interest in rural history; Lucien Febvre, who was in the noblest sense of the term a "peasant" of France, as his friend the novelist Léon Wirth called him, withdrew into the background without regret. Transferring the fields, tilled lands, trees, meadows, and villages to Marc Bloch, he went on to other tasks. These last were not lacking in a review for which only two persons plus five or six friends were at work. In 1937, when I joined their Committee, the *Annales* was a small group that could be contained with ease—despite the advent of the "new men," Henri Brunschwig, Ernest Labrousse, Jacques Soustelle, and myself—in Lucien Febvre's combined salon and office in the rue du Val-de-Grâce, known to us intimately as "au Val." But, to resume the language of Traian Stoianovich, are innovation and the construction of a new paradigm not always the work of a tiny group? How sweet, how fruitful that long-ago France of the interwar years! In spite of its worries, one of the most intelligent of a long line of intelligent Frances.

After the heinous gash of the Second World War, the *Annales*, in 1945, succeeded in mustering its strength and reconstituting itself as a team. Traian Stoianovich believes that the decisive shaping and definition of the historiographical model began only then, as the traditional forces of opposition fell one by one and the University opened itself up to the supporters of the new history, allowing the inception of an "expansive Establishment phase." I hold a somewhat different view.

It was certainly a new period. But the second *Annales* generation added nothing essential to the lot of ideas put into circulation by the first. None of us newcomers, Charles Morazé, Georges Friedmann, and I, contributed any really new idea or concept to the existing arsenal of theory. Formulas, yes; examples and confirmations, yes; but innovations, no, and again no. Instead, between 1945 and 1968 the *program* became reality. It is a fact that a whole new generation of historians chose their "thesis subjects," that is, their line of future work and endeavor, within the framework of *Annales* thought. I therefore envisage that period as one of translation into practice, as a time of confrontation of the *Annales* model with the huge reality of history, through a blossoming of admirable works all related to one another, although dispersed across time and space. But theory had preceded these realizations, which were but tests of the theory.

Moreover, hardly apparent until the Sixième Section's collections began to appear in rapid order during the 1950s and 1960s, this productive élan, it must be understood, was realized only through the rallying of the young historians—those of the *future* University, certainly not of the existing University. In those years, we remained, in effect, marginal men and *heretics,* still very far from the Establishment.

Lucien Febvre and Marc Bloch had not escaped the Sorbonne's wary surliness before the war. Defeated in a shameful election to the Quatrième Section of the Ecole des Hautes Etudes and sidestepped by the Collège de France, even as Henri Berr had been excluded previously, Marc Bloch obtained appointment to the Sorbonne in 1937 by a stroke of luck. There simply was no other candidate sufficiently qualified to seek to succeed Henri Hauser in the chair of economic history, the only chair of economic history in the French university system! Do not say, my dear Traian Stoianovich, that by 1945 these events were an old story, an antiquated quarrel, for, without drum and trumpet and with a thousand nice-sounding words in my ear, I, too, was excluded from the Sorbonne in 1947. When I defended my thesis that year, one of the judges suavely said to me: "You are a geographer, let me be the historian." I was named indeed to the Collège de France in 1949, but the Collège is and always has been marginal to the University. In the same year I was designated to chair the history section of the national program of teacher certification (*président du jury d'agrégation d'histoire*) but only by the individual will of Gustave Monod, Director General of Secondary Education, who in an effort to reform this venerable system of competition was eager to turn the house upside down. I was not remiss in my duties but, in 1954, I was ousted, and the Sorbonne took the operation back into its own hands. If, in those years, Lucien Febvre and I were included in the commissions of scientific research, to which we were elected by the *entire group* of French historians, we were a minority in them: heading the list came the right-thinking persons, and one year, indeed, I was blackballed by the electors.

But, you may ask, what of the Sixième Section of the Ecole des Hautes Etudes and the Maison des Sciences de l'Homme? The Sixième Section for the *Annales* movement assuredly is the miracle, for its creation hung by a thread in 1947, the skillfully devised plot, so to speak, of Lucien Febvre and Charles Morazé. Allowed to be born only because the Ecole des Hautes Etudes, like the Collège de France, did not have the right to grant university degrees, the Sixième Section developed, slowly and with difficulty, as a marginal institution equipped only for the purpose of research. That it knew how to turn this restriction into its strength, into the basis of its autonomy, and into the very motor of its expansion, is another matter. In any case, the more successful it became the more opposition and hostility it met from the traditional University—along with, it is true, examples of exceptional friendship. We also succeeded in doing useful creative work at the Maison des Sciences de l'Homme, which, at the initiative of a great Director of Higher Education, Gaston Berger, was charged with the task of coordinating research in the human sciences, but again outside the University. Moreover, this institution at its inception was a last refuge to which we resorted only after the University had blocked our plan for an experimental faculty of economic and social sciences. Yes, we were heretics until almost 1968, ever more numerous and stronger perhaps but compelled, willy-nilly, to fight ceaselessly for each concession.

The troubles of May and June 1968 changed everything, and Traian Stoianovich rightly uses them as the starting date of a new period. By an irony of fate, this was for me the Establishment period. After collapsing at one blow in 1968, the citadel of the Sorbonne was divided into a dozen different institutions of higher learning. From the reforms that followed, a new life began to take hold, and more than one innovation was meritorious. As a conclusion to these reforms, the Sixième Section in 1975 lost its numerical rank and honored name, to become the Ecole des Hautes Etudes en Sciences Sociales, with degree-granting rights. It continues as a research institution but has become at the same time a university. In the meantime, the *Annales*, whose direction I gave up years ago to younger historians, has achieved an immense success. To publish an article in that review, indeed, is the first step in the normal *cursus honorum.*

Is this triumph a good thing? The presence of vigilant opponents, prompt to attack and not necessarily wrong in every case, is a useful guarantee against falling asleep on one's so-called laurels. A guarantee perhaps also against the dangerous yearning for novelty at any price: when one is the target of the attacks of tradition, one knows oneself, or at least one believes oneself, to be among the innovators. There is, then, no need to chase after fashion.

In the final pages of his book, Traian Stoianovich describes in detail the historiographical conjuncture as it is being shaped in Paris in 1975. It is a muddled situation, certainly, a turbulent sea on which travel is not easy. The nonhistorians, the philosophers, first among them the most brilliant and most likable, Michel Foucault, are the ones who speak out on history with the greatest vehemence. Confronting the philosophers, who declaim loudly, perhaps even too loudly, today's historians, it seems to me, are afraid to utter their own tongue, the language of an old craft that must be formed close down to the earth. New methods allow better employment of the tools, but the tools are the old tools. The future of the historical discipline depends, nevertheless, on the historians. It is for them to break with yesterday's paradigms if they have the strength, the courage, and the intelligence.

I believe that they will be assisted in that by a new fact of immense importance: today the fate of the *Annales* "paradigm" is being played out not only in France but on a worldwide scale. It seems impossible to me that a new debate will not issue from this enlarged confrontation of ideas. Such, at least, is the optimistic conclusion that I draw from the reflective, attentive, and fruitful book of Traian Stoianovich. I thank him from deep in my heart for having written it.

FERNAND BRAUDEL

Saint-Gervais-les-Bains (Haute-Savoie)

≽ Preface

For the last three decades (since 1946–1949) there has been no more prestigious and important school of history than that of the *Annales*, whose name is taken from the first word of the title of a review founded in 1929 by Lucien Febvre and Marc Bloch and continued in 1956 under Fernand Braudel's direction. The present study is not a history of the *Annales* review, however, but of the *Annales* movement, of the ideas of the scholars who have been inspired primarily, and sometimes secondarily, by the historical methods of the review's founders and their successors. It is thus not a study of a formal institution, nor is it a sociological study, although I try to indicate some of the questions that ought to be raised by a sociology of the *Annales* movement and of its formal institutions. It is, rather, an essay in the social history of ideas—more specifically, about the *Annales* network of historiographical and methodological conceptions. It is an inquiry into the attempt by French scholars to adapt economic, linguistic, sociological, geographic, anthropological, psychological, and natural-science notions to the study of history and to infuse an historical orientation into the social and human sciences. The movement's leaders and adherents were first thought to be—and they themselves thought they were—hostile to political and diplomatic history. But they were antagonistic only to a political history, or any kind of history, that failed to go beyond a superficial examination of events, or that sought an explanation based on a succession of *heterogeneous* events. Their later identification with the cause of "serial history" clearly indicates that they were not opposed to the study of events as such but only to the study of events in a methodologically dubious way.

This book is limited for the most part to the period since 1946, that is, to the period since the movement's institutionalization in a new section (Sixième Section) of the Ecole Pratique des Hautes Etudes, one of France's most influential schools of graduate studies. I shall concentrate on its evolution since 1946 because its firm institutionalization in that year signified its triumph over the narrative historical method (of Germanic type). The latter, unable to compete with other disciplines in providing guidance for a time of economic crisis and political peril, had become for many persons a useless mode of history. A second reason for focusing on this period is that the *Annales* group developed a recognizable—recognizable, it is true, only if one probes deeply into their methods—paradigm, or autonomous disciplinary matrix, only between 1946 and 1972. This study attempts to define that matrix. It also holds that some of the seemingly contradictory approaches of the *Annales* movement's diverse partisans are, in fact, largely complementary. By means of a brief introduction to the other main modes of historical inquiry—the other paradigms, or disciplinary matrices—I seek to emphasize how profoundly different the *Annales* methodology is. Moreover, as the reader progresses from chapter to chapter, the reasons for the *Annales* movement's prestige, for the wide geographic diffusion of its methods, and for the failure of ideological frontiers to act as a barrier against their partial penetration, should become increasingly evident.

The definition of *Annales* methodology as developed here is the product of many years of research and thought. The book itself grew out of a long paper on *Annales* methods for a meeting sponsored by the American Historical Association and the *Journal of Social History*, held in New York on December 30, 1971.

I have benefited greatly from the criticisms of the commentators at this meeting—Natalie Z. Davis, Elizabeth Fox-Genovese, and

George Huppert. On April 17, 1972, I spoke on some aspects of the *Annales* methodology to the Social History Group of the Rutgers University colleges in New Brunswick. In preparation for this faculty seminar, I developed in embryonic form the idea, since then much modified, of the third chapter, "Hermes and Hidden Hestia." I have profited, too, from the formal and informal comments of other readers of an earlier version—the *Annales* historians André Burguière, José-Gentil Da Silva, and Jean-Jacques Hémardinquer, my former colleague Peter N. Stearns, my colleagues Rudolph M. Bell, Warren I. Susman, and Donald Weinstein, and the two perceptive readers for Cornell University Press. Although their statements were often brief, they were always useful, and I am grateful to them for helping me to rethink my ideas. As scholars, they will surely understand why I have been unable to accept their suggestions invariably. The diligent editing and astute remarks of copy editor Jeanne Duell have similarly helped to produce a better book. I am especially grateful to my wife, Marcelle Caffe Stoianovich, for advice consonant with the nuance and vision of an artist. For the typing of the final manuscript I am glad to acknowledge the financial aid of the Rutgers Research Council.

Readers may be surprised at the omission of a bibliography. A thorough bibliography would double the size of the book, however, making it both less wieldy and costlier. Since, moreover, there is in the present case no sufficiently meaningful rationale to justify including some items and excluding others, I abandoned the thought of a selective bibliography. Serving the function of a bibliography, nevertheless, is a Subject and Reference Index. All works included in the footnotes are listed in the index under the author's name. The page reference immediately following a title locates the full citation. The footnotes provide complete bibliographical data, including translations.

Product of an *Annales* author—or, rather, of an author informally affiliated with that group but generally physically distant from it—this book is the work also of a person immersed throughout his teaching career in the milieu of American scholarship, and is thus a response to the interaction of two cultures. No one has made a greater contribution to my intellectual development, however, than my mentor, Fernand Braudel. Because of my exposure to the Sixième Section and the Sorbonne of 1949 to 1952 —not only to Fernand Braudel but to C.-E. Labrousse, Georges Lefebvre, Ruggiero Romano, Pierre Renouvin, and V.-L. Tapié— the book reflects my personal familiarity with the *Annales* School, a personal familarity maintained, renewed, and constantly extended since then. Happily, Fernand Braudel's foreword (which I have translated) is not of the usual kind. In the central tradition of the *Annales* School, it constitutes, in effect, a friendly debate with the author, a powerful vehicle of "intellectual pleasure." I am grateful to Fernand Braudel not only for the debate but also for his enrichment of the book by the new data that he provides, based on his own experiences and intimate knowledge, even personification, of the *Annales* movement.

TRAIAN STOIANOVICH

Metuchen, New Jersey

French Historical Method
The *Annales* Paradigm

1 The Three Paradigms

The quest of human societies for consensus on the most economical or utilitarian forms of research into the perceived events of social action has culminated in the development of three main forms of history—exemplar, evolutionary, and functional-structural. Most human societies that moved from mythological to historical thought retained the exemplar form until the nineteenth or twentieth century. European societies, on the other hand, discovered the developmental form and, embryonically, the functional-structural type of history in the eighteenth century. In the nineteenth century, however, the developmental type prevailed over the incompletely understood functional-structural type. After it was improved in the twentieth century, the functional-structural approach obtained wider currency.

No group of historians has played so important a role in assuring the ascendancy of the functional-structural approach as the group of scholars who welcomed the initiatives of the French historical journal *Annales: Economies, Sociétés, Civilisations*. I therefore propose to deal with the achievements of the *Annales* historians and especially with their constitution as three interacting generations of scholars. I propose, in effect, to examine the problem of the formation of a relatively well-defined third historical paradigm, or disciplinary matrix, with a substantial body of professional opinion supporting it, with the ability to impose its presence on other scholars.

To explain the third paradigm it is necessary to explain its

predecessors. According to George H. Nadel, who has designated
the first paradigm as "exemplar history," its object was "training
for public service." For its proponents history was a guide to
action.[1] This kind of history would include the "traditional piety"
of the Chinese, the hagiography of the Christian Middle Ages,
and the conventional "archaic and hieratic" vision that may prevail among historians (as in fifteenth-century France) when
society is changing too quickly for them to empathize with it.[2]
The history of Thucydides is sometimes excluded from the
general category of exemplar history because of his conception
of history as inquiry and of his desire to distinguish it from fable.
Both his goals required a clear and reliable account of events. In
Book I, Chapter 22, of his *Peloponnesian Wars*, however,
Thucydides unequivocally gave priority to exemplar history:
identification and explication of the types of events likely to occur
again and thus to possess significance for the future, a forever
"useful" history, "an everlasting possession, not a prize composition that is heard and forgotten."[3] The function of this type of
history is to select the relevant example (*paradeigma, exemplum*),
in the didactic sense of being illustrative of what the society,
through the historian, desires to inculcate and what it wants to
warn against. The function of Clio in exemplar history is to

1. George H. Nadel, "Philosophy of History before Historicism," *Studies
in the Philosophy of History: Selected Essays from "History and Theory,"*
ed. George H. Nadel (New York: Harper & Row, 1965), pp. 49–73. First
published in Mario Augusto Bunge, ed., *The Critical Approach to Science
and Philosophy: Essays in Honor of Karl R. Popper* (New York: Free
Press of Glencoe, 1964), and reprinted in *History and Theory*, III, 3
(1964), 291–315.
2. Robert Marichal, "La Critique des textes," in Charles Samaran, ed.,
L'Histoire et ses méthodes, "Encyclopédie de la Pléiade" (Paris: Gallimard,
1961), pp. 1327–40 (1247–1366). The page numbers in parentheses will refer
henceforth to the complete pagination. If no parentheses appear in the
first citation, the pages given will correspond to the complete pagination.
3. Thucydides, *The Peloponnesian Wars*, trans. Benjamin Jowett, revised
and abridged with an introduction by P. A. Brunt (New York: Washington Square Press, 1963), B. I, Chap. 22, pp. 12–13.

discard the trivial and embrace the glorious[4] or, contrarily, to
draw attention to errors and horrors. According to Herodotus,
it was his duty as historian "to preserve the memory of the past
by putting on record the astonishing achievements both of our
own and of the Asiatic peoples."[5] It was all the more imperative
to keep such records in view of the Greek conception of truth
as lying outside the confines of time, which alternately was not,
is, and is no more.[6] If venerable and despicable memories are not
recorded, time will quickly erode them.

In the context of Western historical experience—and as early
as classical antiquity—exemplar history evolved through three
different forms of expression: from history as narration or
chronicle, or as a discourse on events or conditions but without
a formal or systematic explanation of the connection between
events and conditions (Herodotus),[7] to history as systematic
explanation (Thucydides), and then to "the *methodical applica-*
tion of the systematic human studies to the *explanation* of the
historical context," as illustrated by the writings of Polybius.[8]

4. Alfred Stern, "The Irreversibility of History," *Diogenes*, No. 29
(Spring 1960), p. 13 (1–15). For an unexpected definition of history as
exemplar history by an *Annales* scholar, see Maurice Crubellier, "Enseignement de l'histoire et formation humaine," *Recherches et débats du
Centre Catholique des Intellectuels Français*, No. 47 (June 1964), pp. 66–
67 (63–76), colloquium of Feb. 22–23, 1964.

5. Herodotus, *The Histories*, translated with an introduction by Aubrey
de Sélincourt (Baltimore: Penguin Books, 1954), B. I, par. 1, p. 14.

6. Kostas Papaioannou, "Nature and History in the Greek Conception of
the Cosmos," *Diogenes*, No. 25 (Spring 1959), p. 23 (1–27).

7. For a definition of "chronicle" in this sense, see Morton White, "The
Logic of Historical Narration," in Sidney Hook, ed., *Philosophy and History: A Symposium*, proceedings of the fifth annual New York University
Institute of Philosophy, held at Washington Square, New York, May 11–
12, 1962 (New York: New York University Press, 1963), pp. 5–6 (3–31).

8. Wilhelm Dilthey, *Pattern and Meaning in History: Thoughts on His-
tory and Society*, edited and introduced by H. P. Rickman (New York:
Harper & Row, 1962; published originally in London, 1961, by Allen and
Unwin, under the title *Meaning in History*), pp. 142–44, drawn from Vol.
VII of Dilthey's collected works in twelve volumes. The italics are in the
original.

Chronicle, narrative, and critical-explanatory history constitute different aspects or stresses of the same general exemplar paradigm. Since some degree of explanation, connection, or evaluation is contained in each, there is little need, at least for the purposes of the present essay, to underline the differences among the three. In any event, they are alike in their predilection for examples. At the same time, it should be noted that the critical-explanatory approach, with its obvious concern for soundness of explanation as well as for accuracy of detail, allowed and encouraged the identification of history in the fifteenth and sixteenth centuries as a discipline independent of rhetoric,[9] as in the writings of Niccolò Machiavelli and Francesco Guicciardini. But on winning autonomy, instead of discarding the classical Ciceronian notion of the need for elegance and eloquence in historical expression, the discipline was imbued in addition with the Ciceronian fervor for *explanatory* narrative.[10]

Machiavelli, Guicciardini, Jean Bodin, and Francis Bacon were exponents of exemplar history. Such is "the multiplicity and disorder of human activities," insisted Bodin, "that unless the actions and affairs of men are confined to certain types," unless "similar instances of memorable matters" are "placed in a certain definite order," the historian will fail to bring forth, and his readers will fail to discover, "a variety of examples to direct our acts." Chief among the examples to be set forth and identified, moreover, are such as are directed toward the defense of the "common society," that is, which teach man to control himself, his family, and his state, for one must "impose upon oneself the rule of reason" before one may "rule a wife, children, and ser-

9. Based on a reinterpretation of Beatrice Reynolds, "Shifting Currents in Historical Criticism," *Journal of the History of Ideas*, XIV (October 1953), 471–92.

10. Bernard Guenée, "Histoire, annales, chroniques: Essai sur les genres historiques au Moyen âge," *Annales: Economies, Sociétés, Civilisations* (hereafter cited as *Annales ESC*), XXVIII (July–August 1973), 1012–15 (997–1016).

vants, and one must control the family before he can control the state."[11]

Not until the eighteenth century was the historical discipline redefined and given a developmental sense. But the developmental thought of historians—the second paradigm—took two directions. It examined the particular with the object of discovering the general, or universal, laws of human development, but it also focused on the particular aspects of change for their own sake or, increasingly in the nineteenth century, because of their usefulness in illustrating the principles of national and cultural autonomy.

The universalistic developmental orientation was occasionally allied to a functional-structural approach and it was generally rooted in the realization that culture or civilization (both terms were used in France and England from about the middle of the century) embraces more than just politics or the values, institutions, and other works and behavior patterns of political elites. Voltaire thus perceived a need not only for a history of battles and of dynastic quarrels but also for a history of customs (*moeurs*) and cultures. Giambattista Vico furthered the new trend by his conception of the true and the fabulous, in the words of Hayden White, as "simply *different* ways of signifying the relationship of the human consciousness to the world it confronts in different *degrees* of certitude and comprehension."[12]

11. Jean Bodin, *Method for the Easy Comprehension of History*, trans. Beatrice Reynolds (New York: Columbia University Press, 1945), Chap. III, "The Proper Arrangement of Historical Material," pp. 28, 31. See also Julien Freund, "Quelques aperçus sur la formation de l'histoire de Jean Bodin," in Horst Denzer, ed., *Jean Bodin: Verhandlungen der internationalen Bodin Tagung in München. Proceedings of the International Conference in Munich. Actes du colloque international Jean Bodin à Munich* (Munich: C. H. Beck, 1973), 105–22; Donald R. Kelley, "The Development and Context of Bodin's Method," in *ibid.*, pp. 123–50. See also Kelley's *Foundations of Modern Historical Scholarship: Language, Law, and History in the French Renaissance* (New York: Columbia University Press, 1970).

12. Hayden White, "The Irrational and the Problem of Historical

While this did not involve a rejection of political history, it did require the historian to immerse himself in the problem of myth. The explanation of the structures and functions of myth thus became indispensable to a general historical explanation. The understanding of events and the ascertainment of their reliability sank to a level of secondary significance.

A further reaction against exemplar history came in the form of the "Histoire Raisonnée" of some French thinkers and of the history of the Scottish philosophers, called "Natural History" by David Hume and "Theoretical" or "Conjectural History" by Adam Smith's friend Dugald Stewart.[13] This last form of history was the product not only of an awareness of differences between societies, but also of a dim consciousness of the problem of function and structure and of a clearer sense of the operation of directed change within each society and in the world society as a whole. Natural History was the fruit of the triumph of the Moderns, of the new conviction that the modern European cultures were superior even to the most distinguished of the ancient cultures simply because scientific and technological culture is cumulative and thus tends to accrue to the benefit of latecomers. One of the ideas that the exponents of Natural History handed down to the nineteenth century was the notion of progress, which in the thought of Adam Ferguson had assumed a spiral curve—progress, retrogression, progress.[14]

According to Kostas Papaioannou, the "idea of progress as well

---

Knowledge in the Enlightenment," in Harold E. Pagliaro, ed., *Studies in Eighteenth-Century Culture: Irrationalism in the Eighteenth Century,* Proceedings of the American Society for Eighteenth-Century Studies, 2 (Cleveland: Press of Case Western Reserve University, 1972), p. 315 (303–21).

13. Gladys Bryson, *Man and Society: The Scottish Inquiry of the Eighteenth Century* (Princeton, N.J.: Princeton University Press, 1945), p. 88.

14. *Ibid.,* pp. 101, 104; William Christian Lehmann, *Adam Ferguson and the Beginnings of Modern Sociology: An Analysis of the Sociological Elements in His Writings with Some Suggestions as to His Place in the History of Social Theory* (New York: Columbia University Press, 1930), pp. 230–34.

as that of the historicity of man as a fundamental characteristic
of his structure was introduced into philosophy only with
Christianity." We can agree readily with Papaioannou that the
ancient Greeks lacked a notion of progress,[15] but however much
of a notion of progress there may have been in Western philosophy under the influence of Christianity, there was none in
the historical discipline—or only very little—until the end of the
seventeenth century, indeed until the eighteenth century. Then,
as George H. Nadel and other scholars have remarked, it entered
into usuage through the attempt to reconstruct unknown stages
of historical development from known stages by means of a
number of hypotheses concerning society, culture, human nature,
politics, and economics—in other words, through the development
of Natural, Theoretical, or Conjectural History; through the
subordination of the written document to the methical application of theory to a great variety of documentary forms.

The second developmental orientation was in part the consequence of the improvement of critical techniques begun in the
fifteenth century by Lorenzo Valla, and continued by the textual
criticism of the Reformation and Counter-Reformation historians,
by the Benedictines of the congregation of Saint-Maur at the
abbey of Saint-Germain-des-Prés, and by the Society of the
Bollandistes. The division of labor spawned by the utilization and
improvement of critical techniques culminated in the organization
of the historical discipline as a scholarly or professional enterprise.

Among the first historians to give clear recognition to this
tendency was the Parisian abbé Nicolas Lenglet Du Fresnoy, who
looked on Guicciardini as Italy's greatest historical writer and
whose influential *Méthode pour étudier l'histoire,* several times
revised and enlarged, was published in thirteen editions between
1713 and 1772. Oriented toward profane or secular rather than
religious history, Du Fresnoy's *Méthode* subordinated the in-

15. Papaioannou, "Nature and History," pp. 24, 26; Kostas Papaioannou,
"The Consecration of History: An Essay on the Genealogy of the Historical Consciousness," *Diogenes,* No. 31 (Fall 1960), pp. 29–55.

culcation of moral values to the goal of accurate narrative, fully
supported by the evidence. To engage in sound criticism, held
Du Fresnoy, the historian should be neither too credulous nor
too skeptical. Moreover, the requirement of scholarly research
made public experience (the recruiting ground of exemplar history) either insufficient or unnecessary as a qualification for being
an historian. The historian of the second paradigm in its particularist form would rather have to be a professional, and Du
Fresnoy was to further the cause of professionalism by his recommendation that historians extend their documentation from published narrative accounts to public archives and to family papers.[16]

In practice, the professionalization of history was postponed
to the post-Napoleonic or even post-Romantic era, whereafter
the particularist form was put to more effective use than developmental history in its universalistic form, which was more largely
the choice of nonprofessional generalists who failed to develop
its notions of function and structure beyond the embryonic form.
Unlike the followers of "Histoire Raisonnée," the new professional historians, sometimes identified as exponents of historicism
(a term used in a variety of senses) or as members of the Historical School, were swayed by a concern not for historical
generalization but for the infinite variety of historical experience.
Products of the era of the theory of nationality, they sought to
underline that the experiences of peoples were dissimilar. Their
object was to depict history as the expression of a particular
evolution or development—to show, in Leopold von Ranke's oft-
quoted words, "wie es eigentlich gewesen." Their attention was
directed to history as an illustration of the particularities of change
or development, of the vast variety of choices (freedom) available to individuals and human societies, of the operation of the
principle of national and cultural autonomy.[17] Exponents of de-

16. Lester A. Segal, "Nicolas Lenglet Du Fresnoy and Change in French
Historiographical Thought in the Early Eighteenth Century," *Studies on
Voltaire and the Eighteenth Century*, XCVIII (1972), 69–117.
17. Hajo Holborn, "Greek and Modern Conceptions of History," *Journal*

velopment and often of the notion of linear progress—at least for Western European cultures—the Historical School believed in general that freedom would culminate in the nation-state, which they tended to regard in turn as the perfect vehicle of progress.

Before the end of the nineteenth century, however, the short-lived idea of progress itself began to be questioned by some intellectuals even as it was diffused to the working and popular classes. One way in which this questioning occurred was through the perception of the significance for mankind of the second principle of thermodynamics: the hypothesis that the amount of *free* energy, that is, energy transformable into work, is diminishing constantly. As a result of this principle, it was easier to perceive a clear distinction between "earlier" and "later" and to reject the notion of a reversible world of repeated identical cycles. But a second consequence was the stimulation of an awareness of the absurdity of the notion of progress.[18]

This last conclusion was plausible, however, only if men and women, cultures and societies, were subject to the same logic as nature. In their zeal to escape or refute a monolithic logic, German historians took the lead in proposing a shift from Natural History to *Kulturgeschichte*, from historicism to *Geistesgeschichte:* that is, to a conception of history either as an experience (and as a discipline dealing with the experience) of changing cultural types or patterns or as a discipline wholly independent of natural science—as one of a group of autonomous cultural sciences (*Geisteswissenschaften*).

Karl Lamprecht, for example, embraced *Kulturgeschichte*. For Lamprecht, history was "primarily a socio-psychological science,"

of the History of Ideas, X (January 1949), 11 (3–13); Hans Meyerhoff, "History and Philosophy: An Introduction," *The Philosophy of History in Our Time: An Anthology,* selected and with an introduction and commentary by Hans Meyerhoff (Garden City, N.Y.: Doubleday, 1959), pp. 9–10 (1–25); Isaiah Berlin, "Foreword" to Friedrich Meinecke, *Historism: The Rise of a New Historical Outlook,* trans. J. E. Anderson (London: Routledge & Kegan Paul, 1972), pp. ix–xvi.

18. Stern, "The Irreversibility of History," pp. 6–11.

and he interpreted the European historical experience in terms of
three psychic epochs—an epoch of "symbolism," characterized
by a high valuation of hierarchical roles, an integrative epoch of
"individualism," and a disintegrative epoch of "subjectivism" and
"mixed sensations." Like the French philosopher and psychologist
of a later period Michel Foucault, he did not believe that the
values of a later epoch evolve from those of the previous one,
but rather conceived of each epoch and each system of values
as the product of a cultural leap, break, or discontinuity. He was
thus able to entertain the belief that Europe could move from the
epoch of mixed sensations to a fourth epoch governed by the
"idealism of the psychic authority of man over the outer world."[19]

Wilhelm Dilthey opted for *Geistesgeschichte*. In Dilthey's
view, the cultural sciences possess a logic entirely distinct from
that of the natural sciences, for their point of departure for
understanding others or *the other* is autobiography or self-
knowledge. They are grounded in the principle of phenomeno-
logical relativism, or of the autonomy of phenomena, that is, of
the existence of different patterns of perception and behavior
and of different mind sets in different societies.[20]

From science, technology, business, and the new cultural
sciences, however, the notion of the meaninglessness or irrelevance
of history spread to an ever larger circle of people during the
twentieth century even as (and in part because) the number of
historians continued to grow (the process of professionalization

19. Karl Lamprecht, *What Is History? Five Lectures on the Modern
Science of History*, trans. E. A. Andrews (New York: Macmillan, 1905),
pp. 3, 44–45, 49–50, 71, 79, 123–24, 130, 133–34. First published in Freiburg,
Germany (1904), as *Moderne Geschichtswissenschaft*.

20. Dilthey, *Pattern and Meaning in History*, pp. 68–71; Meyerhoff, "History and Philosophy," pp. 12–25; Georg G. Iggers, *The German Conception of History: The National Tradition of Historical Thought from Herder
to the Present* (Middletown, Conn.: Wesleyan University Press, 1968), pp.
133–44, 240, 246–47; Nathan Rotenstreich, *Between Past and Present: An
Essay on History* (New Haven: Yale University Press, 1958), pp. 246–50;
Henri-Irénée Marrou, *De la connaissance historique*, 5th rev. ed. (Paris:
Editions du Seuil, 1966), p. 205 (first published in 1954).

seemed irreversible). For some persons, history became irrelevant because it was insufficiently mythical. For others, it became irrelevant because it was insufficiently rational.[21] As Foucault has remarked, the extension of historicity to a host of phenomena, including political economy (economics), literature, grammar, and nature, led to the "dehistoricization" of societies as each discipline acquired an autonomous existence.[22] Whether practiced by German or by other historians, *Kulturgeschichte* and *Geistesgeschichte* failed to stem the tide from relativism to nihilism or, more generally, simply to a disinterest in the meaning of history.

Relativism need not terminate in nihilism, however, so long as societies continue to react to "the imagined happenings of the past," even if for no other reason than to try to determine what is useful, beautiful, or good in their own imagined experience—to profit from the exemplar function of history. Such societies will rethink and rewrite their history as it changes. As Raymond Aron has observed, "The past is never definitively fixed except when it has no future," when the present ceases to take the initiative, when it misinterprets the need for "a constant reinterpretation of the past" as a sign of the irrelevance of history.[23] But the very fact that relativism has culminated in nihilism, anguish, and despondence suggests that historians may become functionless—even though professionalization greatly slows down that process—unless they are able to develop a mode of historical inquiry that can cope with the complexities and transformations of their own simultaneously highly rigid and highly plastic societies.

21. For a suggestion of this, see the Canadian philosopher Fernand Dumont, "La Fonction sociale de l'histoire," *Histoire sociale, Social History*, No. 4 (November 1969), pp. 5–16.

22. Michel Foucault, *The Order of Things: An Archaeology of the Human Sciences* (New York: Pantheon, 1971), pp. 367–73. This is a translation of *Les Mots et les choses: Une archéologie des sciences humaines* (Paris: Gallimard, 1966).

23. Raymond Aron, "Relativism in History," in Meyerhoff, *The Philosophy of History*, pp. 153–62, taken from Aron's "The Philosophy of History," *Chambers's Encyclopaedia*, VII (1950), 147–49; new rev. ed., VII (1967), 150–54.

Historians have begun indeed to undertake this task, and Murray G. Murphey, one of the few philosophers of history to know history as a contemporary discipline rather than as a discipline of Thucydides, Polybius, Guicciardini, Voltaire, or Ranke points out how they have proceeded. One of the chief distinguishing characteristics of history (as a discipline of any paradigmatic type), Murphey notes, is that it often investigates objects that no longer exist or exist only as vestiges, and it describes and analyzes events that the historian cannot recall because he has not experienced them. It is consequently important to bear in mind that historians investigate the past in order to explain the present. Since they must always examine current evidence about the past (including currently existing narratives and contemporary human science theory), they are always concerned with contemporary objects and with contemporary ways of viewing those objects.[24] In effect, the discipline of history is the study of present data relating to experience in another temporal context (traditionally past but conceivably future) as a means of conveying a particular image or group of images to contemporary society and to future generations. Even the attempt to understand the past in its own terms is "presentist" to the extent that it is founded on what contemporary science and bias lead us to believe to have been its own terms. Every past in its own terms is thus a hypothesis or theoretical construct, particularly since the plasticity of the past cannot be eliminated unless a society has become utterly static in every important detail. Historical facts are thus not given. They are rather postulates designed to explain the characteristics of contemporary data relating to the past or future.[25]

The facts, postulates, "interpretations," or "explanatory gen-

24. Murray G. Murphey, *Our Knowledge of the Historical Past* (Indianapolis and New York: Bobbs-Merrill, 1973), pp. 6, 14, 26–27. See also Edward A. Tiryakian, "Structural Sociology," in John C. McKinney and Edward A. Tiryakian, eds., *Theoretical Sociology: Perspectives and Developments* (New York: Appleton-Century-Crofts, 1970), p. 120.

25. Murphey, *Our Knowledge of the Historical Past*, p. 64.

eralizations" of the historian normally relate, however, to "a specific spatio-temporal domain."[26] Historians are therefore especially competent in analyzing an individual society or culture, or a particular social or cultural component, during a specific and limited period of time, and they generally affirm that sociological generalization to all societies on the basis of theory applicable to a particular spatiotemporal domain is likely to be without cogency. But they are skillful in showing how individual cultural traits change even as an overall culture is maintained and transmitted from one biological cohort to another. They may thus succeed in making feasible a comparative study of cultures.[27]

On the subject of comparative method, however, there is a modicum of disagreement. One of the early leaders of the *Annales* School, Marc Bloch, held that "there is no true understanding without a certain range of comparison; provided, of course, that comparison is based upon differing and, at the same time, related realities."[28] On the other hand, the cultural anthropology of Claude Lévi-Strauss, who has disciples in the *Annales* School, teaches that a comparative method is rarely likely to be useful since the data introduced for purposes of comparison may be temporally or spatially so close that one cannot be sure of dealing with separate phenomena, or the allegedly related realities may be so heterogeneous that they in fact involve a comparison of incomparable things.[29]

Historians have begun to participate nevertheless in a third historical paradigm. In its individual aspects, this paradigm is the discovery of many different historians and national cultures, for

26. *Ibid.*, pp. 101–2.
27. *Ibid.*, pp. 122–23, 154.
28. Marc Bloch, *The Historian's Craft*, introduction by Joseph R. Strayer, trans. Peter Putnam (New York: Knopf, 1953), p. 42. Originally entitled *Apologie pour l'histoire ou Métier d'historien*, "Cahiers des Annales," 3 (Paris: Armand Colin, 1949).
29. Claude Lévi-Strauss, "Le Champ de l'anthropologie," *Anthropologie structurale deux* (Paris: Plon, 1973), pp. 21–22 (11–44), inaugural lecture at the Collège de France, January 5, 1960.

it is, at least in part, the probable product of the inner dialectic of developmental history, or of the confrontation between the universalistic (with elements of a functional-structural approach) and particularistic developmental modes. But just as the dominant —particularistic—mode of developmental history was perfected by one national culture—namely, by German historians—so the third paradigm has been in large measure the accomplishment of French historians and of students of the French historical method, that is, of the *Annales* School. By means of their broad conception of communication and their serial, functional, and structural approaches to history, they have made substantial inroads into the exemplar and developmental paradigms. Action is thus no longer simply an example. It is also a function. Change is perceived not as progress, regular development, or continuity, but in terms of a need for other functions, or as part of a process of structuring, destructuring, and restructuring. More precisely, a distinction is made between two major types of change—one that proceeds along evolutionary lines, and another that represents a deviation, discontinuity, or mutation. More than storytelling, the task of the historian of the third paradigm embraces problem-solving and puzzle-solving.[30]

If, in conclusion, it appears that we have provided no place for the Marxist historical method in the scheme of historiographical types, it is not because we regard it as unimportant but because Marxist historians have opted variously for each of the three paradigms—the exemplar, the developmental in both of its main aspects, and the functional-structural. Marxist historiography would thus require analysis in terms of all three paradigms. A proper treatment of that subject would necessitate a different orientation and

30. David Hackett Fischer, *Historians' Fallacies: Toward a Logic of Historical Thought* (New York: Harper & Row, 1970), pp. xii, xv; Margaret Masterman, "The Nature of a Paradigm," in *Criticism and the Growth of Knowledge,* ed. Imre Lakatos and Alan Musgrave, International Colloquium in the Philosophy of Science, Bedford College, 1965 (Cambridge: University Press, 1970), p. 70 (59–89); Thomas S. Kuhn, "Reflections on My Critics," in *ibid.,* pp. 270–71 (231–78).

a different kind of book. The present book aspires to indicate, of course, how Marxist historical method(s) and functional-structural history impinge upon each other. Its principal concern, however, will be to show how the *Annales* School has transformed the discipline of history generally, particularly in the period, between 1946/1949 and 1968/1972, during which a full-blown *Annales* paradigm emerged.

2 Third Generation

The elaboration and clarification of the third paradigm perhaps could not have been undertaken in Germany because German historians had perfected the second, or developmental, paradigm, at least in its particularist form. Another culture had to be the agent of innovation simply because, both psychologically and for reasons of material self-interest, people are generally less reluctant to transform or give up a way of doing things of foreign inspiration—or regarded as such—than to surrender one that they regard as inalienable. Innovation was necessary if the historical discipline was to survive the sharp criticisms directed against it, or against its inadequacies, after 1890 or 1900, by the dynamic new social sciences. After 1905, however, Germany was apparently incapable of carrying out such a change.

Some Western European and American historians, on the other hand, began to subject their discipline to an agonizing reappraisal during the early decades of the twentieth century. In France, where the self-questioning was particularly intense,[1] the crisis of historical consciousness was resolved through a four-part series of acts. The first part took the form of a general reaction against German historical method[2] and witnessed the successive founding

1. Ernst Robert Curtius, *The Civilization of France*, trans. Olive Wyon (New York: Macmillan, 1932; Vintage Books, 1962), p. 90.
2. Maurice Aymard, "The *Annales* and French Historiography (1929–1972)," *Journal of European Economic History*, I (Fall 1972), 495 (491–511). Aymard refers to a forthcoming article by Marina Cedronio, "Profilo Storico delle 'Annales,'" which I have been unable to locate.

of the *Annales de géographie* (1891), *L'Année sociologique* (1896–1898), and Henri Berr's *Revue de synthèse historique* (1900). In the second group of acts, situated mostly in the 1920s, were the appearance of the early volumes of Berr's collection "L'Evolution de l'Humanité"; the organization of his Centre de Synthèse and of the annual colloquium "Semaine de Synthèse"; the conception of a topically rather than alphabetically ordered *Encyclopédie Française;* and the launching in 1929 of Lucien Febvre's and Marc Bloch's *Annales d'histoire économique et sociale.* During this second phase, which continued until World War II, the advocates of transforming the historical discipline succeeded in extending their control of the institutional structure, waging a battle of words in favor of their own habits and patterns of perception against those of the older and still well established school that continued to be enamored of German historical method, and striving to modify institutional arrangements to favor their own predominance. At once institutional and combative, this phase was succeeded between 1946 and 1968 by a spurt of creative activity during an expansive Establishment phase. Aided by Nazi Germany's military and political demise, the postwar *Annales* no longer had to confront vigorous resistance from French partisans of German historical method. As the opposition was partly or wholly mollified or as it went, so to speak, underground, the innovating *Annales* cohorts entered "a period of almost bureaucratic consolidation." The transitional years 1968–1975, signaled by the "Events of May" (1968 student revolt), by financial pressures, by Braudel's retirement from the Chair of Modern Civilization at the Collège de France, by eclecticism and some loss of direction, and by the elevation, in 1975, of the Sixième Section to the status of an Ecole des Hautes Etudes en Sciences Sociales, with the right to grant both the doctorate *de troisième cycle* and the state doctorate, may constitute the beginning of a fourth phase.[3]

3. Hugh R. Trevor-Roper, "Fernand Braudel, the *Annales,* and the Mediterranean," *Journal of Modern History,* XLIV (December 1972), 472

In a preliminary way at least, several scholars have already explored the first two phases.[4] For this reason, but also because the disciplinary matrix of *Annales* methods was not fully defined

(468–79), for the view of a period of "bureaucratic consolidation." For the decree of January 23, 1975, by means of which the Sixième Section obtained the status of Ecole des Hautes Etudes en Sciences Sociales, see the *Journal Officiel de la République Française*, Jan. 25, 1975, a copy of which was communicated to me by Joseph Goy.

4. Martin Siegel, "Henri Berr's Revue de Synthèse Historique," *History and Theory*, IX, 3 (1970), 322–34; Karl Erich Born, "Neue Wege der Wirtschafts- und Sozialgeschichte in Frankreich: Die Historikergruppe der *Annales*," *Saeculum*, XV, 3 (1964), 298–309; Jean Glénisson, "L'Historiographie française contemporaine: Tendances et réalisations," in Comité Français des Sciences Historiques, *Vingt-cinq ans de recherche historique en France (1940–1965)*, I. *L'Enseignement et la recherche, les publications* (Paris: Centre National de la Recherche Scientifique, 1965), pp. xv–xvii (ix–lxiv); H. Stuart Hughes, *The Obstructed Path: French Social Thought in the Years of Desperation, 1930–1960* (New York: Harper & Row, 1968), especially "The Historians and the Social Order," pp. 18–64, in which he chides Lucien Febvre for his "peremptory and hortatory tone" and Fernand Braudel for having moved "a further step away from clarity of thought and presentation," for the "sprawling and invertebrate" character of his work, for its lack of "a discernible focus," for his erratic flights "between the statistical and the poetic," for his failure to establish "a tight relationship among the various strands of his accounts." For a more favorable brief analysis of the *Annales* and related currents, see Frank E. Manuel, "The Use and Abuse of Psychology in History," *Daedalus*, C (Winter 1971), 187–213 (pp. 193–96 on psychological trends in the *Annales* School). A more thorough study is Hans-Dieter Mann, *Lucien Febvre: La Pensée vivante d'un historien*, "Cahiers des Annales," 31 (Paris: Armand Colin, 1971). See also the papers for the session on historical studies in France, American Historical Association, Chicago, December 28, 1974: William R. Keylor, "A New Academic Discipline in the Sorbonne, 1875–1900"; Martin Siegel, "Toward a Prehistory of the *Annales:* Henri Berr and the Search for a New History, 1900–1929"; and Hilah F. Thomas, "Innovation and Continuity in the *Annales d'Histoire Economique et Sociale:* The Directorship of Marc Bloch and Lucien Febvre, 1929–44." Hilah Thomas is preparing a dissertation at Columbia University, "Theory and Practice in the Work of Marc Bloch and Lucien Febvre: The Historiography of the Early *Annales* Movement." Samuel Kinser of Northern Illinois University is also working on *Annales* subjects: "Braudel and Vilar: The 'Structuralism' of the *Annales* School," colloquium paper, University of California, Berkeley, February 1974; "Structural History: A Theory and Its Practice by Braudel," monograph in preparation.

and elaborated until the third phase, this book will focus on the methodological premises and artifacts of the phase of consolidation.

After having circulated briefly under two other titles—*Annales d'histoire sociale* and *Mélanges d'histoire sociale*—the review was renamed in 1946. Its new name, *Annales: Economies, Sociétés, Civilisations,* was apparently designed to emphasize that it would not confine itself to social and economic history, but would rather pursue the ambitious goal of a comprehensive science of history or even of a science of the human sciences.

The new authority of the *Annales* School was given force by several rites of passage, among them Braudel's appointment to the *Agrégation* (national program of teacher certification) and Febvre's to the board of directors of the Centre National de la Recherche Scientifique and to the chairmanship not only of the UNESCO Committee of French Historians but also of the Committee for the History of World War II. Another momentous event was the addition to the Ecole Pratique des Hautes Etudes, by means of an initial grant from the Rockefeller Foundation, of a Sixième Section.

Regularly funded thereafter by the Ministry of National Education, the Sixième Section was conceived as a graduate but non-degree-granting center at which scholars associated with the *Annales* journal and other distinguished or promising scholars would train advanced students and carry on discourse with them in the methods and problems of social and economic history, of economics, and of the behavioral or communications sciences. Set up under the Section almost from the start was a new Centre de Recherches Historiques under Braudel and a Centre de Recherches Economiques under Charles Morazé.[5]

In the late 1950s, France's Director General of Higher Education, Gaston Berger, issued a call to put all research units, or departments, of the "human sciences" under a single roof. A

5. Lucien Febvre, "Vingt ans après," *Annales ESC,* IV (January–March 1949), 1–3.

subsequent Ford Foundation grant and an allocation of funds
from the Ministry of National Education facilitated the establishment, in 1963, of a Maison des Sciences de l'Homme. The
Maison's component parts remained physically dispersed, however, until the inauguration, in 1970, of a new multistoried
building of steel and glass as the site of an integrated Maison,
with Braudel as President Administrator.[6]

All human science and social science units were not authorized
to move into the building at that time, and the Maison had to limit
its goals in view of the government's inadequate financial resources to develop research units (such as the units in the Maison)
and teaching departments (in the universities) simultaneously.
This deficiency has imposed a special hardship on the money-
consuming disciplines of economics, sociology, and psychology.
For the human sciences "à petit moteur," such as history and
geography, whose financial needs are more modest, the problem
has been less serious. Despite a low budget, affirms Braudel, the
"French school of economic and social history" has fared brilliantly, not only at home but internationally.[7]

First under Lucien Febvre's pilotage and then, in effect, under
Braudel's (1956-1968),[8] *Annales* themes and methods have been

6. Fernand Braudel, "Gaston Berger, 1896-1960," *Annales ESC*, XVI
(January-February 1961), 210-11; Marie-Raymonde Delorme, "Une Maison
des Sciences de l'Homme: pour quoi faire?" *Psychologie: Comprendre, savoir,
agir dans le monde d'aujourd'hui*, No. 14 (March 1971), pp. 14-15, 18, accompanied by the photographic report of André Dorka.

7. Sarah Peltant, "Conversation avec Braudel, Professeur au Collège de
France, Directeur de la Maison des Sciences de l'Homme," in *ibid.*, pp. 16-
18, 21.

8. In his "Personal Testimony," *Journal of Modern History*, XLIV
(December 1972), 461 (448-67), Fernand Braudel writes: "From 1946 to
1956 Lucien Febvre was in fact the sole editor of the *Annales*; from 1956
to 1968 I was, in fact, sole editor in my turn." From 1946 to mid-1967 the
editorial board was composed of the same three persons and, Febvre apart,
no others: Braudel, Charles Morazé, and Georges Friedmann. On the
continuity of key personnel in the *Annales*, see the perceptive remarks of
Jack Hexter, "Fernand Braudel and the *Monde Braudellien*," in *ibid.*, p. 487
(480-539). Devoted to the general theme "History with a French Accent,"

disseminated widely among French historians. They have exerted an important peripheral impact on Mediterranean, Iberian, Latin American, Western European, and French Canadian historians. Even a portion of the United States intellectual community emulates some of its practices and embraces some aspects of its outlook. They have made a similar impress on Marxist historians not only in France and Western Europe but also in Poland and other countries of the socialist West.[9]

With a difficulty understandable in that they represent an outlook very different from that of the German Historical School, they have been diffused in watered-down form to German advocates of *Strukturgeschichte*, such as Theodor Schieder, Werner Conze, and Fritz Wagner. But the chief concern of *Strukturgeschichte* has been with the problem of historical discontinuity between the period preceding 1933 and the period since 1945, which they explain in terms not of political and ethical, or spiritual, shortcomings, but of the general emergence of a technological and bureaucratic mass society. While interested in the identification of impersonal forces and "typical processes," they have generally lacked the highly innovative qualities of the *Annales* School.[10] Braudel further writes of Otto Brunner, another pro-

---

this issue of the *Journal of Modern History* also includes an article by H. R. Trevor-Roper, "Fernand Braudel, the *Annales*, and the Mediterranean," pp. 468–79. On the concept of generational pilot and on generations and teams (*équipes*) of writers, see Robert Escarpit, *Sociologie de la littérature*, "Que sais-je?" 777 (Paris: Presses Universitaires de France, 1964), pp. 31–40.

9. On Polish interest in the *Annales*, see Robert Mandrou, "Les *Annales* en Pologne," *Annales ESC*, XV (March–April 1960), 328–29. Many *Annales* articles are by Polish scholars.

10. Georg G. Iggers, "The Dissolution of German Historism," in Richard Herr and Harold T. Parker, eds., *Ideas in History: Essays Presented to Louis Gottschalk by His Former Students* (Durham, N.C.: Duke University Press, 1965), pp. 324–25 (288–329); Iggers, *The German Conception of History*, pp. 262–65; George H. Nadel's review of Fritz Wagner, *Moderne Geschichtsschreibung: Ausblick auf eine Philosophie der Geschichtswissenschaft* (Berlin: Duncker und Humblot, 1960), in *History and Theory*, I, 3

ponent of *Strukurgeschichte,* that he "is in no way indebted to the *Annales*" and that "the givens of his reasoning or experience, his props and his conclusions, are not ours." Brunner's history is too static. His "two-dimensional geometry," a history of Europe from the eleventh century to the eighteenth century that is reduced at first simply to the social dimension (household and kinship) and then to the political (the affirmation of states), fails to satisfy Braudel's demand for conjunctures (oscillatory movements) and events as well as structures—for a conception of history in terms of "*n*-dimensions."[11]

Since the Establishment period of *Annales* scholarship was a time of mingling of three generations—that of the two founders of the review, that of the continuers and pilot of the second half of the Establishment phase, and that of the more numerous generation of historians born mostly in the 1920s—readers may wonder whether the younger scholars have given heed to Braudel's admonitions against a history that is simply structural,

---

(1961), 297–305. According to Nadel, Wagner fails to engage "in much philosophical analysis" in his chapter "Undecided Methodological Dispute in the French Historical Profession." Unavailable to me before the termination of my book was Georg G. Iggers, *New Directions in European Historiography,* with a contribution by Norman Baker (Middletown, Conn.: Wesleyan University Press, 1975).

11. Fernand Braudel, "Sur une conception de l'histoire sociale," *Annales ESC,* XIV (April–June 1959), 308–19, reprinted in Fernand Braudel, *Ecrits sur l'histoire* (Paris: Flammarion, 1969), pp. 175–91. This article is a review of Otto Brunner, *Neue Wege der Sozialgeschichte: Vorträge und Aufsätze* (Göttingen: Vandenhoeck und Ruprecht, 1956). While critical of Brunner's static *Strukturgeschichte,* Braudel admires Wilhelm Abel's penchant for a history of structures traversed by the woof of mobile conjunctures of long duration, such as the fluctuations in European population and consumption patterns since the thirteenth century. Abel's classic *Agrarkrisen und Agrarkonjunktur: Eine Geschichte der Land und Ernährungswirtschaft seit dem hohen Mittelalter,* 2d rev. ed. (Hamburg: Paul Parey, 1966), was thus included in French translation in Braudel's Flammarion series "Nouvelle Bibliothèque Scientifique," under the title *Crises agraires en Europe, XIIIe–XXe siècle* (Paris: Flammarion, 1974). See also Wilhelm Abel, *Massenarmut und Hungerkrisen in vorindustriellen Europa* (Hamburg and Berlin: Paul Parey, 1974).

without other dimensions. The answer to this question is that they possess in large measure the mental gear of an interwar and Depression generation which—unlike many of the German historians—has sought not to blot out the details of its experience but rather to recall them. Even more than their predecessors, perhaps under the conscious or unconscious influence of the Saint-Simonian notion of "critical" and "organic" epochs, they have oriented their research toward problems of conjuncture and crisis not unlike those of the postwar period and war of their childhood and youth.[12]

A disciple of Ortega y Gasset sagely warns, however, against equating generation and age category: "Two men of nearly the same age may gravitate toward different social groups, one joining a younger group, the other an older. The reason for this is that, despite the temporal proximity of the two men, they are separated by a generational demarcation line."[13] It therefore would be helpful to know what in addition to age draws together a given generation and distinguishes it from its predecessors and successors. In the present case, it would be especially desirable to define the characteristics of the third generation of *Annales* scholars. Such an undertaking might or might not run against the grain of *Annales* thought, depending on how it is done. Lucien Febvre, for example, at one time (1929) considered the notion of generation "useless" and "parasitical." On another occasion (1939), however, he affirmed that it could be useful if it

12. For the widespread concern of twentieth-century historians with problems of crises, see Randolph Starn, "Historians and 'Crisis,'" *Past and Present*, No. 52 (August 1971), pp. 3–22. For the specific concern of *Annales* historians with crises and economic fluctuations, see Pierre Chaunu, "L'Economie: Dépassement et prospective," in Jacques Le Goff and Pierre Nora, eds., *Faire de l'histoire*, 3 vols. (Paris: Gallimard, 1974), II, *Nouvelles approches*, 55–61 (51–73). Braudel's conceptualization of a quasi-immobile history, according to Chaunu, was itself a response to the crisis of the 1930s, without which Braudel may not have opted in favor of "geohistory."

13. Julián Marías, *Generations: A Historical Method*, trans. Harold C. Raley (University, Ala.: University of Alabama Press, 1970), p. 172.

was carefully conceived and not confused with an age category, and he himself had the sense of belonging to a distinct generation.[14]

It eventually should be possible to subject the community of *Annales* and Sixième Section scholars to sociological analysis in order to determine precisely what they do, what forms of puzzle-solving or problem-solving they pursue, what they sometimes say in private as well as what they write for public consumption, who they are as persons, what their social and economic origins are, and what their material possessions have been. It is no easy task, however, to subject an institution to an empirical sociological analysis, for some of its members will be secretive and the institutional structure itself is likely to have more than one reason (sometimes legitimate) for not wanting to divulge some types of information.

In an effort to cope with this problem to some extent, I circulated a brief questionnaire during the winter and spring of 1972 to about sixty persons, including members of the *Annales* staff, regular contributors, and members of the Sixième Section. Ideally, a survey of this kind should have been conducted jointly by the *Annales* journal and the Sixième Section, for no one is better placed than they to enforce an effective inquiry. My own quickly devised and deficient survey may provide, nevertheless, a few valid clues. It will serve its purpose if it goads these deservedly renowned, interlocking institutions to engage in some quantitative and psychological self-analysis.

Of the twenty-eight respondents to my questionnaire, fourteen stated that they had either taught or studied in the Section.[15] Of

14. Lucien Febvre, "Générations (Projets d'articles du vocabulaire historique)," *Revue de Synthèse historique*, XLVII (1929), 36–43; Lucien Febvre, "Avant-propos" to "Education et instruction," *Encyclopédie Française*, XV (1939), 15.02–1 to 15.02–6; Mann, *Lucien Febvre*, p. 24; Allan B. Spitzer, "The Historical Problem of Generations," *American Historical Review*, LXXVIII (December 1973), 1355–59 (1353–85).

15. The fourteen persons are Charles Morazé, Pierre Goubert, Marc Ferro, Anouar Abdel-Malek, José-Gentil Da Silva, Robert Mandrou, Julien

these fourteen, two had been students, two others had both studied and taught in the Section, and ten had been appointed Section teachers without a prior apprenticeship in it. If the sample is representative, it would signify that the Section presently recruits about 85 per cent of its teaching personnel from other schools. In other words, it has in no sense succumbed to the danger of institutional incest.

Three-quarters of the respondents indicated that they were or had been at one time members of a research team (*équipe*), that is, of a form of intellectual enterprise that the *Annales* and the Sixième Section have encouraged unremittingly. Three out of four historians and social scientists in team research is a high percentage. The French define "team," however, in a variety of ways. It may comprise the seminar members who examine different aspects of a common theme and communicate their tentative results through a collective publication. It may mean the joint publication of a book. It includes participation in collective research in one of several research centers and institutes. But few of the teams appear to be organic units that are likely to be maintained beyond the period required for the completion of a limited project. Eleven respondents—two out of five scholars—indicated that they have participated in more than one team. Two of the respondents made it known that they have never been members of a research team except to the extent that work with research assistants may be a team endeavor. One of them, Pierre Goubert, emphasized that he regarded himself as pretty much a self-made man. *Annales* scholars would thus appear to appreciate team research highly but they do not value it universally.

Brancolini, Jean Bouvier, Denis Richet, François Furet, Geneviève Bollème, Jean-Louis Flandrin, Alessandro Fontana, and Daniel Roche. Of the other persons who sent answers, most are linked directly or indirectly to the *Annales,* although several are in some respect hostile to it. They are Frédéric Mauro, François Crouzet, Georges Duby, Louis Althusser, Robert Escarpit, Roland Mousnier, Albert Soboul, Henri-Irénée Marrou, André Varagnac, Georges Dumézil, Maurice Tournier, Jean Ehrard, Claude Mazauric, and Henry Zalamansky. I am grateful to everyone who replied.

The sample, if representative, would suggest further that in 1972 two-fifths of the Sixième Section's teachers were born in Paris, a third in other parts of France, and the rest in other countries, especially of the Mediterranean region. If there is a sense none the less in which this diversity is misleading, it derives from the Section's location in Paris, from Paris's role as the birthplace of many of its teachers, and from the likely fact that two-thirds of the Section's teachers teach beforehand in other schools in the Paris region. But how peculiar is this to the Sixième Section? May it not reflect a situation prevalent also in other higher schools and research units in Paris?

It is nevertheless significant that the Sixième Section's cultural-geographic composition was primarily Parisian and secondarily Mediterranean in 1972, whereas the precursors and early *Annales* leaders—Henri Berr, Lucien Febvre, Marc Bloch, and Fernand Braudel—had been men "from eastern France," true continentals, although one of them, Braudel, was drawn by the magic of the Mediterranean, which like so many other northerners and continentals, he learned to love ardently. The *Annales* itself had been inaugurated in Strasbourg, "next door to Germany and to German historical thought,"[16] an advantageous position from which to filter into the rest of France those aspects of German scholarship that it found acceptable and from which to react vigorously against other aspects. The journal, too, moved quickly to Paris, however, and Braudel later noted that France lives through its capital, "a kind of hothouse outside of which fruits fail to ripen, or ripen less rapidly."[17] Indeed, a recent analysis by several scholars unaffiliated with the *Annales* School arrives at the more striking conclusion that the major social science achievements of the twentieth century have been the work of elites confined to a few key cities of the world.[18]

16. Braudel, "Personal Testimony," p. 467. See also Paul Leuilliot, "Lucien Febvre à Strasbourg," *Annales ESC*, XIII (April-June 1958), 209–13.

17. Peltant, "Conversation avec Braudel," p. 17.

18. Karl W. Deutsch, John Platt, and Dieter Senghaas, "Conditions Favoring Major Advances in Social Science," *Science*, Feb. 5, 1971, 450–59.

Proceeding to another aspect of a sociology of the *Annales* third generation, one may think it odd, in view of their own known predilections for contemporary history, culture areas and civilizations, and ethnocultural and nonconsensual interpretations, that *Annales* scholars have shown so little interest thus far in the role of various religious and ethnic traditions and reference group antagonisms as sources of inspiration for contemporary scholarship in general, and for contemporary historiography in particular. Catholics, Protestants, Jews, Moslems, and other religious groups and traditions are not prone to be intrigued equally by the same themes, nor is it at all certain that they have a propensity for precisely the same methods, and it is quite clear that scholars of different cultural and ethnic identities do not ask the same questions. While several *Annales* scholars, among them Fernand Braudel, Emmanuel Le Roy Ladurie, Nathan Wachtel, and Jacques Le Goff, have shown some concern in their works for a differential ethnosociology and ethnohistory—Le Goff entitles one chapter section of a book, "The Proscripts: Heretics, Lepers, Jews, Sorcerers, Sodomites, Cripples, Foreigners, Outcasts"[19]— *Annales* scholars in general have demonstrated a remarkable disinclination to examine the interrelations between cultural and ethnoreligious affiliations on the one hand and contemporary scholarship on the other.[20]

Especially regrettable is the lack of an ethnosociology and an ethnohistory of contemporary Jewish scholarship in view of the fact that, since the end of World War II, no one ethnocultural or ethnoreligious group of scholars in the Western world has been either quite so eminent or quite so numerous as that of the

19. Jacques Le Goff, *La Civilisation de l'Occident médiéval* (Paris: Arthaud, 1964), pp. 387–96.

20. A notable exception is the Cairo-born Marxist lecturer in the Sixième Section, Anouar Abel-Malek, some of whose views are discussed in a later portion of this book. But Abdel-Malek comes from a non-Western ethnocultural group. For the evolution of some aspects of ethnohistory in the United States, see Richard L. McCormick, "Ethno-Cultural Interpretations of Nineteenth-Century American Voting Behavior," *Political Science Quarterly*, LXXXIX (June 1974), 351–74.

Jews. As for the applicability of this problem to France, despite
the circulation of rumors for several years to the effect that
unidentified French official circles have been distressed by the
allegedly high proportion of Jews in the Sixième Section, *Annales*
scholars do not seem to have considered the subject of Jewish
scholarship worthy of scholarly attention. Even at the risk of
being misunderstood, therefore, let me try to justify the urgency
of such an inquiry.

One need but turn to Braudel. Under the title "One Civilization against All the Others: The Destiny of the Jews," Braudel
wrote a wholly new section of twenty-one pages (11,000–12,000
words) for the revised and enlarged edition of *La Méditerranée
et le monde méditerranéen à l'époque de Philippe II* (1966).
Absent from the first edition (1949), this section was perhaps in
part a reaction against Arnold J. Toynbee's view that Jews have
not constituted a separate civilization. Braudel, on the other hand,
maintains that the Jews of Europe and the Mediterranean have
held a strange advantage over the numerically superior peoples
around them—the other civilizations: "One prince might persecute
them, another would protect them. One economy might betray
them, another would reward them copiously. One civilization
might reject them, another would give them ample welcome." To
complicate matters, he adds, "The Jews, wherever they are to
be found, seem to the historian to adjust very well to the
ambient milieu. They are good pupils of other cultures regardless of whether the encounter is brief or drawn out." But they
remain a separate civilization, with its own underlying *basic
personality*. Jewish civilization is like all civilizations in its
propensity to accept certain cultural traits, to erect barriers
against others, and in the process to reassert its own integrity.
It differs from all others in its constitution as "the foremost
mercantile network in the world," and it differs from most in
its lack of stable territorial or geographic limits, that is, in its
constitution as a culture of the diaspora, or linear, rather than
territorial type.[21]

21. Fernand Braudel, *La Méditerranée et le monde méditerranéen à*

Is it conceivable that Charles de Gaulle, President of the French Republic, overlooked Braudel's world-famous *Méditerranée* and consequently this discourse on the Jews? Or was this discourse one of the sources of inspiration for his denunciation of Israel's Six Days' War in his famous press conference—*gros événement*, to use the language of Lucien Febvre—of November 27, 1967? His definition of the Jews, in any case, as a people "scattered hitherto, but who had remained what they had always been, that is an elite people, self-assured and domineering . . . ,"[22] shows a striking analogy to Braudel's.

The situation of the Jews has been altered, of course, since 1789 by their acquisition of the right to citizenship, by other manifestations of secularism, by the unprecedented magnitude of the horror of the Nazi policies of genocide, and by the Jews' ability, since the creation of Israel in 1948, to take pride simultaneously in a Jewish state (and potential homeland) with a definable territorial base and political authority, in some other nation-state, and in their continuing existence as an ubiquitous civilization of the diaspora, or linear, type. In this confusion of identities, accusations of anti-Semitism were not slow in being directed against de Gaulle, and in view of "the abominable persecutions of the Jews" by Nazi Germany and of "their ancient misfortunes" (de Gaulle's own terms), the outcry was doubtless a normal reaction.

Statements such as de Gaulle's became taboo, and Braudel's tableau of Jewish civilization has been (conveniently?) ignored by and large. In any event, *Annales* scholars have not undertaken to examine the question from the point at which Braudel left off in 1966. On the other hand, an American historian, H. G. Koenigsberger, criticizes *The Mediterranean*'s neglect of the con-

---

l'époque de Philippe II, rev. ed., 2 vols. (Paris: Armand Colin, 1966), II, 135-55. The translation is my own. For the authorized translation, see *The Mediterranean and the Mediterranean World in the Age of Philip II*, 2 vols., trans. Siân Reynolds (New York: Harper & Row, 1973), II, 802-26.

22. Raymond Aron, *De Gaulle, Israel, and the Jews*, trans. John Sturrock (New York: Praeger, 1969), "Preface to the English Edition," p. 9.

tributions to Spanish literature (especially the picaresque novel), and to law, philosophy, and religious thought and practice, of the *conversos*, or "converted" Jews (Marranos). Koenigsberger similarly censures Braudel, in an otherwise generally admiring critique, for "personifying abstractions such as civilisations, and ascribing will and volition to institutions." Indeed, he rhetorically rejects not only Braudel's tableau of Jewish civilization but the very notion of civilizations. If, on the other hand, Braudel's observations and conclusions fit the sixteenth century, may they be extended with equal propriety to the twentieth? Certainly not without caution, since a well-conceived "sociology of the Jews" is still lacking. It is difficult to determine what "Jewishness" includes and what it excludes, and how varying degrees of integration with other cultural and institutional entities alter Jewishness.[23] Jewishness may not be as homogeneous or integral as it appears sometimes to Jews and non-Jews alike, for persons "commonly called Jews by reason of their membership in an ethnic-religious group are also at the same time members of many other groups."[24]

23. H. G. Koenigsberger, "Fernand Braudel and the Mediterranean," *The Listener*, Jan. 3, 1974, pp. 10–12, review of the English translation. For an approach to the problem of a sociology of the Jews, see Otto Klineberg, "Toward a Sociology of the Jews," in American Jewish Committee, *Aspects of French Jewry* (London: Valentine, Mitchell, 1969), pp. 1–9; Centre National des Hautes Etudes Juives (Brussels) and Institute of Contemporary Jewry of the Hebrew University of Jerusalem, *La Vie juive dans la vie contemporaine, Jewish Life in Contemporary Europe: Actes du Colloque tenu à l'Institut de Sociologie de l'Université Libre de Bruxelles du 19 au 21 septembre 1962* (Brussels: Institut de Sociologie de l'Université Libre de Bruxelles, 1965), especially the following contributions: Abraham Moles, "Sur l'aspect théorique du décompte du populations mal définies," pp. 81–88; Charlotte Roland-Lowenthal, "Sociologie juive, méthode d'une expérience en cours," pp. 297–307; Abraham Moles, "Sur le contenu d'une sociologie juive," pp. 311–14. Each paper is followed by an abridgment in English. In "Capitalisme et marchands marranes à Hambourg et auprès des cours princières," *Annales ESC*, XVI (November–December 1961), 1208–11, Léon Poliakov, a Sixième Section teacher and frequent contributor to the *Annales*, is highly critical of Werner Sombart for the carelessness with which he defined Jews as well as for his alleged anti-Semitism.

24. Fischer, *Historians' Fallacies*, p. 144.

One should seek to determine, however, not only whether a general Jewish civilization exists today but also whether an ethnohistory (or ethnosociology), preferably with quantitative (thus qualitative) foundations, of contemporary Jewish scholarship is feasible. Must not Jewish scholarship, moreover, be partly ubiquitous and linear—of the diaspora type—if contemporary Jewish civilization is partly ubiquitous and linear? Is there no relationship between the localization of the major social science achievements of our century in a few key cities of the Western world and the presence, in large numbers, of Jews and Jewish scholars in those same cities and their institutions?

To approach such questions one may refer with profit to an article written in 1919 by Thorstein Veblen, who suggests, in effect, that the intellectual pre-eminence of Jews in Europe in his own time was the result of their "skeptical frame of mind," produced by their release from the dead hand of conventional reality through their exposure to two worlds, Jewish and gentile. Maintaining further that the intelligent among them with a secular education took their cue not from "traditional interpretation" but "from the run of the facts," Veblen regarded Jewish intellectuals and Jews in the so-called liberal professions as being "in a peculiar degree exposed to the unmediated facts of the current situation."[25] Whatever Veblen's attitude toward Jews was in other studies, no anti-Jewish sentiment was expressed in this article even though readers sometimes consider it present. The

25. Thorstein Veblen, "The Intellectual Pre-eminence of Jews in Modern Europe," *Political Science Quarterly*, XXXIV (1919), 33–42. For more recent conceptualizations of the secularized Jewish intellectual along similar lines, see John Murray Cuddihy, *The Ordeal of Civility: Freud, Marx, Lévi-Strauss, and the Jewish Struggle with Modernity* (New York: Basic Books, 1974); Stanley Diamond, *In Search of the Primitive: A Critique of Civilization* (New Brunswick, N.J.: Transaction Books, 1974), pp. 321–31, on the contribution of Claude Lévi-Strauss's Jewishness to the formation of a structural anthropology that attributes an equally valid logic to the primitive mind as to the civilized. Cuddihy regards structural anthropology as one of several ideological remedies adopted by Jewish intellectuals who have been emancipated into the modern world but continue to have feelings of guilt for their emancipation, modernization, secularization, and westernization.

article, indeed, is a useful guide to the psychology of those Jews who, superficially at least, have been "emancipated" into the West and are thus furthest withdrawn from an assumed Jewish civilization—those with a secular (here-and-now) education and thus a passion for innovation, for novelty and fad, for the mediation of "the unmediated facts of the current situation." If Veblen's hypothesis is correct, there may be a positive correlation between the culture of the secularized Jew—whether European or American—and a particular methodology or intellectual approach. There may be a connection, for example, between the growing participation of secularized Jews in the Sixième Section and the trend in *Annales* scholarship toward contemporary (current) and extra-European problems. Some aspects of this trend are as old as the *Annales*, but heavy Jewish participation may have reinforced it, perhaps to the benefit of the full formulation and clarification of the *Annales* paradigm.

Another important contribution to the character of the *Annales* School may have been made by the various institutions of learning through which *Annales* scholars pass earlier in their careers. It has been suggested to me privately, for example, that what characterizes the present group of Sixième Section scholars and teachers is an experience as students at the Ecole Normale Supérieure and their consequent manifestation of an *esprit normalien*. But of the twenty-four persons who answered that part of my questionnaire regarding former school experience, only five replied that they had studied at the Ecole Normale Supérieure in Paris and two at its sister institution in Saint-Cloud. Only three of these seven persons went on to teach in the Sixième Section. It is therefore very doubtful that more than one out of four or five Sixième Section teachers was a *normalien* in 1972. The founders of the *Annales*, on the other hand, were both graduates of the Ecole Normale Supérieure in Paris.[26]

26. Lucien Febvre, "Vivre l'histoire: Propos d'initiation," *Mélanges d'histoire sociale*, III (1943), 5–18, reprinted in Febvre, *Combats pour*

Twenty or twenty-five per cent (if indeed the proportion is so high) is not overwhelming, but it is not without significance. The trend, however, may have been in fact toward a declining proportion of *normaliens* in the Sixième Section. This is suggested at least by the lists of the Ecole Normale graduates for the years 1950–1969, very few of whose names have appeared thus far among the teachers of the Sixième Section.[27] But since the percentage may have been higher among the members of the third *Annales* generation, as suggested by the 1972 sample figures, it may be desirable to ascertain the meaning of the term *esprit normalien*.

Among the characteristics attributed by former graduates to the select students—often future teachers—of the Ecole Normale Supérieure in Paris are an extra-ordinary capacity for work, a tendency to divide into numerous friendship groups and coteries or *turnes*, a propensity for skepticism, criticism, and liberalism (more recently, radicalism), a "deep conformism" hidden beneath a "superficial originality" (Marc Soriano, a literary folklorist in the Sixième Section), and a penchant to form a kind of "Casa nostra" or "secret society with its own coded language, signs of recognition, a solidarity among members apparently stronger than the divisions of politics or religion" (Thierry Maulnier). According to Gaston Roupnel, an historian admired by Febvre and

l'histoire (Paris: Armand Colin, 1953), p. 18 (18–33), three inaugural lectures given at the Ecole Normale Supérieure in 1941; Lucien Febvre, "Souvenirs d'une grande histoire: Marc Bloch et Strasbourg," *Combats pour l'histoire*, pp. 391–92 (391–407), published originally in Strasbourg, Faculté des Lettres, *Mémorial des années 1939–1945* (1947).

27. I am grateful to Monsieur J. Bousquet of the Ecole Normale Supérieure in Paris for this list—a photocopy of the relevant pages of the annual of the Association des Anciens Elèves de l'Ecole Normale Supérieure. Of all the persons graduated from the Ecole Normale Supérieure, rue d'Ulm, 1950–1969 inclusive, only six—André Miquel (1950), Pierre Bourdieu (1951), Christian Metz (1951), Lucien Bianco (1952), Marc Augé (1957), and Daniel Pécaut (1957)—are listed in the 1974–1975 *Programme d'Enseignement* of the Sixième Section, Ecole Pratique des Hautes Etudes, among the 226 teachers, thus less than 3 per cent of the total teaching staff.

Braudel alike, the Ecole was "more Normale than Supérieure."[28]
Such a harsh evaluation does not solve the problem of the
precise relationship between *esprit normalien* and *esprit de
Sixième Section*, however, unless one prematurely identifies the
Sixième Section as a graduate unit of historians, economists,
behaviorists, and other social scientists with a penchant for the
very same things that the students of the Ecole Normale are said
to be inclined to. The question of the effect of the Ecole Normale
on the Sixième Section, like the question of that of Jewish
scholarship, must therefore be left in abeyance.

The present chapter does not—cannot—aspire to provide a
sociology and social history of the *Annales* School. I have done
little more than to suggest a few of the questions that such an
inquiry would have to raise if social change is understood as a
function of social organization. But as Lucien Febvre once emphasized, very little has been done to take the discipline of history
in this direction.[29] More has been accomplished since Febvre's
time, and the day may not be far off when a social history and
sociology of the *Annales* School at last will be possible.

If, at present, one is at a loss to identify the *Annales* paradigm
clearly and unambiguously in a sociological sense, one may
define it, nevertheless, as instrumentation, artifact, or construct. A
definition of the sociological aspects of the paradigm doubtless
would clarify some now obscure relationships. Fortunately, we
do not need a perfect understanding of the paradigm as a sociological phenomenon in order to determine precisely what the

28. Alain Peyrefitte, *Rue d'Ulm: Chronique de la vie Normalienne*, introduction by Georges Pompidou, rev. ed. (Paris: Flammarion, 1963), pp.
354, 358–60, 383–85. For a study of the Ecole Normale during the period
1890–1904, while Lucien Febvre was a student there and in the years of the
Dreyfus affair, see Robert J. Smith, "L'Atmosphère politique à l'Ecole
Normale Supérieure à la fin du XIXe siècle," *Revue d'histoire moderne et
contemporaine*, XX (April–June 1973), 248–68.

29. Lucien Febvre, "Vers une autre histoire," *Combats pour l'histoire*,
p. 438 (419–38), originally published in *Revue de métaphysique et de
morale*, LVIII (1949).

Annales paradigm *does.*[30] One may easily conclude from the available evidence, for example, that the journal has sought to refine and enrich the notion of communication, develop a dialogue with the other "sciences of man," and rid scholars of pernicious ethnocentric biases (but not of an interest in ethnocultural questions). The *Annales* of the sixties and early seventies also gave heed to the appeal made by Lucien Febvre and Marc Bloch in the first issue of their journal (January 15, 1929) for collaboration between historians and students of "contemporary societies and economies."

But as Braudel shrewdly observed in 1956, in a eulogy to Lucien Febvre, the multiple forces that had driven first-generation Febvre and second-generation Braudel toward new ways would accelerate and ultimately impel the third generation to perpetrate "a profound upheaval of the very foundations of science and culture." It behooves them, he consequently warned, to direct that transformation toward a workable "new humanism" instead of simply yielding to, and thus provoking, the ineluctable destruction of old values.[31]

Despite premonitions and precautions, however, an older generation may be caught momentarily unprepared. Under the impetus of the partly "absurd" but crucial Events of May 1968— again, *gros événement*—Braudel had to cut short his stay at the University of Chicago, return to Paris, and summon quickly an extraordinary session of "friends, collaborators, and directors of the *Annales*" to re-examine "the hierarchy of present urgencies." As a result, starting with the third number in 1969, the review was given a larger format. To the probable end of opening its doors to more contributors and drawing a larger and younger

30. I have borrowed the ideas presented above from Margaret Masterman, "The Nature of a Paradigm," pp. 65–66, 69–70.

31. Fernand Braudel, "Lucien Febvre et l'histoire," *Annales ESC,* XII (April–June 1957), 177–82, published originally in *Education Nationale,* Dec. 13, 1956.

readership, hence promoting the circulation of elites, there was also a change of rubrics and of emphasis.

The focus on contemporary history and the sociology of contemporary societies was made sharper. Under the rubric "Inter-Sciences," a special section was reserved for the methods and modes of inquiry of the numerous disciplines at history's doors, including linguistics, semiotics, and comparative mythology. Moreover, the internally restyled journal was thereafter to devote from time to time, at least once each year, a whole or partial number to some general interdisciplinary theme or to a special historical theme. The ten themes chosen between the end of 1969 and the end of 1974 have dealt successively with biological (and demographic) history and society, history and urbanization, prosopography, history and structure, family and society, nonwritten (archeological, symbolic, cinematic, oral) history, reinterpretations of the ancien régime and French Revolution, immobile or slow-changing history and environmental history, sexuality, and heresy and the "religious field." The new rubric "History Less Europe" (*L'Histoire Moins l'Europe*) was quickly retitled "History Save Europe" (*L'Histoire Sauf l'Europe*), perhaps in reflection of an underlying ambivalence and of a subconscious hope that history (either as process or as discipline) would save Europe, enabling it somehow to maintain its cultural identity and distinction.

After having won their way to positions of intermediate scholarly authority between 1956 and 1968, the third generation of *Annales* scholars began to fill the top posts. Braudel thereupon voiced the hope that the new generation of "young directors" would lend an attentive ear to outside counsels and know tomorrow, if necessary, how to make a "new new *Annales*."[32]

A few years later, however, a third-generation *Annales* collaborator and teacher at the Institut Français in Naples expressed

32. Fernand Braudel, "Les 'Nouvelles' *Annales*," *Annales ESC*, XXIV (May–June 1969), 1.

doubt that the *Annales* had been able to retain its old intellectual power and rigor of analysis. He was afraid that *Annales* history as it had evolved might be "less able than ever to satisfy all those who expect from it a rational, stringent, and dialectical ordering of the past," since its concept of a model is still undefined and since "its structures waver between true mathematical formalization and empirically established *topoi.*"[33]

One might reply to this skepticism that the concept of "model, like that of structure," generally hesitates between abstraction (mathematical or not) and the miniature representation or abbreviation of a larger concrete reality or controllable experiment.[34] On the other hand, the philosopher Gilles Gaston Granger affirms that the situation described above is inevitable because knowledge tends to be represented in one of two basic ways, depending upon the treatment of time. Those disciplines that aspire to expel time from their calculations may seek mathematical expression. Those that deal with concrete things in space and time will be historical.[35] If this view is correct, history would have no option for mathematical formulation.

The view that will emerge from this book is that history, whether capable or not of mathematical formulation, can be improved as a discipline to the extent that it subjects problems to an intelligent quantitative analysis. *Annales* scholars have moved consistently in this direction, and the third generation has accentuated the trend. If the *Annales* errs or falters in the future, it has performed at least the highly useful function of redefining history and its methods and making it easier for other historians to carry on its work.

33. Aymard, "The *Annales,*" p. 510.

34. Roger Bastide, "Colloque sur le mot 'structure,'" *Annales ESC,* XIV (April–June 1959), 351–52; Marc Barbut, "Sur le mot et le concept de 'modèle,'" *Annales ESC,* XVIII (March–April 1963), 383–86. See also Roger Bastide, ed., *Sens et usages du terme structure dans les sciences humaines et sociales* (The Hague: Mouton, 1962).

35. Gilles Gaston Granger, *Méthodologie économique* (Paris: Presses Universitaires de France, 1955), pp. 8–9.

3 Hermes and Hidden Hestia

"Empfangen und Geben: das ist das Leben." To give and to take, such is life. The plants and animals about us, the words we use, the things we eat and drink, the clothes we wear, and even the kind of people we are, affirmed Lucien Febvre and François Crouzet, are in large measure the fruits of cultural diffusion. Art is the common product of the world's peoples. Literature, too, constitutes a "field of influence."[1]

One of the constant goals of the *Annales* has been to deal with problems of communication and exchange. Despite changes in the journal, one basic theme persists. At the bottom of the cover of every issue appears the image of the god Hermes, wearer of the winged cap of liberty and bearer of the magic rod, instrument of transformation. The *Annales* thus honors a messenger god: mediator between gods and men; god of communication with the dead and of access to the earth's underground mineral wealth; god of eloquence and conversation and inventor of the flute and lyre—thus of rational and aesthetic communication alike; inventor, too, of laws and letters and especially of insignia denoting property; god of ambassadors, merchants, shepherds, wanderers, and thieves; god of exchange and of the redistribution of goods; guardian of routes, creeks, passes, gates, public places, palestras, and frontiers; mediator god between collectivities and individuals.[2]

1. Lucien Febvre and François Crouzet, "Der internationale Ursprung einer Kultur: Grundgedanken zu einer Geschichte Frankreichs," *Internationales Jahrbuch für Geschichtsunterricht*, II (1953), 5-31.

2. Jules Toutain, "Hermès, dieu social chez les Grecs," *Revue d'histoire*

Behind or beside the revealed Hermes stands, we presume, an invisible or concealed Hestia, as in classical Greek tradition. As in Greece, too, the Hestia of the *Annales* represents an enclosed, domestic, feminine space, with a fixed center (the hearth), while Hermes represents movement, passage, repeated change of condition, mobile wealth, constant and repeated intercourse with the outside world. The space of human collectivities, in *Annales* thought as in Greek tradition, has a dual aspect—Hermaean and Hestian. It is at once fixed and mobile, autarkic and interdependent.[3] Nor can one stress sufficiently the constant presence of these two aspects in general human experience. In a state of perpetual tension with each other, they are also necessary complements and may have impelled the *Annales* leadership to found such other reviews as *Cahiers du monde russe et soviétique* (1960), *Cahiers d'études africaines* (1960), *Internord* (1961), *Etudes rurales* (1961, under the joint editorship of the geographer Daniel Faucher and the medievalist Georges Duby), *L'Homme: Revue française d'anthropologie* (1961), and *Communications* (1960).[4]

In view of its characteristic preoccupation with problems of communication, it is hardly surprising that the *Annales* should

---

et de *philosophie religieuses*, XII (1932), 289–99; Mann, *Lucien Febvre*, p. 34, n. 19; *The New Science of Giambattista Vico*, trans., from the 3d ed. (1744), Thomas Goddard Bergin and Max Harold Fisch, abridged and revised with a new introduction (Garden City, N.Y.: Doubleday–Anchor Books, 1961), pp. 118, 181–83 (Sec. II, Chap. 6, par. 483; Sec. V, Chap. 2, par. 604–6); Veselin Čajkanović, *O srpskom vrhovnom bogu* [The Serbian Supreme God] (Belgrade: Srpska Kraljevska Akademija, 1941), pp. 12, 88, 153.

3. On the Greek tradition, see Jean-Pierre Vernant, *Mythe et pensée chez les Grecs*, 2 vols. (Paris: François Maspero, 1965), 124–70, chapter entitled "Hestia-Hermès: Sur l'expression religieuse de l'espace et du mouvement chez les Grecs." The book is dedicated to Ignace Meyerson for his contribution to historical psychology.

4. Maurice Aymard, "The [*sic*] Geohistory Faces with [*sic*] the Human Sciences: The Case of *Etudes rurales*," *Journal of European Economic History*, III (Fall 1974), 493–504. On the review *Communications*, see Chap. 8 below.

have chosen Hermes to symbolize its scholarship. As early as the beginning of his career as a specialist in sixteenth-century history, for example, Lucien Febvre had been intrigued by the role of Franche-Comté as "a great route"—a "country of passage, of union, of junction."[5] His interest in the problem of empire and of systems of imperial communication may have been reinforced, consciously or unconsciously, by the partial communality of orientation of the first *Annales* generation with the writers and thinkers known in Spain as the Generation of '98 and in Central Europe as the modernists, a name by means of which its members sought to emphasize involvement in an interacting contemporary world.[6]

The Generation of '98—that of Angel Ganivet, Miguel de Unamuno, and José Martínez Ruiz, alias Azorín—began to sense a difference between the modern and the contemporary (although the contemporary often continued to be called modern, whence the designation modernist). They were ambivalent toward the idea of empire, at once repelled and obsessed by it. Some concluded that Spain's assumption of an imperial function was the wrong path and hoped that the Spanish experience might serve as a lesson to other societies and cultures. As early as 1895 Unamuno asserted that history cannot be understood unless one probes its depths, just as the sea cannot be known simply by its foam. This generation sometimes de-emphasized the ethnocentric

5. Lucien Febvre, *Philippe II et la Franche-Comté: Etude d'histoire politique, religieuse et sociale*, preface by Fernand Braudel (Paris: Flammarion, 1970), pp. 18, 455, published originally by Librairie Ancienne Honoré Champion, Paris, 1911. For the concern with routes, see also Lucien Febvre, in collaboration with Lionel Bataillon, *La Terre et l'évolution humaine: Introduction géographique à l'histoire*, in series "L'Evolution de l'Humanité" (Paris: La Renaissance du Livre, 1922; reprint ed. Albin Michel, 1949), translated by E. G. Mountford and J. H. Paxton as *A Geographical Introduction to History* (New York: Knopf, 1925).

6. On the subject of an interacting contemporary world, see Geoffrey Barraclough, *An Introduction to Contemporary History* (London: C. A. Watts, 1964), Chap. 1, "The Nature of Contemporary History"; Robert L. Delevoy, *Dimensions du XXe siècle 1900–1945* (Geneva: Skira, 1965), pp. 11–12.

focus, but it believed that the meaningful was the durable, hence, stressed the history of people and peoples rather than of notable events or of political action.[7] It thus vaguely anticipated Braudel's *Méditerranée*, whose vision of long duration has been defined by an American historian as "unmistakably post-imperial, shaped by analysis of the failure of French imperial ambitions and of the dogmas which had provided their underpinning."[8]

One of the outstanding personalities of the generation of 1898 in France was Paul Valéry, who arrived at what is tantamount to a scientific distinction between the modern era and its successor, the postmodern or contemporary. The history of the modern era, he held, was a relatively *"melodic* history," characterized by the localization or "isolation of events." Postmodern or contemporary history, on the other hand, is distinguished by the difficulty of localization and subsumes "a plurality of simultaneous and inseparable meanings."[9] Without being able to free himself from the habit of calling the industrial era "modern," the artist Fernand Léger separated it in like manner from the preceding era by designating it as an "epoch of contrasts"—that is, of change in brief time—in contradistinction to the eighteenth-century "epoch of melody,"[10] in which contrasts were products of place more than of time. Léger, too, was a member of that precocious generation of 1900 that sensed how vastly different their world was becoming from all past worlds.

The entire *Annales* movement reflects this contemporary desire

7. Mann, *Lucien Febvre*, pp. 157–64.

8. Richard Mowery Andrews, review of Braudel, *The Mediterranean*, in *New York Times Book Review*, May 18, 1975, pp. 1–3, 42–45.

9. Paul Valéry, *Regards sur le monde actuel* (Paris: Librairie Stock, Delamain et Boutelleau, 1931), "Avant-propos," p. 37, and "De l'histoire," p. 65.

10. Fernand Léger, *Fonctions de la peinture* (Paris: Editions Gonthier, 1965), p. 52. Translated and reprinted by permission of the Viking Press, Inc. An English translation by Alexandra Anderson of Fernand Léger's *Functions of Painting* is published by Viking in both paperback and hardcover (New York: Viking Press, 1973). Published in London, England, by Thames and Hudson, 1973.

not only to see the history of the past as it may have been seen by those who experienced it, as a succession of localized events, but to see it as such and yet give it a new meaning in terms of a plurality of simultaneously reinforcing and contradictory meanings—in terms of the knowledge and insights of the interpreters. In his magisterial doctoral dissertation, *La Méditerranée et le monde méditerranéen à l'époque de Philippe II*,[11] Braudel thus portrays the sixteenth century by immersing himself in it as "a *picaresque* . . . wanderer with the whole Mediterranean world . . . to roam in," by means of a "Rabelaisian embrace" of the entire Mediterranean, by a "Gargantuan . . . delight" in its "largest lineaments" and "most intimate details," and by an "irrepressible appetite for going everywhere, seeing everything, and telling all about it."[12] But he also provides another conception of communication, very close to that of the historical psychologist Ignace Meyerson, who defines a human act or work as a form endowed with temporal, spatial, and social limits; inserted in a series of acts or works; assigned a signification; and having the purpose of perpetuating itself and its signification. Indeed, the object of every act, work, or institution is to communicate itself through time and to maintain or extend its spatial limits.[13] Braudel's *Méditerranée* is, among other things, a study of the work and works of the larger Mediterranean of the later sixteenth century understood as acts of communication.

Braudel's Hermes is thus a god who presides over the multiple forms of collective action and communication—god of the pastoral life, of circulation on country roads and city streets, and of commerce, speech, and conversation; god who surveys relations

11. First published by Armand Colin, Paris, 1949.

12. Hexter, "Fernand Braudel," pp. 522–25, 562.

13. Ignace Meyerson, *Les Fonctions psychologiques et les oeuvres* (Paris: Librairie philosophique J. Vrin, 1948), pp. 9–11, 15, 21–25, 75, 96, 108, 119. See also Meyerson's "Discontinuités et cheminements autonomes dans l'histoire de l'esprit," *Journal de psychologie normale et pathologique*, XLI (July–September 1948), 273–89, reviewed briefly by Braudel, in *Annales ESC*, V (January–March 1950), 127–28.

between one house or family and another, between each family and the external world and among larger collectivities; god of virtually all forms of social communication. By appropriating, during the Hellenistic era, some of the characteristics of even more encompassing Oriental deities and by forcing Hestia into hiding, Hermes became, in addition, god of fecundity and productivity. In sum, he became "the creator god" of civilization, "the Logos."[14] The scholarship of Braudel and *Annales* scholars of the third generation has incorporated many of these Hermaean/ Hestian attributes, including a focus on historical demography and on the problem of civilization.

The *Annales* did not give equal emphasis to all of Hermes' attributes, however, and an American economic historian criticized Braudel's *Méditerranée* for overrating "the monetary-impact feature of François Simiand's theory of economic development."[15] Criticisms of the *Annales* for their overdependence on Simiand and neglect of production and productivity were especially vehement, however, from Marxists. In 1951, at the height of the Cold War, Jacques Blot published a vituperative attack against Braudel and the *Annales* for overemphasizing the exchange phenomenon—calling it their *"fétichisme de la circulation"*—and thus for concentrating, as disciples of Simiand and as dutiful bourgeois, on such things as money, banking, commerce, ships, and the sea, and for their inclination to regard capitalism as a permanent historical category.[16] Another Marxist, Jacques Chambaz, leveled similar criticisms against the *"Annales* current," which he censured further for its neglect of the "relationships between infrastructure and superstructure."[17]

14. Toutain, "Hermès," pp. 297–98.
15. Melvin M. Knight, "The Geohistory of Fernand Braudel," *Journal of Economic History*, X (1950), 212–16.
16. Jacques Blot, "Le Révisionnisme en histoire ou l'Ecole des *Annales*," *La Nouvelle Critique: Revue du Marxisme militant*, III (November 1951), 46–60.
17. "Le Marxisme et l'histoire de France," one of the sessions at the University Colloquium on Marx and Marxism, May 25, 1953, in com-

In isolation the Marxist criticisms might have had little effect on *Annales* practices. They were succeeded, however, by a doctoral dissertation of fundamental importance by the *Annales* collaborator René Baehrel, *Une croissance: La Basse-Provence rurale*, which clearly demonstrated that the agricultural (wheat, wine, wool) and other rural production of Marseille's hinterland (Basse-Provence) was far more important than Marseille's international commerce. Exchange, moreover, pointed out Baehrel, may respond to the supply of and demand for money. It responds no less, and probably more, to variations in the production (supply) of goods and in the demand for them.[18]

Perhaps as an ultimate response to Marxist criticisms but more certainly as a follow-up to the suggestions of Baehrel and Pierre Chaunu,[19] and as a consequence of self-criticism and possibly even of an increasing awareness of himself as an "historian of peasant stock" and continental origin (born in a little village between Champagne and Barrois),[20] Braudel's two-volume revised edition of *La Méditerranée* moved farther inland and paid more attention to the rural sector. Since economic cycles (thus the ascendancy of François Simiand) and "the prowesses of

memoration of the seventieth anniversary of Marx's death, published in *La Pensée: Revue du rationalisme moderne* (cited hereafter as *La Pensée*), No. 51 (November 1953), p. 124 (109–43).

18. René Baehrel, *Une croissance: La Basse-Provence rurale fin XVIe siècle–1789*), Ecole Pratique des Hautes Etudes (VIe Section), "Démographie et sociétés," 6 (Paris: S.E.V.P.E.N., 1961); reviewed by Emmanuel Le Roy Ladurie, "Voies nouvelles pour l'histoire rurale (XVIe–XVIIIe siècles)" *Etudes rurales*, No. 13–14 (April–September 1964), pp. 79–95, republished in *Annales ESC*, XX (November–December 1965), 1268–80.

19. Fernand Braudel, "Pour une histoire sérielle: Séville et l'Atlantique (1504–1650)," *Annales ESC*, XVIII (May–June 1963), 541–53, reprinted in Braudel, *Ecrits sur l'histoire*, pp. 135–53, a review of Pierre Chaunu's contribution to Huguette and Pierre Chaunu, *Séville et l'Atlantique 1504–1650*, 8 vols. in 11 tomes, Ecole Pratique des Hautes Etudes (VIe Section), "Ports, routes, trafics," 6 (Paris: Armand Colin; S.E.V.P.E.N., 1955–1959).

20. Braudel, "Personal Testimony," pp. 448–49; Fernand Braudel, *Civilisation matérielle et capitalisme*, I (Paris: Armand Colin, 1967), p. 433.

cities" had "dazzled [him] too much"[21] in the first edition, he added a wholly new section of thirty-seven pages entitled "Can a Model Be Made of the Mediterranean Economy?" The section contains invaluable observations on the interrelationships between production, consumption, exchange and distribution.[22] J. H. Elliott commends it as "an extraordinarily suggestive section, both in its historical approach and technique and in its application of statistical methods to the examination of preindustrial societies. Discussions of this kind make the middle sections of the book a manual for the professional historian, to some extent inevitably at the expense of even the most enthusiastic layman."[23] H. R. Trevor-Roper observes in regard to the middle sections (Part Two)—economies, empires, societies, civilizations, and forms of war—that they constitute "a series of [wonderful] essays loosely held together by the geographic theme."[24] The *Annales* scholar Pierre Chaunu adds that the new edition gives an accounting of the Mediterranean "ten times better than the old."[25]

21. Braudel's remark is in *La Méditerranée*, II, 518, but see I, 255, where he continues to be no less dazzled by the function of cities. Recognizing the importance of agricultural production and productivity, the Sixième Section organized a discussion unit around this theme for a meeting of economic historians. See *IIIe Conférence Internationale d'Histoire Economique, Munich, 1965*, II, *Production et productivité agricoles*, ed. Jean Meuvret, Ecole Pratique des Hautes Etudes (VIe Section), "Congrès et colloques," 10 (Paris, The Hague: Mouton, 1968).

22. Braudel, *La Méditerranée*, I, 383–419.

23. J. H. Elliott, "Mediterranean Mysteries," *New York Review of Books*, May 3, 1973, pp. 25–28, review of Braudel, *The Mediterranean*.

24. Trevor-Roper, "Fernand Braudel," p. 476. For an equally favorable book review of Braudel, see Hugh R. Trevor-Roper, "Capitalism and Material Life," *New York Times Book Review*, Nov. 10, 1974, pp. 31–32.

25. Pierre Chaunu, "La Pesée globale en histoire," *Cahiers Vilfredo Pareto: Revue européenne d'histoire des sciences sociales* (cited hereafter as *Cahiers Vilfredo Pareto*), No. 15 (1968), p. 138 (135–64). See also Pierre Jeannin, "Une histoire planétaire de la civilisation matérielle," *Annales ESC*, XXVII (January–February 1972), 73 (71–79). On the other hand, in "Our Mediterranean," *The Guardian*, Dec. 13, 1973, Peter Laslett concludes, without substantiating his argument, that "none of Braudel's

J. H. Hexter, on the other hand, remarks that the revised work
still contains only "a few pages" on agriculture and the manufac-
turing economy.[26]

The last criticism may seem a bit harsh if one notes that, within
a year of his revised *Méditerranée*, Braudel published the first
volume of his *Civilisation matérielle et capitalisme*, almost one-
fifth of which is concerned with the energy resources of the preindustrial world, methods of production and transportation,
productivity, and aids and obstacles to the diffusion of new
techniques. But his treatment of energy resources, too, has been
criticized, albeit not without admiration. "Ever audacious in his
use of figures," maintains the economic historian Rondo Cameron,
and without citing the "sources of his data (probably there are
none)" and with "only the barest hint of the method of calculation," Braudel computes Europe's energy balance sheet, for the
late eighteenth century, here arranged in tabular form as in
Cameron's thoughtful review:

Energy Source	Horsepower (in Millions)
14 million horses and 24 million oxen	10
firewood	10
waterwheels	1.5–3
50 million workers	0.9
sailing ships (merchant marine)	0.15–0.233
war fleets, riverboats, windmills, charcoal, and coal	(no estimates given)

social analysis, least of all his numerical estimates, carries the conviction
which it had in the 1950s." A more relevant criticism may be Jan de
Vries's observation that Braudel "double-counted all agricultural commodities used as raw materials in industry in his estimate of Mediterranean
'national income.'" See Jan de Vries, "The Classics in Translation," *Reviews in European History*, I (March 1975), 473 (468–73), review of Peter
Earle, ed., *Essays in European Economic History, 1500–1800* (Oxford:
Clarendon Press, 1974). Braudel's model of the Mediterranean economy of
the sixteenth century is nevertheless ingenious.

26. Hexter, "Fernand Braudel," p. 530.

"However astonished one may be even at the thought of such a table," continues Cameron, "however fanciful the figures, they are probably correct in emphasizing that the largest part of Europe's economically useful energy derived from animals and from inefficient, exhaustible timber."[27] If, however, such figures are a risky venture, as Braudel himself admits, they are not as fanciful as they may seem. If Braudel fails to cite his sources and does not provide a bibliography, he offers a good reason with an apology and promise of a remedy: "I have but one regret—not to have cited my references. I shall correct this lack, unavoidable in view of the purpose and norms of this collection, by publishing a list of my sources (some of them unpublished materials) and borrowings as a separate number of the *Cahiers des Annales*."[28] Most important of all, however, he does explain his methods of calculation, although neither with the desired precision nor on the same page as his energy balance sheet.

He estimates, for example, the work capacity of a man at 0.03 to 0.04 horsepower (the power required to raise an object weighing 75 kilograms to a height of one meter in one second) as against 0.27 to 0.57 horsepower for a draft horse and about 0.25 horsepower for oxen and draft horses in combination (presumably in the proportions in which the two were to be found in the eighteenth century). In actuality, he multiplies the estimated fifty million workers not by 0.03 or 0.04 but by 0.018, presumably to take into account the lower work capacity of women, of the less strong, and of the sick, the latter probably more numerous in 1800 than in the twentieth century, to which the work capacity

27. Rondo Cameron, "Europe's Second Logistic," *Comparative Studies in Society and History*, XII (October 1970), 461 (452–62), review of E. E. Rich and C. H. Wilson, eds., *The Cambridge Economic History of Europe*, IV, *The Economy of Expanding Europe in the Sixteenth and Seventeenth Centuries* (Cambridge: University Press, 1967), and of Braudel, *Civilisation matérielle*, Vol. I (three volumes are expected).

28. *Ibid.*, I, 12 n. This explanation does not appear in Miriam Kochan's translation of Braudel's book, *Capitalism and Material Life, 1400–1800* (New York: Harper & Row, 1973).

of 0.03 and 0.04 horsepower doubtless applies. He fails to explain, however, what he has done—Cameron's underlying criticism is thus quite appropriate—and if one were to multiply the estimated European work force of fifty million by 0.03 or 0.04, one would get 1.5 million or 2 million horsepower instead of the 0.9 that he shows. Furthermore, if we multiply the estimated 38 million draft animals by 0.25, we obtain 9.5 (rather than 10) million horsepower. These 38 million horses and oxen have a partly empirical, but largely hypothetical basis. Accepting Antoine-Laurent de Lavoisier's estimate that there were 3 million oxen and 1,781,000 horses in France on the eve of the French Revolution, he multiplies each of these two figures by eight in order to obtain the hypothetical number of oxen and horses in Europe, on the theory that the ratio of draft animals to people in Europe as a whole was then about the same as the ratio in France. As for the energy product of firewood, he calculates this on the basis of France's estimated consumption of 12 million tons in 1830, which he multiplies by ten in order to arrive at the total European consumption around 1800. Unfortunately, he fails to explain why he now uses a multiplier of ten rather than eight. Its use could be defended on two grounds: that the consumption of firewood may have been greater around 1800 than in 1830 and that Eastern and Central Europe (excluding the steppe regions) had a much greater forest coverage than France. But one probably also could demonstrate that Europe's central and eastern regions had a greater proportion of horses and oxen than France. His estimate of the energy product of waterwheels is based on the count in Austrian Poland, at the end of the eighteenth century, of 5,243 watermills to serve a population of two million. If the same proportion prevailed in the rest of Europe, the latter should have had 500,000–600,000 waterwheels (one wheel to a mill). Having made the further assumption that a waterwheel produces 2 to 5 horsepower, he has multiplied the hypothetical 500,000 waterwheels by three and the equally hypothetical 600,000 by five to obtain a minimum waterwheel horsepower of 1.5 million and a maximum of 3 million. Finally, he has estimated that Europe's merchant ships possessed the equivalent carrying capacity of 600,000–700,000 steamship tons. Europe's merchant marine consequently should have contributed 150,000 to 233,000 horsepower, depending on whether the energy required to propel a steamship is set at 0.25 or 0.333 horsepower.[29]

Braudel's conversion of the performance of various power sources and devices into horsepower is not infallible, but it is confirmed in part at least by the estimates of Abbott Payson Usher, who more than a decade earlier had estimated the work capacity of oxen at 0.3 horsepower, of horses at 0.5 horsepower, and of an eighteen-foot overshot waterwheel at 2 to 5 horsepower. It is true that Usher estimated the work capacity of men at the high level of 0.1 horsepower. He maintained none the less that, on the average, men are able to exert only one-fifth to one-eighth as much energy as horses.[30] If we accept the lower figure, the estimated work capacity of men would drop to 0.06, although it still would be larger than all of Braudel's three possible figures. Usher's conversion ratios, however, are more relevant to the latter half of the nineteenth and the twentieth centuries, whereas Braudel's pertain to the eighteenth century.

With all its possible defects, Braudel's energy balance sheet represents a giant step in the right direction—toward a more realistic (if partly hypothetical) quantification of the preindustrial era of human experience. Some of his estimates and conversion rates may have to be revised, but for the time being we may retain the total of 22.6 million to 24.1 million horsepower for the power sources or devices whose performance he attempted to quantify. Making the technical corrections that we have suggested

29. Braudel, *Civilisation matérielle*, I, 254, 267–69, 270, 273, 275, 280, 282. On these technical matters, readers may want to consult the English translation, *Capitalism and Material Life*, pp. 246, 257, 260, 262–63, 265–66, 271, 274.

30. Abbott Payson Usher, "Analysis and Evaluation: The Balance Sheet of Economic Development," *Journal of Economic History*, XI (Fall 1951), 327–28 (323–38).

ld raise the total by a further 0.1 million to 0.6 million horse-
ver. To complete the quantification, however, we should note
audel's firm belief that Europe's war fleets contributed a much
greater horsepower than its merchant fleets (thus much more
than 0.233 million horsepower) and that its windmills, concentrated
largely in the region under the influence of the westerlies from
the North Atlantic to the Baltic, generated less power than its
watermills (thus considerably less than 3 million and perhaps less
than 1.5 million). One thus may infer that these two sources
(navies and windmills) contributed to Europe's use an additional
2 million horsepower. While Braudel does not quantify the total
horsepower derived from coal, we know from other research
that the world production of coal grew from 2.4 million tons
around 1640, with England producing 2 million and France and
China nearly all the rest, to 11 million tons around 1800, with
England's product at 10 million and Europe's as a whole at somewhat under 11 million.[31] Since, as Braudel indicates in a round-
about way, six metric tons of coal are required to produce one
horsepower, we may calculate Europe's (mostly England's)
energy product from coal at about 0.35 million horsepower in
1640 and 1.8 million in 1800. The only empirical information that
Braudel offers on charcoal is to note that Paris's consumption of
firewood in 1830 was twenty-two times as great.[32] Even though the
Mediterranean was the major region of charcoal consumption,
however, his own *Méditerranée* contains only two brief allusions
to the subject, neither very useful for quantifying horsepower.[33]
But if we assume that the consumption of charcoal in Europe
beyond the Mediterranean was unlikely to have exceeded the
Paris ratio, we may risk estimating it for Europe as a whole at 12

31. John U. Nef, *Western Civilization since the Renaissance: Peace, War,
Industry, and the Arts* (New York: Harper & Row, 1963), p. 14; first
published as *War and Human Progress*, Harvard University Press, 1950;
Eric J. Hobsbawm, *The Age of Revolution: Europe, 1789–1848* (London:
Weidenfeld and Nicolson, 1962), p. 43.
32. Braudel, *Civilisation matérielle*, I, 280.
33. Braudel, *La Méditerranée*, I, 81, 472.

million to 24 million tons (one-tenth to one-twentieth of the consumption of firewood). Converting this at the rate of one horsepower to twelve metric tons,[34] we obtain an additional 1 million to 2 million horsepower.

Adding the amounts derived above—4.8 million to 5.8 million horsepower plus the corrections of 0.1 million to 0.6 million—to Braudel's computation of Europe's energy balance sheet, we may estimate Europe's total useful energy product toward the end of the eighteenth century at 27.5 million to 30.5 million horsepower. But we may assume, in addition, on the basis of further (partly impressionistic) data in Braudel's *Civilisation matérielle*, as Pierre Chaunu has observed, that Europe's useful energy resources were then probably twice as great per capita as China's and ten times as great as those of the rest of the world, while Europe's horsepower in draft animals was five or six times as great as China's.[35] Since Europe's estimated population was then 187 million,[36] we may establish the per capita horsepower available to Europeans around 1800 at 0.14 to 0.16. China's per capita horsepower consequently should have been 0.07 or 0.08, that of the rest of the world 0.014 to 0.016. All of this is obviously too exact, and some modifications of the estimates eventually will have to be made. But it is much better to do what Braudel has done—and to continue his work—than to ignore the crucial question of the distribution in the world of useful energy and of energy sources and power devices.

This form of analysis constitutes what the Marxist collaborator of the *Annales*, literary historian Lucien Goldmann, has called a "total model of the economic process."[37] It goes back, indeed, to Physiocracy and especially to its founder, François Quesnay,

34. Braudel, *Civilisation matérielle*, I, 280.

35. *Ibid.*, 282–83; Chaunu, "La Pesée globale," p. 157; Traian Stoianovich, "Theoretical Implications of Braudel's *Civilisation matérielle*," *Journal of Modern History*, XLI (March 1969), 76 (68–81).

36. Braudel, *Civilisation matérielle*, I, 26.

37. Lucien Goldmann, "La Pensée des 'Lumières,'" *Annales ESC*, XXII (July–August 1967), 772–73 (752–79).

se *Tableau économique* did not fail to impress both Karl
x and the free enterprise economists Léon Walras and Joseph
umpeter. The twentieth-century French economist Michel
Lutfalla aptly refers to the *Tableau économique* as the "first
macroeconomic machine,"[38] whose aim it was, according to
Goldmann, to harmonize the highly imperfect existing social
order and avert revolution by channeling capital away from
commerce and manufactures toward agriculture.[39]

A total-model approach was revived in France during the
second half of the twentieth century by French economists—
among them François Perroux, Jean Marczewski, and Jean
Fourastié—under the influence of such American general equilibrium economists as Simon Kuznets. Calling their method quantitative history, these economists study macroeconomic change over
several generations and sometimes several centuries, adapting
national income accounting and applying input-output analysis
to large social aggregates, such as a whole industry, region, group
of cities, nation, or group of countries.[40] Braudel admits his indebtedness to them for his own still more audacious macro-
economic approach.[41]

While *Annales* historians have had to learn to regard production as part of the overall communications system, their conception of territoriality as part of the communications system has
been of longer duration. It is based on their long-standing interest
in the interaction between people and environment and on their

38. Michel Lutfalla, "Modernité du *Tableau économique*," *François
Quesnay: Tableau économique des Physiocrates* (Paris: Calmann-Lévy,
1969), pp. 9–41.

39. Lucien Goldmann, *The Human Sciences and Philosophy*, trans. Hayden
V. White and Robert Anchor, with a new preface (London: Jonathan
Cape, 1969), pp. 120–21. The French edition is *Sciences humaines et philosophie* (Paris: Presses Universitaires de France, 1952). The English translation is based on the edition with a new preface (Paris: Société Nouvelle
des Editions Gonthier, 1966).

40. Jean Marczewski, "Quantitative History," *Journal of Contemporary
History*, III, 2 (1968), 179–91.

41. Braudel, *La Méditerranée*, II, 517.

image of people as a function of their situation on a dynamic Earth, at once acting upon them and acted upon. It has its origins in the "possibilist" geography of Paul Vidal de La Blache, as reinterpreted by Febvre, Bloch, and Braudel.[42]

Under the notion of "the dialectic between space and time (geography and history),"[43] which he once called "geohistory,"[44] Braudel subsumes both ecological and temporal-territorial continuities and transformations. He has examined this dialectic mainly from two angles, however, first envisioning a physical milieu that is almost impervious to other than traditional forms of human action (Hestia),[45] and then looking at that milieu as it is transformed and consumed by an ongoing dialectic of plowmen, graziers, merchants, travelers, and states and their agents against "Space, [Public] Enemy Number One" (Hermes).[46] This in turn has led him to scrutinize that dialectic as a struggle to build more and better roads and land and sea vehicles and to

42. Braudel, *La Méditerranée* (1949), p. 301.

43. Braudel, *La Méditerranée*, I, Preface to the 2d ed., 12.

44. Braudel, *La Méditerranée* (1949), pp. 295–96. The section in which Braudel employs the term "geohistory" is part of the "Conclusion" to Part One ("The Share of the Milieu"), and bears the subtitle "Geohistory and Determinism." There is no corresponding section in the second edition. What roughly may pass for it is a brief passage entitled "Determinism and Economic Life," but this appears in a different context and does not contain the term "geohistory." Pierre Chaunu, on the other hand, continues to use the term in *Histoire, science sociale: La Durée, l'espace et l'homme à l'époque moderne* (Paris: Société d'Edition d'Enseignement Supérieur, 1974), pp. 15, 62. The first use of the term that I have come across occurs in Louis Voinovitch (Count), *Histoire de Dalmatie*, I, *Des origines au marché infâme* (1409), 2d ed. (Paris: Hachette, 1934), a book cited in Braudel's footnotes and bibliography. Voinovitch wrote on the first page: "La Dalmatie est l'expression géo-historique finale d'un grand territoire qui embrasse les rivages de l'Archipel et de l'Euxin." I have been unable to check the first edition of Voinovitch's work.

45. Conceptually a third and quantitatively a fourth of Braudel's *Méditerranée* (Part One) is devoted to what he calls a "quasi-immobile history of man in relation to his milieu." See Braudel, *La Méditerranée* (1949), p. xiii, and Braudel, *La Méditerranée*, I (1966), Preface to the 1st ed., 16.

46. *Ibid.*, I, 326.

develop larger and commercially more active cities. He consequently defines "the immense Spanish Empire" as "a colossal enterprise of transports by sea and by land," requiring an incessant flow of troops, the repeated transfer of precious metals, and an expanding credit economy. "For states, indeed, there is not one, there are ten struggles against space."[47]

Commenting on Georges Lefebvre's *La Grande Peur de 1789*, Lucien Febvre drew attention to another aspect of space and communication—the diffusion of panics. "Strange geography of routes," he observed, for the rural panics of 1789 reveal a Massif Central "remiss in its legendary role as a pole of repulsion." On the contrary, it was "largely permeable to the panics, unlike [such major arteries of communication as] the Loire and Garonne valleys." Highly pleased with Lefebvre's contribution, Febvre recommended the ultimate publication of a new edition with an improved map and an accompanying transparency on which would be indicated not only arrows showing the direction of movement but the date of occurrence of each panic. The new map, he added, should show not only hydrographic features but topographic (mountains and forests), too.[48]

Lucien Febvre came close, indeed, to recommending what Charles Tilly would later call a "quantitative analysis of paths," or currents, and the use of intuitive path analysis for the purpose of defining common, powerful, or persistent links in a complex set of field relationships; comparing different sets of field relationships; and noting the interdependence between each particular form of linkage and the field in which the linkages are made.[49]

47. *Ibid.*, p. 341.
48. Lucien Febvre, "Une gigantesque fausse nouvelle: La Grande Peur de juillet 89," *Pour une histoire à part entière*, Bibliothèque Générale de l'Ecole Pratique des Hautes Etudes (VIe Section) (Paris: S.E.V.P.E.N., 1962), pp. 821–23 (821–28), first published in *Revue de Synthèse*, V (February 1933), 7–15.
49. Charles Tilly, "Quantification in History, as Seen from France," in Val R. Lorwin and Jacob M. Price, eds., *The Dimensions of the Past: Materials, Problems, and Opportunities for Quantitative Work in History* (New Haven: Yale University Press, 1972), pp. 105–6 (93–125).

And if Georges Lefebvre did not engage in a systematic quantitative analysis of the panic paths, he did determine what the Great Fear was not. It *was not* "a series of concentric waves starting from Paris and spreading through the provinces." It *did not* travel "from Paris to Bordeaux *via* the Loire valley and the Poitou gap, or from Paris to Marseille down the Saône and the Rhône." The panics *did not* follow the king's highways or the customary paths of regional and long-distance trade. They rather "developed out of local incidents of chance occurrence."[50] Paris was eccentric to them. As Lucien Febvre observed, the rural panic paths may have coincided even with the mythical or traditional paths of the centuries before the affirmation of centralized government.[51]

As a leading specialist in the French Revolution with a direction of his own to follow, Lefebvre was associated only peripherally with the *Annales* movement. He nevertheless laid the basis for a geohistory of one form of collective sensitivity or psychology—a subject of constant interest to Marc Bloch, Lucien Febvre,[52] and the *Annales* School: contagious or communicable emotion, fear in a rural or semirural environment. But no subsequent study of the subject has been of equal significance, perhaps because of an underlying distrust among historians of the kind of socioscientific methodology initiated by Lefebvre, improved by the recommendations of Lucien Febvre, and given systematic form, many years later, by the sociologist-historian Charles Tilly.

A fate of similar negligence has befallen a tremendously in-

50. Georges Lefebvre, *La Grande Peur de 1789* (Paris: Armand Colin, 1932), pp. 197–231, 165. A second edition was published in 1970. The quotations are from the English translation by Joan White, *The Great Fear of 1789: Rural Panic in Revolutionary France*, introduction by George Rudé (New York: Pantheon, 1973), p. 169.

51. Febvre, "Une gigantesque fausse nouvelle," pp. 825–26.

52. Lucien Febvre, "La Sensibilité et l'histoire: Comment reconstituer la vie affective d'autrefois?" *Combats pour l'histoire*, p. 224 (221–38), first published in *Annales d'histoire sociale*, III (1941), 5–20.

teresting and highly suggestive essay—which lacks the extensive research, however, that went into Lefebvre's book—by the political sociologist André Siegfried on the paths of contagious diseases, ecumenical and missionary religions, political ideologies (and, incidentally, international and interregional commerce).[53] Lefebvre's *Grande Peur* and Siegfried's *Itinéraires de contagions* allow an examination of two very different types of paths and sets of field relationships. By and large, however, scholars have failed to perceive how the two may and should—in order to further our understanding of human societies—be brought together, as Tilly suggests, by a study of the points at which rural panics and routes of commerce, ideology, and epidemics converge, and by a determination of the effect of that convergence on their existence as part of an autonomous set of field relationships, by applying to the Hermaean subject of currents and paths what *Annales* scholars call *histoire ponctuelle* and *sérielle* (Chapter 7).

The curiosity of *Annales* scholars has been extended less grudgingly, on the other hand, to climatic and oceanic paths and currents and to the routes of plant and animal movement—to meteorology, climatology, oceanography, phytogeography, and zoogeography. Emmanuel Le Roy Ladurie, for example, has shown interest in the cultivated plants, in the techniques of vegetal production, and in plant and animal migration in pre-eighteenth-century Languedoc.[54] He similarly has investigated the meteorology of Languedoc[55] and the climate of the northern

53. André Siegfried, *Itinéraires de contagions: Epidémies et idéologies,* preface by Pasteur Valéry-Radot (Paris: Armand Colin, 1960).

54. Emmanuel Le Roy Ladurie, *Les Paysans de Languedoc,* Bibliothèque Générale de l'Ecole Pratique des Hautes Etudes (VIe Section), 2 vols. (Paris: S.E.V.P.E.N., 1965), I, 53–133. An abridged French edition, published in 1969 by Flammarion, has been translated and introduced by John Day, *The Peasants of Languedoc* (Urbana, Ill.: University of Illinois Press, 1974). The last chapter of this translation has been reprinted in Earle, *Essays in European Economic History,* pp. 143–64.

55. Le Roy Ladurie, *Les Paysans de Languedoc,* I, 17–49.

hemisphere during a portion of the historical era, as a result of which he has been able to confirm a "little ice age" between 1200 and 1850, interrupted by a slight amelioration between 1350 and 1550. He conceived the object of his research on climate as the construction of "a pure climatic history free of any anthropocentric preoccupation or presumption," but he also had practical reasons for refusing to relate the history of climate to that of long-term agricultural and economic change. One such reason was that the historian can refer to "excellent meteorological, climatological, and glaciological modes" but to no "fully elaborated ecological ones."[56] Moreover, Le Roy Ladurie was unable to observe any close temporal concordance between climatic change and secular economic change. At the same time, he was able to show that the progressive delay in grape-gathering in certain parts of France was not provoked by a deteriorating climatic condition—even though a slight climatic worsening was an independent reality—but by the desire of specific human communities to give their wines a higher alcoholic content.[57]

Le Roy Ladurie's reluctance to assign primacy to climatic change in the history of long-term social and economic change is shared by other economic historians—among them Karl Helleiner of Canada and B. H. Slicher van Bath of the Netherlands. But it stands in sharp contrast to the views of the Swedish his-

56. Emmanuel Le Roy Ladurie, *Histoire du climat depuis l'an mil* (Paris: Flammarion, 1967), and a revised and updated English translation, *Times of Feast, Times of Famine: A History of Climate since the Year 1000*, trans. Barbara Bray (Garden City, N.Y.: Doubleday, 1971), pp. 22, 100, for the statements attributed to Le Roy Ladurie. The English translation is mistitled since it does not deal with the anthropological problem of times of feast and treats only incidentally the sociological and economic problem of famine. See also Emmanuel Le Roy Ladurie, "Pour une histoire de l'environnement: La Part du climat," *Annales ESC*, XXV (September–October 1970), 1459–70.

57. Emmanuel Le Roy Ladurie, "Histoire et climat," *Annales ESC*, XIV (January–March 1959), 16–26 (3–34), reprinted in Emmanuel Le Roy Ladurie, *Le Territoire de l'historien* (Paris: Gallimard, 1973), pp. 424–55.

..astaf Utterström.[58] It would appear to be at variance, with Braudel's views, for despite his desire to give human societies their due and despite his general unreceptivity to deterministic interpretations of history, Braudel has come to be convinced not only—like Le Roy Ladurie—that climate is global or hemispheric in scope, with a "unitary history,"[59] but also that climatic changes—whether produced by fluctuations in the speed of the jet stream or by some other agent—explain why demographic growth and decline tend in the long run to be simultaneous over large portions of the earth and why the share of the various continental masses in the world's total population tends to remain at a constant level, except when disturbed by transcontinental and transoceanic migrations of peoples, animals, plants, and their viral and other diseases.[60] In fact, however, the difference between Braudel and Le Roy Ladurie may be negligible, for Braudel establishes a correlation between world

58. Karl Helleiner, "The Population of Europe from the Black Death to the Eve of the Vital Revolution," in Rich and Wilson, eds., *The Cambridge Economic History of Europe*, IV, *The Economy of Expanding Europe*, 76 (1–95); Gustaf Utterström, "Climatic Fluctuations and Population Problems in Early Modern History," *Scandinavian Economic History Review*, III, 1 (1955), 3–47; Immanuel Wallerstein, *The Modern World-System: Capitalist Agriculture and the Origins of the European World-Economy in the Sixteenth Century* (New York and London: Academic Press, 1974), pp. 33–35.

59. Braudel, *La Méditerranée*, I, 251–52.

60. Braudel, *Civilisation matérielle*, I, 19, 32–34; Stoianovich, "Theoretical Implications of Braudel's *Civilisation matérielle*," p. 75. Le Roy Ladurie similarly emphasizes the disturbing role in world history of viral diseases, notably in "Un concept: L'Unification microbienne du monde (XIVe–XVIIe siècles)," *Revue suisse d'histoire*, XXIII, 4 (1973), 627–96, an article that deals with the manifestation in certain periods—from the fifth century to the end of the seventh century in the Old World and from the fourteenth to the end of the seventeenth century in Old World and New—of "a common market of microbes." Derived in part from the thought of Woodrow Borah, Sherburne F. Cook, and Lesley Boyd Simpson, Le Roy Ladurie's concept "microbian unification of the world" is also clearly present in Braudel's work.

climate and world demographic change, not between climatic change and change in social and economic structures.

Rondo Cameron, however, is critical of Braudel's attempt to prove one hypothesis (parallel demographic movements and a relatively stable division of the world's fluctuating total population among the several land masses) by another (climatic change).[61] Braudel's hypotheses indeed do need verification. One should add, however, that they were made in terms of the *Annales* conception of history as inquiry and of the corollary that inquiry proceeds by the perception of data, the formulation of hypotheses, the verification of the latter by means of additional data, the rejection or modification of the original hypotheses, and so forth.

Another American historian, John D. Post, directs his criticisms to Le Roy Ladurie. A specialist in environmental history who interprets the post-Napoleonic world economic crisis as the product of agricultural shortages and these, in turn, of a worldwide climatic disturbance, Post contends that historical data are available for some of the greater ecological disasters, such as those of 1315–1317, 1591–1597, 1643–1653, 1687–1700, 1812–1817, and 1845–1847, although he attributes these disasters not to the action of the jet stream—at least not directly—but to major volcanic eruptions. He further believes that Le Roy Ladurie should have been able to find an intimate correspondence between climatic change and economic change.[62] One may argue in Le

61. Cameron, "Europe's Second Logistic," p. 457.
62. John D. Post, "Meteorological Historiography," *Journal of Interdisciplinary History*, III (Spring 1973), 721–32, a review article with a focus on Le Roy Ladurie, *Times of Feast, Times of Famine*. See also Post, "A Study in Meteorological and Trade Cycle History: The Economic Crisis Following the Napoleonic Wars," *Journal of Economic History*, XXXIV (June 1974), 315–49, and his unpublished doctoral dissertation, "The Economic Crisis of 1816–1817 and Its Social and Political Consequences," Boston University, 1969. For a further examination of the relationships among climate, disease, demographic calamities, and economic strains at the end of the eighteenth and in the early nineteenth centuries, see Lucette Valensi, "Calamités démographiques en Tunisie et en Méditerranée orientale

Roy Ladurie's behalf that he does not deny a connection between meteorological fluctuations and short-term economic change and that Post himself discusses the ecological disasters in question not in the framework of the long run but only as short-term phenomena. Moreover, the imprecise and fragmentary nature of pre-nineteenth-century data on agricultural production and productivity would caution prudence to the prudent and avoidance of the hasty linkages that Post would like to state immediately. To his credit, Le Roy Ladurie has achieved his immediate goal of "a pure climatic history."

Pierre Chaunu maintains, indeed, that Le Roy Ladurie's *Histoire du climat depuis l'an mil* is an even more important book than his main doctoral dissertation, *Les Paysans de Languedoc*.[63] It consequently may not be irrelevant to note that one of the main threads in both books, as well as in his articles published under the title *Le Territoire de l'historien*, is the treatment of social facts, in a language at once pithy and learned, descriptive and analytical, as if they were things, along with a readiness to install men (in the generic sense), "eventually quantified, in a geohistorical, biological, and indeed purely physical environment."[64] By simultaneously treating social facts as things and using historical data meticulously, he even succeeds in purifying the environment of history and therefore separating the more enduring from the less enduring.

As for a precise definition of the relationship between climatic history and long-term environmental and economic history, what may have to precede it is an extended *enquête*—a mode of inquiry

---

au XVIIIe et XIXe siècles," *Annales ESC*, XXIV (November–December 1969), 1540–61; M.-H. Chérif, "Expansion européenne et difficultés tunisiennes de 1815 à 1830," *Annales ESC*, XXV (May–June 1970), 714–45.

63. Pierre Chaunu, "Le Climat et l'histoire: A propos d'un livre récent," *Revue historique*, CCXXXVIII (October–December 1967), 365.

64. Comment on the inside flap of the jacket of Le Roy Ladurie, *Le Territoire de l'historien*. On the historiographical conceptions of Pierre Nora, editor of the collection in which this book is included, "Bibliothèque des Histoires," see Chap. 8 below.

used by Lucien Febvre and Marc Bloch to observe history in the process of its construction, often by means of intensive communication with other disciplines. In 1961, indeed, the *Annales* returned to this mode of inquiry, and among the first of the new *enquêtes* was an investigation into "the history of material life and of biological behavior," under which Braudel included five categories of human organization and action—biology and demography, food and nutrition, clothing and shelter, living standards (the kind and quantity of material goods that a society makes available to its various members), and the techniques of production and other forms of interaction between the natural and cultural milieus.[65]

Pursuing this mode of research, an *Annales* team under the direction of Jean-Jacques Hémardinquer and with the aid of Jacques Bertin's cartographical laboratory has undertaken an analysis of the changing geographical distribution of cultivated plants[66] and domesticated animals and has produced a valuable *Atlas of Food Crops*.[67] The Sixième Section's Centre de Recherches Historiques envisages, moreover, a further series of atlases on the circulation of peoples and of plastic and musical art forms in diverse geohistorical settings.[68]

65. Fernand Braudel, "Retour aux enquêtes," *Annales ESC*, XVI (May–June 1961), 421–24; Fernand Braudel, "Vie matérielle et comportements biologiques: Bulletin No. 1," *ibid.*, pp. 545–49, under the rubric "Enquêtes ouvertes."

66. Jacques Bertin, "Principe de l'Atlas," *Annales ESC*, XXI (September–October 1966), 1014–15, followed by the observations on cultivated plants by Jean-Jacques Hémardinquer, Michael Keul, and W. G. L. Randles, pp. 1016–24, all included under the general authorship of the Centre de Recherches Historiques, "Pour un Atlas d'histoire de la vie matérielle: Cartes historiques des cultures vivrières," pp. 1012–24.

67. Jacques Bertin, Jean-Jacques Hémardinquer, Michael Keul, and W. G. L. Randles, *Atlas des cultures vivrières, Atlas of Food Crops*, Ecole Pratique des Hautes Etudes (VIe Section), "Geographical and Chronological Survey for an Atlas of World History" (Paris, The Hague: Mouton, 1971).

68. Centre de Recherches Historiques, "Pour un Atlas d'histoire de la vie matérielle," pp. 1012–14.

Annales scholars have shown an especially keen interest in scrutinizing the relations between a given milieu and its occupational groups—in depicting city, port, village and forest as distinctive forms of environment.[69] More precisely, they have been drawn to the Vidalian notion of *genres de vie* (ways of life and occupation), so threatening to conservative (but not all) Marxists who, despite an evident bent for social questions, manifest only an infrequent concern for cultural (either in the narrow or in the anthropologist's sense) and biological or demographic themes.

The medievalist Maurice Lombard thus sought to create a "retrospective geography" of production and exchange and circulation in the Muslim world by mapping the places of origin of commodities that were scarce in that world—timber, furs, skins, feathers, ivory, and slaves—and the Muslim cities in which such raw materials were traded, consumed, or transformed. He thereupon was able to distinguish between the cities that were principally consumers of naval timber and those that required wood for their sugar mills or for the manufacture of eating and drinking utensils, for their glass and pottery manufactures, or for their decorative crafts. Having dealt with this problem, he was able to perceive that supplies of timber and wood were increasingly more difficult for the Muslim world to obtain as the commercially "useless forest"—to use the terminology of another scholar—of

69. Sixième Section studies of ports are generally published as part of a series called "Ports, routes, trafics." Its studies of rural life usually are included in the series "Les Hommes et la terre," of which the most significant volume may be *Villages désertés et histoire économique, XIe-XVIIIe siècle*, Ecole Pratique des Hautes Etudes (VIe Section), "Les Hommes et la terre," 11 (Paris: S.E.V.P.E.N., 1965). See also Jacques Le Goff and Ruggiero Romano, "Paysages et peuplement rural en Europe après le XIe siècle," *Etudes rurales*, No. 17 (April–June 1965), pp. 5–24. On forests and forest life, see Michel Devèze, *La Vie et la forêt française au XVIe siècle*, 2 vols. (Paris: S.E.V.P.E.N., 1961); Michel Devèze, *Histoire des forêts*, "Que sais-je?" No. 1135 (Paris: Presses Universitaires de France, 1965); Michel Devèze, "Superficie et propriété des forêts du Nord et de l'Est de la France vers la fin du règne de François Ier (1540–1547)," *Annales ESC*, XV (May–June 1960), 485–92.

northern Europe became an increasingly "precious forest,"[70] that is, as Europe developed its own manufactures and shipping soon after the close of the eleventh century.[71]

A scholar who has made a signal contribution to our knowledge of the forest is also the author of a book on the communication of goods, ideas, services, and people (travelers, migrants, and invaders) that depicts eighteenth-century Europe as a group of receiving cultures as well as of donor cultures. Their impact on the rest of the world and the world's influence on them generally varied with the approximate distance of each prospective donor and receiver from the sea.[72] Braudel's own fondness for geography and conceivably his fascination with the idea of two types of society—land-based administrative and sea-based commercial—may have been crucial in persuading him to publish in his own Flammarion collection a French version of Edward W. Fox's brilliant and conceptually provocative *History in Geographic Perspective*.[73]

The *Annales* proclivity for a definition of spatial relationships (Hermes and Hestia) has encouraged collaboration with classicists who have taken note of the custom of ancient Greek society to

70. Bernard Berthet (posthumous), "De la forêt inutile à la forêt précieuse: Dans le Jura au XVe et au XVIe siècle," *Annales ESC*, VI (April–June 1951), 145–53.

71. Maurice Lombard, "Un problème cartographié: Le Bois dans la Méditerranée musulmane (VIIe–XIe siècles)," *Annales ESC*, XIV (April–June 1959), 234–54; Maurice Lombard, "La Chasse et les produits de la chasse dans le monde musulman, VIIIe–Xe siècles," *Annales ESC*, XXIV (May–June 1969), 572–93. See also Maurice Lombard (posthumous), *L'Islam dans sa première grandeur* (*VIIIe–XIe siècle*), in series "Nouvelle Bibliothèque Scientifique" (Paris: Flammarion, 1971), pp. 161–234, and Lombard's collection of articles, *Espaces et réseaux du haut Moyen âge* (Paris, The Hague: Mouton, 1972).

72. Michel Devèze, *L'Europe et le monde à la fin du XVIIIe siècle*, in series "L'Evolution de l'Humanité" (Paris: Albin Michel, 1970).

73. Edward Whiting Fox, *History in Geographic Perspective: The Other France* (New York: Norton, 1971), translated by M. d'Argenson as *L'Autre France: L'Histoire en perspective géographique*, in series "Nouvelle Bibliothèque Scientifique" (Paris: Flammarion, 1973).

give a symmetrical or geometrical organization to their institutions
—to define many relationships in terms of distance and position.[74]
It also has promoted close relations with folklorists and anthropologists, and it has stimulated interest in the Mediterranean distinction between a feminine inner space (kitchen, hearth, house) and
a masculine outer space (public square, men's society known in
Provence as *chambrette,* among others).[75] More recently, it has
enabled Pierre Chaunu to combine in new form the work of
economic anthropology and of such "spatial" economists as
Johann Heinrich von Thünen, Walter Christaller, August Lösch,
Claude Ponsard, François Perroux, Lucien Brocard, and Paul
Claval, and formulate a historical theory of four "circles of
communication."

The fourth circle is barely four or five centuries old: a world
market economy in which, according to Claval, there develops
through standardization a multiplicity of market forms, including
labor markets, land markets, transportation markets, abstract as
well as concrete markets, money markets, security markets,
commodity markets, and service markets. Some parts of the
globe, moreover, were without a third circle of communication—
a regional price-based economy—until after the diffusion of a
world market economy. Limited to a radius of about fifty
kilometers, the second circle was comprised of local markets,
presumably price-based if a third circle existed but probably
functioning in terms of some other criterion of redistribution if
the third circle of communication was absent. Formed by rural
collectivities, the first circle of communication had a radius of

74. Marcel Detienne, "En Grèce archaïque: Géométrie, politique et
société," *Annales ESC,* XX (May–June 1965), 425–41; Jean-Pierre Vernant,
"Espace et organisation politique en Grèce ancienne," *ibid.,* pp. 576–95, a
review of Pierre Lévêque and Pierre Vidal-Naquet, *Clisthène l'Athénien:
Essai sur la représentation de l'espace et du temps dans la pensée politique
grecque de la fin du VIe siècle à la mort de Platon* (Paris: Les Belles-
Lettres, 1964).

75. Lucienne A. Roubin, "Espace masculin, espace féminin en com-
munauté provençale," *Annales ESC,* XXV (March–April 1970), 537–60.

about five kilometers and was able to retain nine-tenths of its production during the major part of its history.[76] Chaunu's theory, of course, needs much elaboration and clarification. Were all societies endowed with one fixed local circle, or did some—hunters, food collectors, pastoralists—lack a fixed circle of small dimension? What societies had only two circles of communication? Were they all peasant societies? Under what conditions was a third circle formed? Is the term "circle" the best possible nomenclature, or is some other designation preferable, such as ring or hexagon?

Hestian preoccupations, moreover, have impelled another *Annales* scholar, Paul Leuilliot, to define the basic principles of local history—that is, of the first and second of Chaunu's circles of communication. According to Leuilliot, local history is essentially qualitative in outlook since it so often lacks adequate reliable data. When available, moreover, local data must be used with great caution, for peasants may exaggerate in one sense while landlords and officials may overstate the case in another sense. To a much greater extent than general history, local history is differential by definition since each community is different from every other. In addition to possessing a differential character, local history is basically sectorial, directing its attention to the sectors for which data are available. But its qualitative, differential, and sectorial aspects dictate that it be concrete, that it deal with daily life and practice, including the invisible and durable aspects of daily life. These four characteristics of local history oblige the local historian to manifest considerable flexibility—to orient his studies around one community or another, one sector or another, around quantitative and qualitative aspects equally or around the qualitative aspects in the main, around one or another aspect of daily life and long duration, visible or in-

76. Chaunu, *Histoire, science sociale*, pp. 188–93; Paul Claval, *Géographie générale des marchés*, "Cahiers de Géographie de Besançon," 10, Annales Littéraires de l'Université de Besançon, LVIII (Paris: Les Belles Lettres, 1962), pp. 40–90.

visible. The very disadvantages of local history may thus be turned into a valuable asset, for local history—the discipline—cannot be conducted in an ivory tower. It consequently may be used to awaken public interest in general history. Moreover, through a confrontation of the concrete, individual, and particular elements of local history with general and theoretical history, the local historian can serve the function of restructuring general and theoretical history, challenging untenable "university" or fashionable Parisian modes, rash or premature historical syntheses.[77]

The Hermaean-Hestian scholarship embraces in addition the "material and figurative objects" and the "signs and symbols" of a society, for the historian must study not only words and artifacts but music and dance forms, posters and billboards, as well as the more conventional works of art, and the multiple languages of science, of the theater, and of the cinema; indeed, all the works and images of art and industry to which a society assigns significations and by means of which it expresses itself.[78] Above

77. Paul Leuilliot, "Préface: Défense et illustration de l'histoire locale," in Guy Thuillier, *Aspects de l'économie nivernaise au XIXe siècle,* Ecole Pratique des Hautes Etudes (VIe Section), Centre d'Etudes Economiques, "Etudes et mémoires," 60 (Paris: Armand Colin, 1966), pp. viii–xix (vi–xxix). For a fine example of the applicability of local history to general history by an *Annales*-influenced American historian, see Jay Harvey Smith, "Village Revolution: Agricultural Workers of Cruzy (Hérault), 1850–1910," Ph.D. dissertation, University of Wisconsin, Madison, 1972.

78. Pierre Francastel, "Histoire de la civilisation: Temps modernes," in Comité International des Sciences Historiques, *IXe Congrès International des Sciences Historiques, Paris 28 août–3 septembre 1950,* I, *Rapports* (Paris: Armand Colin, 1950), pp. 343–45, 354 (341–66). On the function of the historian in the making of historical documentary films, see Annie Kriegel, Marc Ferro, and Alain Besançon, "L'Expérience de 'La Grande Guerre,'" *Annales ESC,* XX (March–April 1965), 327–36; Marc Ferro, "1917: History and Cinema," *Journal of Contemporary History,* III (October 1968), 45–61. The subject of the last two articles is the documentary film "La Grande Guerre," a 1964 Franco-German coproduction, made by Marc Ferro and Solange Peter and under the historical direction of Henri Michel, to commemorate the fiftieth anniversary of the war. On the applicability of

all, perhaps, he must study the cinema, which has given a "fluid" quality to contemporary time and space.[79]

Since Hermes presides over relations between members of the same political unit as well as over relations among states, *Annales* scholarship should have admitted political history into its orbit of concern. But being distrustful of the kind of political history that was little more than a string of political and diplomatic events— *histoire événementielle* or *histoire historisante*,[80] as they derisively called it—they ultimately equated all political history with the rejected form—*histoire événementielle*—even though *Annales* cofounder Marc Bloch was himself the author of a political history—*La Société féodale*—that was not a string of heterogeneous political events but careful "analysis and explication of a [particular] social structure," that is, of "the feudal structure":[81] an explanation of political relationships and structures in terms of social, psychological, technological, and economic factors.

---

graphic methods to the study of images, see Jacques Bertin, *La Sémiologie graphique* (Paris: Gauthier-Villars, 1967); Christian Metz, "Réflexions sur la 'Sémiologie graphique' de Jacques Bertin," *Annales ESC*, XXVI (May–August 1971), 741–67, with a reply by Bertin, pp. 768–70.

79. Edgar Morin, *Le Cinéma ou l'homme imaginaire: Essai d'anthropologie sociologique* (Paris: Editions de Minuit, 1956), reviewed by Robert Mandrou, "Histoire et cinéma," *Annales ESC*, XIII (January–March 1958), 140–49.

80. Fernand Braudel, "Histoire et sciences sociales: La Longue durée" (hereafter cited as "La Longue durée"), *Annales ESC*, XIII (October–December 1958), 728–29 (725–53). First translated by Sian France as "History and the Social Sciences: The Long Term," *Social Science Information, Information sur les sciences sociales*, IX (February 1970), 145–73, and then as "History and the Social Sciences," in Peter Burke, ed., *Economy and Society in Early Modern Europe: Essays from "Annales"* (London: Routledge & Kegan Paul, 1972; Harper Torchbooks, 1972), pp. 11–42. The Sian France translation has been reprinted, with a shortened section on communication and social mathematics, in Fritz, Stern, ed., *The Varieties of History: From Voltaire to the Present*, 2d ed. (New York: Meridian Books, 1972).

81. Marc Bloch, *La Société féodale*, 2 vols., in series "L'Evolution de l'Humanité" (Paris: Albin Michel, 1939–1940), I, 7.

As a whole, however, so long as it was made up mostly of
sixteenth-century and seventeenth-century specialists, and of few
medievalists and equally few specialists of antiquity and of the
eighteenth, nineteenth, and twentieth centuries, the *Annales*
School neglected political history, subordinated it to economic
and social history, failed to take note of the partly autonomous
character of political action, or were thought to be doing—and
often thought themselves to be doing—any one or all of these
things. Some historians from outside the *Annales* circle and some
philosophers, sociologists, and political scientists were upset by
the decline of political history in France,[82] but the general
tendency to shy away from political history continued among
French scholars from 1941 to about 1960.

In 1961, however, the medievalist Philippe Wolff called for
the systematic study of the interaction between political factors
or functions and economic, social, and intellectual functions.[83]
In 1963, partly in response to Raymond Aron's attempt, in *Paix
et guerre entre les nations* (1962), to develop a theory of international relations, Braudel opened the pages of the *Annales* to a
debate on the prospects of a "scientific politicology."[84] A year

82. Marrou, *De la connaissance historique*, p. 62; Pierre Renouvin, "Histoire des faits politiques: Epoque contemporaine," in Comité International
des Sciences Historiques, *IXe Congrès International des Sciences Historiques*, I, 572–92; René Rémond, "France: Work in Progress," in Walter
Laqueur and George L. Mosse, eds., *The New History: Trends in Historical
Research and Writing since World War II* (New York: Harper & Row,
1967), pp. 34–47; first published, along with the other articles in the book,
as Volume II, 1 (1967), of the *Journal of Contemporary History;* René
Rémond, "L'Histoire, science du présent," *Revue de l'enseignement
supérieur*, No. 44–45 (1969), 90–95.

83. Philippe Wolff, "L'Etude des économies et des sociétés avant l'ère
statistique," in Samaran, ed., *L'Histoire et ses méthodes*, pp. 866–67 (847–
91).

84. Raymond Aron, *Paix et guerre entre les nations* (Paris: Calmann-
Lévy, 1962), translated by Richard Howard and Annette Baker Fox as
Peace and War: A Theory of International Relations (Garden City, N.Y.:
Doubleday, 1966); "Pour ou contre une politicologie scientifique," *Annales
ESC*, XVIII (January–February 1963), 119–32; XVIII (May–June 1963),

later the medievalist Bernard Guenée made a vigorous plea for the study of political states in the context of the relations of each state with its society's symbolic, economic, and social functions. He further recommended that in place of "political history," scholars adopt Henri Pirenne's and Marc Bloch's term "history of the state," at least so long as existing prejudices continued to envenom the older nomenclature.[85]

Since the mid-1960s, *Annales* scholars themselves have begun to bemoan the neglect of political history, and one of them criticized Braudel for his alleged failure to show the interdependence between "economic conjunctures" (cycles) and "political conjunctures."[86] Soon thereafter, the *Annales* editor who succeeded Braudel as head of the Centre de Recherches Historiques in 1972, Jacques Le Goff, evaluated *La Méditerranée* as "the greatest book produced by the *Annales* school" but found fault with it for its conception of political history as a "history of events," which were relegated to the book's third part. Consequently, scoffed the medievalist Le Goff, "far from being the culmination of the work," the third part "is more like the bits and pieces left over. Once the backbone of history, political history has sunk to being no more than the atrophied appendix: the parson's nose of history."

475–98, with a brief introduction by Fernand Braudel (p. 119) followed by the comments of François Chatelet, Annie Kriegel, Victor Leduc, Pierre Renouvin, Bertrand de Jouvenel, Alain Touraine, and Raymond Aron.

85. Bernard Guenée, "L'Histoire de l'Etat en France à la fin du Moyen âge vue par les historiens français depuis cent ans," *Revue historique*, CCXXXII (October–December 1964), 331–60; Glénisson, "L'Historiographie française contemporaine," p. xxxvii. For later conceptualizations by Bernard Guenée of political organization in the Middle Ages, see his "Espace et Etat dans la France du bas Moyen âge," *Annales ESC*, XXIII (July–August 1968), 744–58; "Y a-t-il un Etat des XIVe et XVe siècles?" *Annales ESC*, XXVI (March–April 1971), 399–406.

86. Frédéric Mauro, *Le XVIe siècle européen: Aspects économiques*, "Nouvelle Clio," 32, 2d rev. ed. (Paris: Presses Universitaires de France, 1970), pp. 308–9, 355. The first edition (1966) does not contain this criticism.

Le Goff failed to allude, however, to the analytical chapters in the second part of both *Méditerranée* editions on polemology or The Forms of War and on The Empires—the relationship between the size of states and their chances of success under different historical conditions of organization of state finances, prebends, and transportation. What he argued instead was that Braudel should have applied his framework of three time cateogories—episodic, conjunctural (cyclical), and structural—to political history as well as to the other types, and he reasoned that if political history need no longer serve as the "backbone" of history, it must remain nevertheless as its "nucleus." To allow it to play such a role, however, historians must be able to represent it as a study of power relationships.[87]

One way to achieve this, suggested Le Goff, is to examine the message systems (he does not use the term itself) by means of which a society comprehends power both ideally and in practice —for example, in terms of Georges Dumézil's three Indo-European "functions," force, production-reproduction, and sovereignty or the right to regulate spatial and temporal limits—[88] and to

87. Jacques Le Goff, "Is Politics Still the Backbone of History?" trans. Barbara Bray, *Daedalus*, C (Winter 1971), 1–19, entire issue entitled "Historical Studies Today." For Le Goff's own prior application of his recommendations, see his *La Civilisation de l'Occident médiéval.*

88. Georges Dumézil's studies include the following among many others: *Jupiter, Mars, Quirinus: Essai sur la conception indo-européenne de la société et sur les origines de Rome* (Paris: Gallimard, 1941); *Naissance d'archanges* (Paris: Gallimard, 1945); *L'Idéologie tripartie des Indo-Européens* (Brussels: Latomus, 1958); *Heur et malheur du guerrier: Aspects mythiques de la fonction guerrière chez les Indo-Européens* (Paris: Presses Universitaries de France, 1969), translated by Alf Hiltebeitel as *The Destiny of the Warrior* (Chicago: University of Chicago Press, 1970). See also S. Scott Littleton, *The New Comparative Mythology: An Anthropological Assessment of the Theories of Georges Dumézil* (Berkeley and Los Angeles: University of California Press, 1966), and Pierre Smith and Dan Sperber, "Mythologiques de Georges Dumézil," *Annales ESC*, XXVI (May–August 1971), 559–86. The same issue of *Annales*, pp. 639–52, contains an article by the American Byzantinist Dean A. Miller, "Royauté et ambiguïté sexuelle," on the tripartite basis of Byzantine society. On the

scrutinize its political semiological system, its signs and symbols of political communication (political vocabulary, rites, behavior, and public opinion).

Le Goff contends, moreover, that there are no immobile societies and that there is no necessary opposition between supposedly immobile structures, more mobile conjunctures (crises), and highly mobile events.[89] Political realities, too, are ever changing. As anthropologists Georges Balandier and Catherine Coquery-Vidrovitch have noted, political power may be defined as a hierarchy of unequal but ambiguous and unstable authoritarian and proprietary relationships that are simultaneously revered and hated or successively accepted and contested.[90]

Political history may thus acquire a new legitimacy among *Annales* historians. It may do so more easily indeed than social history, toward which *Annales* spokesmen have long been ambivalent. Despite Bloch's commitment to the analysis of social structures, for example, Lucien Febvre explained the presence of the term "social" in the several titles of their review simply in terms of contingency. The word is useless, he wrote, to the

---

possible transition in Europe from the three functions to the three estates, see John Batany, "Des 'Trois Fonctions' aux 'Trois Etats'?" *Annales ESC,* XVIII (September–October 1963), 933–38.

89. Jacques Le Goff, "Histoire et ethnologie: L'Historien et l'homme quotidien,'" in *Mélanges en l'honneur de Fernand Braudel,* II, *Méthodologie de l'histoire et des sciences humaines* (Toulouse: Edouard Privat, 1973), p. 243 (233–43), published in English as "The Historian and the Common Man," in Jérôme Dumoulin and Dominique Moïsi, eds., *The Historian Between the Ethnologist and the Futurologist: A Conference Sponsored by the International Association for Cultural Freedom, by the Giovanni Agnelli Foundation, and by the Giorgio Cini Foundation, Venice, April 2–8, 1971* (Paris, The Hague: Mouton, 1973), pp. 204–15. The latter book was published in French under the title *L'Historien entre l'ethnologue et le futurologue,* Ecole Pratique des Hautes Etudes (VIe Section), Sciences Economiques et Sociales, "Le Savior historique," 4 (Paris: Mouton, 1972).

90. Georges Balandier, *Anthropologie politique,* 2d rev. ed. (Paris: Presses Universitaires de France, 1969), pp. 38–39, 42–50, 92–103; Catherine Coquery-Vidrovitch, "Anthropologie politique et histoire de l'Afrique Noire," *Annales ESC,* XXIV (January–February 1969), 143–44 (142–63).

extent that it means too many things. Since all history is social,
there is no such thing as social history. The term is nevertheless
useful because of its very ambiguity.[91]

A similar ambivalence is reflected in Braudel's readiness, on the
one hand, to recommend that scholars study social conjunctures
and structures[92] and, on the other, to criticize the notion of
societies for its extreme vagueness. Braudel proposes instead a
history of "socio-économies,"[93] which (under the name "Eco-
nomico-Social History") Pierre Léon conceives as a study of the
"intimate and perpetual interference between the Economic and
the Social." Likewise favorably disposed toward a history of
what he calls "économies-sociétés" is Le Roy Ladurie, who applies
nevertheless to the quasi-immobility of Western Europe between
1300/1320 and 1720/1730 the label of "traditional eco-demo-
graphic" history on the ground that the economic fluctuations
of the preindustrial era were more likely to be inspired by demographic forces than the other way around.[94] Yet another *Annales*
scholar, Frédéric Mauro, rejects the notion of social structure
altogether on the premise that "every social organization is
political or economic." How, therefore, can there be an autonomous social history?[95]

On the other hand, social historian Adeline Daumard argues
that economic factors should no more be accorded a privileged
position in industrial societies than in preindustrial ones, since
they tend to compartmentalize historical factors that need to be

91. Lucien Febvre, "Vivre l'histoire: Propos d'initiation," *Combats pour
l'histoire*, pp. 19–20 (18–33), reprinted from *Mélanges d'histoire sociale*,
III (1943), 5–18.
92. Braudel, "Sur une conception de l'histoire sociale," p. 318.
93. Braudel, *Civilisation matérielle*, I, 436.
94. Pierre Léon, "Histoire économique et histoire sociale en France:
Problèmes et perspectives," in *Mélanges en l'honneur de Fernand Braudel*,
II, 303–15; Emmanuel Le Roy Ladurie, "L'Histoire immobile," *Annales ESC*,
XXIX (May–June 1974), 673, 689 (673–92), Collège de France inaugural
lecture, Nov. 30, 1973.
95. Mauro, *Le XVIe siècle européen*, pp. 310, 330–53.

brought together. The integrating or totalizing function belongs to social history.[96] Pierre Chaunu, who shares Braudel's and Léon's belief in the fundamental necessity to link économies and sociétés, acknowledges nevertheless that the social tends in practice to be dissolved in the economic simply because it is far less well defined. Regarding economic history as the first major conquest of historians, he identifies social history as an incomplete second conquest because of the inability of its practitioners to quantify the social. This defect will be remedied, however, as social history improves its links with economic history and extends them to an emergent quantitative history at a "third level" —collective psychology.[97]

Despite these divergent attitudes, *Annales* scholars can move on toward the goal of a sound social history by means of the elements of a general communications theory taken over by Braudel from Claude Lévi-Strauss and adapted to the needs of the historian. In particular, Braudel has espoused Lévi-Strauss's view that communication proceeds at three levels of expression— the exchange of women (the level of kinship and other social arrangements), the exchange of goods and services, and the exchange of other types of messages.[98] Like Lévi-Strauss, moreover, he distinguishes between conscious and unconscious forms, although he fails to mention whether the unconscious forms exist at all three levels of expression. Distinguishing, too, between three units of temporal measure—the time of structures, the time of

96. Adeline Daumard, "Données économiques et histoire sociale," *Revue économique*, No. 1 (January 1965), pp. 69, 75–79, 85 (62–85). Medievalist Philippe Wolff, on the contrary, sees no desirable way of separating the social from the economic in "L'Etude des économies et des sociétés avant l'ère statistique," in Samaran, ed., *L'Histoire et ses méthodes*, pp. 850–52 (847–92).

97. Pierre Chaunu, "Les Entraves au changement dans les sociétés et les mentalités en Amérique latine au XVIIIe siècle," *Revue d'histoire économique et sociale*, LI (1973), 57 (54–68).

98. Claude Lévi-Strauss, *Anthropologie structurale* (Paris: Plon, 1958), 326.

conjunctures, and the time of events—he envisions each as operating both at conscious and at unconscious levels.[99]

If we accept the full implications of Braudel's conceptualizations, we must conclude that a systematic analysis of the general communications system of a given collectivity would require the identication of at least eighteen (3 x 2 x 3) subsystems. If full allowance was made for interactions between subsystems, however, and matters were not complicated by the production of configurations that were not equal to the sum of their components, the resulting number of subsystems would be 256. This last number is obtained by raising 2 (interaction exists, interaction does not exist) to the eighth power (3 + 2 + 3).

Annales scholars do not seem to have pronounced themselves, however, on the general theory of communications of the anthropologist Edward T. Hall, who divides the overall communications system of society into ten different primary message systems —symbolic interaction, association, subsistence, bisexuality, territoriality, temporality, learning, play, defense, and the use or exploitation of materials. Hall further maintains that each message system is expressed at three levels—formal (structured), informal or situational (unstructured), and technical (under which would be included art, religion, science, and the like)— and in terms of three components—isolates (such as the sounds of a spoken language), sets (such as words), and patterns (hierarchically ordered sets).[100]

One may argue with Hall over the adequacy of the names for some of the proposed message systems. In the place of subsistence, for example, one may prefer consumption, including under it

99. Braudel, "La Longue durée," pp. 725–53.

100. Edward T. Hall, *The Silent Language* (Greenwich, Conn.: Fawcett Publications, 1959), pp. 45–62, 66, 94–98. Hall identifies four modes of temporality—the time of cultural messages, a longer time of personal messages, a still longer time of political messages, and a fourth temporal mode, of the longest duration, that operates at the level of whole societies and civilizations. Braudel's three modes of temporal reference are logically more satisfying than Hall's *particular* four modes.

food, clothing, shelter, and fashion (ostentation).[101] Perhaps, too, a new message system of goods and service exchange should be added, while Hall's defense system might be separated into two parts, the organization and distribution of power and defense against disease. Braudel's treatment of time, moreover, seems more plausible, and space or territoriality might be treated in part in the manner suggested by anthropologist Robert T. Anderson, who has discovered—much as has Edward W. Fox, despite differences of detail—that an adequate explanation of Western European civilization between 1000 and 1800 would require the study of "a complex of three essentially different cultures"— aristocratic, bourgeois, and peasant—each with its own separate territorial base.[102]

If one combines the Lévi-Strauss–Braudel–Hall–Anderson interpretations, one may have to conclude that the systematic treatment of certain types of historical problems requires the conceptualization of three kinds of time, three kinds of space, two poles of awareness—with the elements at the unconscious end possibly rising to a more conscious level as one passes from the brief time span of striking and fleeting events to the longer one of conjunctures and the still longer time span of structures[103] —and ten different message systems (a modification of Hall's ten by the removal of temporality and territoriality, the separation of defense into two systems, and the addition of goods and service exchange). The analysis of an overall communications system thus might call for the identification of 180 ($3 \times 3 \times 2 \times 10$) different subsystems. A further breakdown into formal, informal, and technical expressions, and into isolates, sets, and patterns

---

101. Lévi-Strauss, *Anthropologie structurale*, pp. 67–68; Roland Barthes, "Pour une psycho-sociologie de l'alimentation contemporaine," *Annales ESC*, XVI (September–October 1961), 977–86, reprinted in Jean–Jacques Hémardinquer, ed., *Pour une histoire de l'alimentation*, "Cahiers des Annales," 25 (Paris: Armand Colin, 1967), pp. 307–15.

102. Robert T. Anderson, *Traditional Europe: A Study in Anthropology and History* (Belmont, Calif.: Wadsworth, 1971), pp. 15–16.

103. Braudel, "La Longue durée," pp. 739–40.

might raise the number of subsystems to 1,620 (180 × 3 × 3). But if one makes allowance for interactions, and further assumes that the interactions will always be equal to the sum of their parts, the resulting number of subsystems would be 2 (interaction exists, interaction does not exist) to the eighteenth power (3 + 3 + 2 + 10) in the first case and 2 to the twenty-fourth power (3 + 3 + 2 + 10 + 3 + 3) in the second—that is, respectively, 262,144 and 16,777,216 subsystems.

With the aid of the computer, it should be possible to analyze even 16,777,216 variables. One problem remains, however. Who would read the enormous number of printouts?[104] As Charles Péguy observed, "To exhaust the indefiniteness, the infinity of detail required to know the whole reality," may be the supreme folly[105]—at least until new forms of human organization have evolved and the human mind itself has been vastly improved.

It is not folly, however, to pursue a Hermaean-Hestian approach and to quantify whenever quantification is feasible and likely to be useful. No historian has produced thus far a more complete system of communications analysis than Braudel, and no group of historians has honored Hermes (and hidden Hestia) with a greater eloquence of deed than the *Annales*. While avoiding the supreme folly, however, it should be possible for the *Annales* and like-minded historians everywhere to go forward toward a still more conscious, explicit, and audacious definition of the communications paradigm. This, however, would necessitate going much beyond the research teams of artisanal enterprise, vaunted time and again by the *Annales*, toward a wholly

104. In making these computations, I have followed the helpful advice of my colleague Rudolph M. Bell.

105. Charles Péguy, *Le Choix de Péguy: Oeuvres choisies 1900–1910* (Paris: Gallimard, copyright 1952), pp. 144–45, on what he calls "la méthode de la grande ceinture." See also Charles Péguy, "Clio: Dialogue de l'histoire et de l'âme païenne," *Oeuvres en prose 1909–1914*, avant-propos and notes by Marcel Péguy (Paris: Gallimard, copyright 1957), pp. 146–50 (93–306). Péguy's "Clio" is available in English translation in *Temporal and Eternal* (London: Collins, 1958).

new type of integrated research—responsive to mass data, quantification, and *prospective* and interdisciplinary orientations[106]—
under the direction of research institutions like the former
Sixième Section (1946–1974) and the Maison des Sciences de
l'Homme. It is doubtful that the discipline of history can afford
to remain a modest "science à petit moteur." To prove its utility
for today's needs and tomorrow's, historians must make it useful
for today and tomorrow.

106. Michel François, "Organisation collective de la recherche historique,"
in Samaran, ed., *L'Histoire et ses méthodes,* pp. 1454–64.

4 An Impossible *Histoire Globale*

Communications analysis with a temporal perspective is often confused with another *Annales* method and goal—*histoire globale* or, as it was known at first, *histoire totale*. The confusion may arise from a certain overlapping and from the consequent failure of *Annales* scholars to distinguish carefully between the two.

Histoire globale is also equated sometimes with universal history, or history on a global scale. One of the most prolific historians of the twentieth century, Pierre Chaunu, thus hailed the first volume of Braudel's *Civilisation matérielle et capitalisme,* calling its embrace of the rule of "global" or "planetary weight" (*pesée globale* or *pesée planétaire*) "the great epistemological event of the social sciences." Chaunu subsumes under the rule of global weight the determination of explicit or implicit relationships between individual cultural traits and whole cultural complexes (societies, economies, civilizations), and a conception of time and space that results in a history of the unity and diversity of cultures and civilizations that have been kept apart or made to mingle by continental and oceanic obstacles and aids.[1]

Histoire globale is not attained, however, simply by examining problems in a world-historical framework, nor even by viewing them in terms of the total communications spectrum. It does require discarding the notion of an *event* as a visible and tangible

1. Chaunu, "La Pesée globale," p. 139.

historical "atom" that is given meaning by its chronological situation beside other historical atoms regardless of how these differ from one another.[2] It also demands the study of whole units of human action as social or cultural networks of dynamic— that is, neither wholly coherent nor wholly incongruous—relationships.

The prelude to the innovation of histoire globale was the rejection of a history of heterogeneous events, followed by Lucien Febvre's definition of a fact, in 1933—at his Collège de France inaugural lecture in the new Chair of Modern Civilization —as an operational construct. An historical fact, too, is an invention or construct, with a basis in the observer's orientations and in the general state of knowledge. Its reliability consequently will vary from time to time, depending upon how well it can be confirmed by men's multifarious ways of symbolizing—written, oral, verbal, mathematical, gesticulative, monumental or commemorative, aesthetic, and technical—and by the fluctuating state of knowledge. If we define a fact as a construct, moreover, we shall have to concur with Philippe Ariès—for whom an historical fact is similarly "a construction of the historian"—that total history "eliminates neither political nor military fact. It distrusts only the notion of isolated" and heterogeneous events.[3]

An historical fact may be an event, that is, an action or ensemble of actions characterized by novelty, suddenness, short duration, narrow spatial limits,[4] and the absence of repetition and triteness.[5] But all historical facts, maintained Lucien Febvre, are not of this type. Some have an unconscious basis, and some are of long duration and broad spatial dimension, thus ascertainable only by reference to geography, demography, ethnography,

2. Marrou, *De la connaissance historique*, pp. 304–5.
3. Philippe Ariès, *Le Temps de l'histoire* (Monaco: Editions du Rocher, 1954), pp. 280, 305.
4. Henri Lévy-Bruhl, "Une notion confuse: Le Fait historique," *Recherches philosophiques*, V (1935–1936), 264–74.
5. Braudel, *Civilisation matérielle*, I, 434.

linguistics, economics, technology, psychology, and other disciplines. Properly defined, an historical fact is not simply the kind
of construct that we call an event. It is any kind of historical
construct or abstraction.[6]

It is doubtful, however, that Febvre would have regarded the
later "counterfactual" constructs of American cliometricians, or
"new economic historians," as acceptable historical facts. Nor is it
even certain that he would have admitted Max Weber's ideal types
under this rubric. But following Febvre's own basic argument that
history, like chemistry (the discipline), creates its own object, that
wing of the *Annales* School which disapproves of narrowly
monetary and cyclical explanations of economic development has
welcomed the attempt of American cliometricians to formulate

6. Lucien Febvre, "De 1892 à 1933: Examen de conscience d'une histoire
et d'un historien" (Collège de France inaugural lecture, Dec. 13, 1933),
Combats pour l'histoire, pp. 3–17, reprinted from *Revue de Synthèse*, VII
(June 1934), 93–106. Febvre reaffirmed his 1933 views in "Les Recherches
collectives et l'avenir de l'histoire," *Revue de Synthèse*, XI (February
1936), 7–14, reprinted in *Combats pour l'histoire*, pp. 55–60; in a communication of July 20, 1949, "Vers une autre histoire," *Combats pour
l'histoire*, pp. 419–38, reprinted from *Revue de métaphysique et de morale*,
LVIII (1949); and in his "Avant-propos" to Charles Morazé, *Trois essais
sur histoire et culture*, "Cahiers des Annales," 2 (Paris: Armand Colin,
1948), pp. v–viii. Carl Becker defined an "historical fact" somewhat
analogously not as a "past event" but as a "more or less appropriate . . .
symbol, a simple statement which is a generalization of a thousand and one
simpler facts which we do not for the moment care to use, and this generalization itself we cannot use apart from the wider facts and generaliza-
tions which it symbolizes." See Carl L. Becker, "What Are Historical
Facts?" *Western Political Quarterly*, VIII (September 1955), 327–40. One
of Becker's students, Leo Gershoy, has taken a similar stand: "Pragmatically
speaking, historical facts, however numerous and detailed, did not take
on significance for me until by using them and not ignoring them, I made
them come to life. In that figurative sense I created them. Their existence
could not be denied, but it was my selection that brought them into the
world of history by lodging them in my mind for the purposes to which
I intended to employ them." "Some Problems of a Working Historian," in
Hook, ed., *Philosophy and History*, pp. 62–63. Whereas Becker and
Gershoy arrive at a moderate relativism, members of the *Annales* School
sought to cope with problems of globality, functionality, and dysfunction.

problems more precisely and to apply econometric methods to historical interpretations. Through one of its representatives, Maurice Lévy-Leboyer, it nevertheless has been critical of the new economic history for its narrow temporal framework, for its failure to seek a "global interpretation," and for its excessive reliance on "historical simulation."[7] *Annales* criticism is directed thus less against the method than against the shortcomings of its applications. It is similar indeed to the criticism of the American economist Wassily W. Leontief, who has called for greater use of models susceptible of empirical verification instead of the continued elaboration of model types that defy empirical testing.[8] It resembles most of all, however, the self-criticism of the new economic historians themselves. They acknowledge that the new economic history "will never be literature," that it sometimes has applied "irrelevant models to history," that it "has been too narrowly focused in space and time," and that it has put too much stress on problems of growth and efficiency and too little on distribution and equity. They agree, furthermore, that its range of theoretical constructs has been too narrow, since it has tried to exploit neither multisector general-equilibrium models nor "models which involve the interrelationship among economic, political, and social variables."[9]

However Lucien Febvre might have reacted to the new eco-

7. Maurice Lévy-Leboyer, "La 'New Economic History,'" *Annales ESC*, XXIV (September–October 1969), 1035–65.

8. Wassily W. Leontief, "Theoretical Assumptions and Nonobserved Facts," *American Economic Review*, LXI (March 1971), 1–7 (presidential address, 83d meeting of the American Economic Association, Detroit, Michigan, Dec. 29, 1970).

9. Lance E. Davis. "'And It Will Never Be Literature'—the New Economic History: A Critique," *Explorations in Entrepreneurial History*, 2d ser., VI, 1 (1968), 75–92; Albert Fishlow and Robert W. Fogel, "Quantitative History: An Interim Evaluation, Past Trends and Present Tendencies," *Journal of Economic History*, XXXI (March 1971), 31. For a critique of counterfactual history by a nonpractitioner, see Fritz Redlich, "Potentialities and Pitfalls in Economic History," *Explorations in Entrepreneurial History*, 2d ser., VI, 1 (1968), 93–115.

nomic history that was only beginning at the time of his death, he was convinced that an historical product acquires deeper meaning through its capacity for endurance and that a construct may be made more significant by being situated formally in a series. Once these things occur, even the formulation of historical laws may be possible. In no event, however, should the historian start out with a system. If a system results, it should be the product of carefully laid constructs. It should be subject also to constant revision, correction, and rejection.[10]

Despite Febvre's valuable contribution to the definition of fact and historical fact, there was no histoire globale until after the adoption of the concept of social structure by Marc Bloch (Lucien Febvre preferred other terms), the completion of Braudel's *Méditerranée*, and the diffusion among *Annales* historians of the concept of economic structure. The term "economic structure" had already been in use among economists by the late 1930s, but the concept itself was clarified only in the late 1940s and early 1950s through the work and thought of such economists as François Perroux, Jean Lhomme, René Clémens, Henri Guitton, André Marchal, and Alexandre Chabert. Clémens, for example, distinguished between the oscillatory variations of cyclical change and the mutational variations of structural change. Guitton saw a close relationship between structural disparities and regional (spatial) disparities. Marchal sought to rehabilitate the "long period" in economic analysis. Some structural variables, he held, may play the role of "motor forces" to a greater extent than others:

But the mechanism is complex. The diverse structures evolve independently, some more rapidly than others and in one direction or

10. Lucien Febvre, "L'Individualité en histoire: Le Personnage historique," in Centre International de Synthèse, *L'Individualité*, Troisième Semaine Internationale de Synthèse (Paris, 1933), p. 133 (123–46); Lucien Febvre, "De la création en histoire: A la mémoire de Georges Jamati" [deceased, a former literary director of the Centre National de la Recherche Scientifique], *Annales ESC*, XI (July–September 1956), 292–95; Mann, *Lucien Febvre*, pp. 29–32.

another, even in opposite directions, generating the maladjustments that simultaneously account for the "crisis" or "alteration" of the system and the "mutation" or "passage" from one system to another. These maladjustments finally cause the system to "snap" [*craquer*] and thus give the lie to our conception of it as a "coherent complex of structures." For there is a certain "accountability" of structures that prevents maladjustments from reaching undue proportions or lasting too long. One day a new adjustment will be made, and there will come into being a new "coherent complex of structures," a new system.[11]

On the basis of the research of these scholars, we may define an economic structure as the organization of a given economic variable, its relative significance to the overall economic system, and its precise relationship to each of the other economic variables—cost, prices, income, money, interest rates, and so forth—in the same space-time, when factors of cyclical or oscillatory movement (conjunctures) have been discounted. Economic structures are of unequal plasticity. To the extent that an economic structure is the product of very slowly changing, or relatively stable, noneconomic natural (climate, geography, natural resources, and demography) and cultural (religion, morality, psychology) factors, it is likely to be endowed with a long life. But since it is also the product of interacting political, economic, and technological factors, it will possess some degree of instability, especially in societies founded on the principle of change and, above all, in those founded on the principle of economic growth. Where prices, costs, income, money, and interest rates are given approximately equal weight and where they bear a similiar relationship to one another over a long period of time, a common set of economic structures may be said to exist. Where there is a common set of economic structures, one often will find a common set of social structures.[12]

11. André Marchal, "Prise de conscience: Structure et concept de période," *Revue économique*, No. 6 (November 1954), p. 924 (917–25).
12. François Perroux, *Cours d'économie politique* (Paris: Domat-Montchrestien, 1941), I, 78; François Perroux, *Les Comptes de la nation:*

Even before the notion of economic structure had matured, however, and contributing to its maturation, Braudel's elaboration of his conception of total history appeared in *La Méditerranée*. This was followed in 1958—under the influence of a large body of thought, including the work of the economists mentioned above, concerned with the problem of structure—by a still more systematic explanation of his views on temporal frames of reference, historical structures, and total history in a justly famous article entitled "La Longue durée":

For social observers, structure means organization, coherence, and relatively stable relationships between social masses and other realities. For historians, it similarly signifies an assembly and an architecture, but it also defines a reality that time alters little and conveys well. Certain structures persist for so long that they become the stable elements of many generations. They encumber history. They hamper, therefore command, its outflow. Other structures molder more quickly. But all are simultaneously props and obstacles. As obstacles, they form boundaries (or *envelopes*, in the mathematical sense) from whose authority people are hardly ever able to free their experiences. Just think how hard it is to shatter certain geographical

---

Apparences et réalités dans notre comptabilité nationale (Paris: Presses Universitaires de France, 1949), pp. 13–14, 151–55; Henri Guitton, "Théorie des cycles et théorie des espaces," *Economia Internazionale: Revista dell' Istituto di Economia Internazionale*, V (November 1952), 748–59, with résumés in Italian, English, German, and Spanish; René Clémens, "Prolégomènes d'une théorie de la structure économique," *Revue d'économie politique*, LXII (November–December 1952), 971–1001; Jean Lhomme, "Matériaux pour une théorie de la structure économique et sociale," *Revue économique*, No. 6 (November 1954), pp. 843–80; Jean Lhomme, "Essai de comparaison entre les structures économiques et les structures sociales," *Revue économique*, No. 5 (September 1956), 689–708; André Marchal, "De la dynamique des structures à la dynamique des systèmes," *Revue économique*, No. 1 (January 1955), pp. 1–34, with a résumé in English; Alexandre Chabert, *Structure économique et théorie monétaire: Essai sur le comportement monétaire dans les pays sous-développés* (Paris: Armand Colin, 1956), pp. 6–11, 23, 68–74. The entire issue of *Revue économique*, No. 6 (November 1954), is devoted to the subject of economic structure, with articles by Jean Lhomme, Johan Åkerman, Manlio Resta, Maurice Flamant, and André Marchal.

frames, biological realities, barriers to increased productivity, and even spiritual constraints. For mind sets, too, are prisons of long duration.[13]

While Braudel's view of structures is similar to that of the economists who conceive of structure in terms of space-time-action relationships, it puts greater emphasis on human action as a function simultaneously of temporal relationships and of spatial relationships. The spatial or topological aspect receives full stress through the Hermaean-Hestian approach to history. The temporal aspect receives its full share through histoire globale.

One prerequisite to histoire globale, then, is the definition of a fact as a construct, and another is the notion of structure. A third—overlapping in point of time with the second—is Braudel's conception of three main arrangements of duration: duration at a quasi-immobile level of structures and traditions, with the ponderous action of the cosmos, geography, biology, collective psychology, and sociology; a level of middle-range duration of conjunctures or periodic cycles of varying length but rarely exceeding several generations; a level of short duration of events, at which almost every action is boom, bang, flash, gnash, news, and noise, but often exerts only a temporary impact.

Among the three levels, rhythms, or modes of action and organization in Braudel's model of temporality exist many correspondences. He admits even an order among the thousands of heteroclite traits of a given culture or civilization, however much some of the traits may appear like strangers to one another.[14] But it may not always be possible to determine a precise correspondence. In that event, we should speak only of coexistence. His object, according to the conclusion of the second edition of La Méditerranée, was therefore to write a history on three successive rolls, or registers, at three levels, on the basis of three different temporal schemes; to apprehend not only the points at

---

13. Braudel, "La Longue durée," p. 731.
14. Braudel, *Civilisation matérielle*, I, 435.

the different times of a culture converge but also those at they diverge the most, or at which there are interferences intradictions. He concedes the model's shortcomings by recognizing that reality comprises not just three temporal schemes but a throng—ten, a hundred, or a good many dozens, each with its own special history. To transcend the model stage, histoire globale must seek to perceive all the multitudinous forms of duration (durée).[15]

Jack Hexter observes, however, that "the most remarkable and successful works of historians within the orbit of the Annales school have not been constructed in precise emulation of La Méditerranée." Indeed, hardly any other Annales scholars have ordered their data systematically into three different temporal schemes, and they have not done so, according to Hexter, because Braudel's work

falls short of its author's intention in one major respect; it does not solve the historiographical problem that it poses: how to deal with the perennial historiographical difficulty of linking the durable phenomena of history with those that involve rapid change. First, the tripartite division of durées may better be referred to as the residual trinitarianism of a mentalité once Christian than to any inherent rational necessity. In the crunch Braudel himself recognizes that between the Platonic poles of total stability and instantaneous change there are durées of the most varied length—"ten, a hundred." Second, the three durées are somewhat arbitrarily attached to the specific subject matters—longue to the geographic, social, and cultural; moyenne to the economic and sometimes the social; courte, in fact if not in theory, to the political.[16]

The objection to Braudel's use of the ternary model is unreasonable on at least two grounds. First, as Braudel himself care-

---

15. Braudel, La Méditerranée, I, 12–17; II, 516–20; Braudel, Civilisation matérielle, I, 10–12, 433–37; Braudel, "Histoire et sociologie," Écrits sur l'histoire, pp. 106, 112 (97–122), article published originally as a chapter in Georges Gurvitch, ed., Traité de sociologie, 2 vols. (Paris: Presses Universitaires de France, 1958–1960), I, 83–98.

16. Hexter, "Fernand Braudel," pp. 532–33.

fully explains, correspondences between durable, intermediate, and rapidly changing historical phenomena should be sought but will not necessarily always be found. Second, Braudel does not confuse the model with reality, but rather utilizes it to get closer to the realities.

Because his model has much in common with Marx's model of interacting levels of society,[17] it has won the sympathy of some of France's foremost Marxist historians. C.-E. Labrousse, for example, distinguishes, much as Braudel does, between quick change in the economic sphere, the slower change of social structures, and the very slow change of mental structures;[18] and Pierre Vilar diverges little from Braudel in his contention that *total history* "comprises not only all factors but all types of historical time. Histories of ideas, no less than social and economic histories, fulfill a needed function primarily insofar as they reconstruct the mutual relations, and above all the hierarchical and dialectical interdependence, between '*économies, sociétés, civilisations.*' " It is the historian's duty, adds Vilar, to take advantage of the methods of psychology and of other disciplines to effect an historical synthesis. Historians will succeed, however, only to the extent that they neither dehumanize history by confining their focus to the long run nor impede the perception of

17. Eric J. Hobsbawm, "Karl Marx's Contribution to Historiography," *Diogenes*, No. 64 (Winter 1968), p. 45 (37–56).

18. Ernest Labrousse, "Introduction" to *L'Histoire sociale, sources et méthodes: Colloque de l'Ecole Normale Supérieure de Saint-Cloud (15–16 mai 1965)* (Paris: Presses Universitaires de France, 1967), p. 5 (1–5), and Labrousse's comment at a session "Structure et mouvement en histoire," in *Structuralisme et marxisme* (Paris: Union Générale d'Edition, 1970), p. 157 (articles and debates published during 1967–1968 in *Raison présente*). Non-Marxist medievalist Georges Duby similarly believes that a value system changes more slowly than economic, demographic, or power structures. See Georges Duby, "L'Histoire des systèmes de valeurs," *History and Theory*, XI, 1 (1972), 15–25, translated as "History of Systems of Values," in Dumoulin and Moïsi, eds., *The Historian Between the Ethnologist and the Futurologist*, pp. 216–27.

the subtleties, intricacies, and differences in the rates and qualities
of change by limiting their sights to the very short run.[19]

Marxists put a greater stress than Braudel, however, on dialectical forces. Robert Mandrou, a former *Annales* editorial secretary
who seems subsequently to have taken a Marxist path, thus
defines "total history" (*histoire totale*) as "a dialectical history"
of ceaseless interaction among the political, economic, and cultural, as a result of which the "whole society" (*société globale*)
is ultimately transformed.[20] Albert Soboul similarly defines structure (which like other Marxists he generally calls social structure)
not only as "an organic ensemble of simultaneously economic,
social, and psychological relations and coherences of long duration," but also as "a tissue of contradictions" that should be
scrutinized in its dynamic, violent, or dialectical, as well as static,
aspects. Soboul, indeed, makes a distinction between structuralist
analysis and historical analysis. Structural analysis, he contends,
proceeds on the principle that structures will remain intact if
they are left to themselves, whereas historical analysis espouses
the hypothesis that structures contain in themselves from the
start the constituent elements of their own ultimate destructuring.[21]

The Marxist philosopher Louis Althusser has taken another
line, criticizing Febvre, Braudel, and Labrousse for concentrating
on a whole society as an expression of different temporal rhythms

19. Pierre Vilar, "General History and Economic History," typescript
translation by David R. Ringrose of "Historia general e historia económica,"
Moneda y crédito, No. 108 (March 1969), pp. 3–21.

20. Robert Mandrou, interviewed by Antoine Casanova and François
Hincker, "Histoire sociale et histoire des mentalités," *La Nouvelle Critique*,
n.s., No. 49 (230) (January 1972), pp. 41–44. Mandrou was *Annales*
editorial secretary from 1954 to 1962.

21. Albert Soboul, "Description et mesure en histoire sociale," in *L'His-
toire sociale*, pp. 14-22 (9–25, and discussion, 26–33); Albert Soboul, *La
Civilisation et la Révolution française*, I, *La Crise de l'Ancien Régime*
(Paris: Arthaud, 1970), pp. 33–36; Pierre Vilar, "Histoire marxiste, histoire
en construction: Essai de dialogue avec Althusser," *Annales ESC*, XXVIII
(January–February 1973), 166 (165–98).

rather than as a representation of hierarchical relationships, and thus for failing to grasp "the structure of the whole." This is not to say that Althusser rejects the notion of different types of time. He finds indeed not only visible but *invisible* temporal rhythms as well in politics, technology, ideology, philosophy, and so on, which must be constructed since they cannot be perceived directly. But the visible and invisible temporal realities and constructs and the various lags between one rhythm and another must be explained. Even if one accepts the hypothesis of the relative autonomy of each kind of time, one should go beyond a mere juxtaposition of time levels to a determination of the reasons for the interferences, lags, and correspondences.[22]

Althusser infers, in effect, that Braudel's humanist scheme lacks Montesquieu's law of totality and unity. In other words, while accepting the idea of a whole society, Braudel has not adopted Montesquieu's view that every state (and inferentially every society) is guided by its own internal "adequate" or "contradictory" reason—adequate if viewed as a static model, contradictory if conceived as a dynamic model of historical evolution.[23]

The absence of a law of totality and unity in Braudel's work is no accident, however. It results from the *Annales* School's horror of system and from the journal's pragmatic and unphilosophical quality (one way in which the *Annales* differed from Henri Berr's *Revue de synthèse historique*). Although ready to derive a general outlook from its constructs, the School is reluctant to base its constructs on a system. The absence of such a law

22. Louis Althusser, "Esquisse du concept d'histoire," *La Pensée*, No. 121 (May–June 1965), pp. 3–21. Born in Algiers in 1918, Althusser has taught philosophy at the École Normale Supérieure in Paris since 1948. For a Marxist defense of the philosophical outlook of Febvre, Labrousse, and Braudel, as opposed to Althusser's and Michel Foucault's, see Vilar, "Histoire marxiste," pp. 165–98. By focusing on Althusser's conception of history as a variety of "histories," however, Vilar misses the essence of Althusser's criticism of the *Annales* School of history.

23. Louis Althusser, *Montesquieu: La Politique et l'histoire* (Paris: Presses Universitaires de France, 1959), pp. 37, 42–46.

has a basis also in Lucien Febvre's hostility to the very term "structure," despite Marc Bloch's early use of it, and in Fernand Braudel's own ambivalence toward a mathematical conceptualization of structures.[24]

At the height of Braudel's success in the United States, following the translation into English of *La Méditerranée* and *Civilisation matérielle*, Richard Mowery Andrews evaluated the *Annales* and Braudel's accomplishments as "a revolution in historical thought, the only one commensurate with our century and its global necessities." Earlier evaluations, however, had sometimes been different, especially in the United States. An American historian and an Italian alike, for example, had seen in the first edition of *La Méditerranée* not "a revolution" in historical method but an eloquent summary and analysis of a large body of knowledge divided into three parts. His American critic, Bernard Bailyn, had reprimanded Braudel for his failure to relate the parts to a central problem—for confusing "a poetic response to the past" with the identification of a problem.[25] A French sociologist had further censured Braudel for the impreciseness of his notion of structure,[26] while a New World historian was taken aback as late as 1971 by the "vague theorizing" in Braudel's articles.[27]

Braudel has replied that the historian should avoid defining a

24. Braudel, "Histoire et sociologie," *Ecrits sur l'histoire*, pp. 108–9; Braudel, "Lucien Febvre et l'histoire," *Annales ESC*, XII (April–June 1957), 180 (177–82), reprinted from *Education Nationale*, Dec. 13, 1956.

25. Richard Mowery Andrews, review of Braudel, *The Mediterranean*, in *New York Times Book Review*, May 18, 1975, pp. 1–3, 42–45; Bernard Bailyn, "Braudel's Geohistory—A Reconsideration," *Journal of Economic History*, XI (Summer 1951), 277–82. An Italian reviewer was, like Bailyn, struck by the lack of integration between the events of the third part and the first two parts of Braudel's book: Giuseppe Martini, "Una 'geo-historia' del Mediterraneo," *Belfagor: Rassegna di varia umanità*, VI, Jan. 31, 1951, 70–80.

26. Claude Lefort, "Histoire et sociologie dans l'oeuvre de Fernand Braudel," *Cahiers internationaux de sociologie*, XIII (1952), 123 (122–31).

27. See J. H. M. Salmon's review of Braudel's *Ecrits sur l'histoire*, in *History and Theory*, X, 3 (1971), 354 (346–55).

structure with too much exactness. The historian's structuralism should lead not to "mathematical precision" but to the apprehension of "the very sources of life in life's most concrete, most everyday, most indestructible, most anonymously human manifestations."[28] Histoire globale—as he referred increasingly to the new historical goals and methods—should aim at bringing people and individuals to the center of attention and noting all the realities that impinge on them, including their own collective realities, and all the realities that they in turn affect. Braudel may have indeed opted for the term "histoire globale" over "histoire totale" because of his discomfort at the thought that a total history conceived as *histoire-structure*—history with long duration as the single temporal dimension or history with a penchant for the discovery of a society's internal cohesion, consensus, or reason—was too "totalitarian" and might act to remove people from the scene. In any event, Braudel prefers Voltaire to Montesquieu not only because he believes Voltaire to have been endowed with a more critical spirit but also because Montesquieu gave little heed to persons.[29]

Braudel may be a structuralist by temperament as he claims, but his structuralism is that of a poet, painter, theatrical director, or music conductor. He communicates not only with the logic of words but with the poetry and music of words as well, and with the total effect of his tableaux and orchestrations. In the work of such an historian, even geographic entities such as the sea may be "raised to the rank of historical personages."[30] For this historian, the world is theater, and he as director must reconstruct whole spatial, visual, sonic, rhetorical, and dramatic

28. Braudel, *La Méditerranée*, II, 520.

29. Fernand Braudel, "Histoire et sciences humaines," lectures et Collège de France, Jan. 12 and Mar. 2, 1966.

30. Lucien Febvre, "Un Livre qui grandit: *La Méditerranée et le monde méditerranéen à l'époque de Philippe II*," *Pour une histoire à part entière*, p. 169 (167–79), a review of the first published version of Braudel's *Méditerranée*, published originally in *Revue historique*, CCIII (April–June 1950), 216–24.

units. In the final analysis, however, the director must return to the actors, without whom there would be no theater.[31]

Without ever having dealt directly with the issue, contends J. H. Hexter, Braudel has been guided by "two mutually exclusive aspirations," two different conceptions of history—"histoire totale" and "histoire-problème." In practice, however, his choice appears to have gone to histoire totale, which travels "under the standard of abundance." The world of Braudel and of the Sixième Section is characterized by "a deluge of information and documentation," by "a torrent of words," by "abundance at the risk of surfeit."[32]

These last comments reflect Roland Mousnier's acrid critique, in 1965, of the trend in the character of the main thesis for the *doctorat ès lettres*. Proposing a reduction of the principal thesis to 300–500 pages, Mousnier denounced the "plump books" (*livres dodus*) of a thousand and even three thousand pages and more that passed for theses despite their lack of systematic and rigorous analysis. Written in "an abundant and tumultuous style, characterized by a torrent of words, by numerous violent images, by a luxury of metaphor, by the aim to excite the imagination and nerves and by the quest for sensation and the 'sensational,'" they call to mind "advertising and propaganda techniques but for their lack of the terse, summary style of advertising."[33] By implication, these statements seem to have been aimed also at the *Annales* School. Braudel anticipated at least one of Mousnier's objections, however, with his own criticism of the otherwise excellent work of Pierre Chaunu for its excessive length and discursive style, thus for having sacrificed dramatic unity to the goal of length. Within three years of Mousnier's chiding remarks, Braudel re-

31. Braudel, "La Longue durée," pp. 730–31; Braudel, "Histoire et sociologie," *Ecrits sur l'histoire*, p. 106.

32. Hexter, "Fernand Braudel," p. 511.

33. Roland Mousnier, "Notes sur la thèse principale d'histoire pour le doctorat ès lettres," *Revue historique*, CCXXXIV (July–September 1965), 123–27.

turned to the theme, citing Pierre Vilar's three-volume doctoral dissertation, *La Catalogne dans l'Espagne moderne*, to prove his point that quality depends not on shortness or length but is rather a function of other critical variables.[34] During the same year Le Roy Ladurie reflected on the irony of the fact that the educational reform designed to give earlier recognition to young scholars (by means of the more elementary thesis *de troisième cycle*) had worked in fact to delay fulfillment of the requirements toward the *doctorat d'Etat*. Candidates further aggravated the matter by their unswerving belief that a thesis would be judged inadequate unless it was, in the current slang, a *brique* (brick) or *pavé* (cobblestone), comprising several volumes of more than two kilograms each. Arguing that the late age at which many candidates were granted the state degree was both economically wasteful and morally demeaning, Le Roy Ladurie proposed, prior to more fundamental reform to be undertaken later, that deserving persons be awarded the state doctorate on the basis of other accomplishments—a book, articles, pedagogical achievements.[35]

Mousnier's and Hexter's criticisms of the "plump books" and of a history that travels "under the standard of abundance" have, in part at least, a different objective: to defend the case of history-as-problem against total history. In Hexter's words, history-as-problem is preferable by far because it "proceeds under the sign of elegance. It is the point in the constellation of its forms

34. Braudel, "Pour une histoire sérielle," *Ecrits sur l'histoire*, pp. 151–53; Braudel, "La Catalogne, plus l'Espagne, de Pierre Vilar," *Annales ESC*, XXIII (March–April 1968), 375 (375–89). At least one book inspired by Fernand Braudel and *Annales* thought—my own—is notable, however, for its brevity, a mere 232 pages: Traian Stoianovich, *A Study in Balkan Civilization* (New York: Knopf, 1967). But this work perhaps fails to conform to Braudel's model of history since it deals with structures and destructuring and restructuring over a very long period instead of going from the long time span to the short or from the short to the long.

35. Emmanuel Le Roy Ladurie, "Apologie pour les damnés de la thèse," *Le Monde*, Sept. 19, 1968, reprinted in Le Roy Ladurie, *Le Territoire de l'historien*, pp. 537–42.

where history comes closest to mathematics. For elegance of demonstration is a mathematic conception and criterion; the elegant solution enjoys the minimum number of steps."[36]

If conflict does exist in the work of Braudel and other members of the *Annales* School between the aspiration of histoire globale and the goal of history-as-problem, that conflict is not, however, inevitable. The two goals are likely indeed to be complementary when the historian represents acts and works as signs endowed with temporal, spatial, and social significations and capable of being inserted in a series. In that case, there is no essential difference between history-as-problem and histoire globale, for the inquiry extends then to an historical problem in its holistic aspects, and that in effect is what histoire globale is about. Braudel's history differs from this only in one notable respect. It is—or may be—histoire globale with theater. History-as-problem properly executed is histoire globale limited to the investigation of a single general historical fact, usually without the benefit of theater.

Histoire globale risks remaining a vague and confusing concept, however, unless it is perceived as a product of at least three different, if not unrelated, traditions. It represents, for example, the extension to history of a tendency manifest in epistemology, biology, field-theory physics, and Gestalt, or configurationist, psychology, during the 1920s and 1930s, to replace "the earlier purposive view with that of wholeness."[37] But total history derives also from Marx's conception of the "total man" and "total society"—that is, from his belief in the potential presence of a whole society in an individual man or individual human reality, in consequence of which he rejected both the materialistic con-

36. Hexter, "Fernand Braudel," p. 537.

37. Ernst Cassirer, *The Problem of Knowledge: Philosophy, Science and History since Hegel*, trans. William H. Woglon and Charles W. Hendel (New Haven: Yale University Press, 1950), pp. 212–13. See also William Morton Wheeler, "Present Tendencies in Biological Theory," *Scientific Monthly*, XXVIII (February 1929), 104–5 (97–109).

ception and the alienating subjectivist notion of society as an ideal type or transcendental category, different from the individuals who comprise it, in favor of a total view of all things that affect man and that man affects.[38] A third tradition comes from the anthropology of Marcel Mauss, which maintains that a "total social fact" is expressed socially, psychologically, and historically, and that the observer is included in each observation, just as the symbolic system of the unconscious is contained in each fact observed. The family, for example, becomes a total social fact when it is scrutinized in terms of the totality of its functions and of all the scientific disciplines that can illuminate it—in other words, when it is viewed as a particular form of juridical, economic, religious, political, aesthetic, and morphological (endowed with the ability to change form temporarily or regularly) action and organization.[39] Mauss did not remove "the whole man" (*l'homme complet*) from his analysis, but he did redirect attention to the *functions* of a total social fact. More than this, he was intrigued by the relationships among the various social facts in a given society—between mental and social forms, for example.

More recently, Claude Lévi-Strauss has expressed doubt that all structures (total social facts) in a given society are part of the same system, and Lucien Sebag has affirmed categorically that a society is not a unified or coordinated totality, but rather is made up of "the juxtaposition of logics with only partial reference to

---

38. Georges Gurvitch, "La Sociologie du jeune Marx," *La Vocation actuelle de la sociologie: Vers une sociologie différentielle* (Paris: Presses Universitaires de France, 1950), pp. 581–84 (568–602). See also pp. 27 and 91–93 for Gurvitch's comments on Marx's and Mauss's concepts of totality.

39. Marcel Mauss, "Essai sur le don: Forme et raison de l'échange dans les sociétés archaïques," *Sociologie et anthropologie* (Paris: Presses Universitaires de France, 1960), pp. 143–279 but especially 273–79, published originally in *Année sociologique*, n.s., I (1923–1924), 30–186, translated by Ian Cunnison as *The Gift: Forms and Functions of Exchange in Archaic Societies*, with an introduction by Edward Evan Evans-Pritchard (London: Cohen and West; New York: Free Press, 1954).

one another."[40] Lévi-Strauss's conception of structural analysis, moreover, calls for the reduction of variables to the smallest possible number and for the examination of each structure, for disciplinary purposes at least, as part of a closed system. He further insists that a structure is identifiable not in terms of its exposed contents but rather in spite of them. A structure, he maintained—in his inaugural lecture in the Chair of Social Anthropology at the Collège de France (January 5, 1960)—is not simply the visible arrangement of parts, as claimed by the English anthropologist A. R. Radcliffe-Brown, but the internal cohesion normally inaccessible to simple empirical observation. It is not part of empirical reality but rather exists at the level of the unconscious categories present in the myths, rites, and religious representations of societies and their institutions.[41] Lévi-Strauss's goals and methods are thus both complementary to and, in some respects, at variance with the demands of histoire globale.

Other scholars, however, have been attracted to the adjective "global" and to the notions it subsumes. The psychologist Ignace Meyerson, for example, has pinpointed the major direction of anthropologist Lucien Lévy-Bruhl's research as "the whole mental fact" (le fait global de la mentalité).[42] And at least as early as 1950, the sociologist Georges Gurvitch employed the term "société globale," drawing within the scope of his definition of "whole society" not only those social groups and facts that are in harmony with the whole society's hierarchical principles and provisions for altering hierarchical arrangements, but also those secret, proscript, and scapegoat groups and (by inference) taboos that are contained negatively or are included in some ways while

40. Jean Viet, Les Méthodes structuralistes dans les sciences sociales, Maison des Sciences de l'Homme—Service d'Echange d'Informations Scientifiques, Publication Série D, "Méthodes et techniques," 1 (2d ed.; Paris, The Hague: Mouton, 1967), pp. 128–30; Lucien Sebag, Marxisme et structuralisme (Paris: Payot, 1964), p. 153.

41. Lévi-Strauss, Anthropologie structurale deux, pp. 28, 99–100, 322–23, 353.

42. Meyerson, Les Fonctions psychologiques, p. 127.

being excluded in others. Some groups of this last type even enjoy autonomies that the whole society may not normally violate.[43] Gurvitch also clearly distinguished between concrete societies and types of whole society. Whole social structures (*structures sociales globales*), he held, characterize a type of whole society from which a concrete society may diverge through the manifestation of astructural and nonstructured traits.[44]

No later than 1958, under the influence of the thought of Marcel Mauss and perhaps of Ignace Meyerson but especially of Georges Gurvitch, Braudel adopted the term "global" to describe his own approach to history. Calling history "an extraordinary holistic science of man" (*une impossible science globale de l'homme*) and identifying history and sociology as the only holistic social sciences, the only sciences able to "stretch their curiosity to any aspect of the social,"[45] he thereafter tended to designate his own conception of history "histoire globale,"[46] whereas Marxists attuned to *Annales* thought have clung more tenaciously to the term "total history."

Histoire globale comprises, in effect, the study of whole social units and of whole societies along the directions pointed out by Mauss and Gurvitch but with Braudel's added dimension of social totality in terms of all the forms of duration contained therein—a "precarious equilibrium" of structures, conjunctures, and events. Braudel thus rhetorically asks, "Who would maintain that at each *synchronic* slice of its history the social in its totality does not enter the fray with its becoming and therefore evoke a constantly different image despite the repetition of a thousand former details and realities? That is why the idea of a holistic structure [*structure globale*] of society fazes the historian and makes him uneasy, even if allowances are made—as they should

---

43. Gurvitch, *La Vocation actuelle de la sociologie*, pp. 321–38.

44. Georges Gurvitch, "Les Sociétés globales et les types de leurs structures," *Traité de sociologie*, I, 216–35.

45. Braudel, "Histoire et sociologie," *Ecrits sur l'histoire*, pp. 103, 106.

46. Braudel, "Pour une histoire sérielle," *ibid.*, p. 138.

be—for a considerable gap between holistic structure and whole reality."[47] That is why, in discussing forms of mentality, Ignace Meyerson perceives a need to examine both "simultaneous diversity" and "successive variations."[48]

Braudel's histoire globale demands an inquiry into diverse durations. Apart from Braudel himself, however, few members of the *Annales* School (Le Roy Ladurie and Pierre Chaunu are among the notable exceptions) have undertaken this practice. Instead, in the mid-1960s, even as Le Roy Ladurie emerged as a visible advocate of "very long duration," Adeline Daumard proposed that, until social history attains greater maturity, historians limit their chronological scope to the biological and cultural cycle of an individual "active and lucid life"—consequently to some fifty years—or at most to a period of three generations, or about a century. She justified her maximum chronological scope of three generations on the ground that "each individual benefits from the experience of his parents and participates in that of his children."[49]

Daumard's interpretation may have an indirect foundation in the view of the nineteenth-century philosopher-mathematician Antoine-Augustin Cournot that each generation learns customarily not only from its own members but from the immediately preceding and the immediately succeeding generations. Because there is a mix of ages in society, differences between successive generations sometimes are not easily perceived. But if societies are reviewed at intervals of approximately one century, it may be found that the society imposing its institutions over a given space at one time is quite dissimilar from that occupying the same territory a century later.

Cournot's discerning comments on generations, on a *siècle* as a series of three successive generations, and on centuries as dis-

47. Braudel, "Histoire et sociologie," *ibid.*, pp. 114–15.
48. Meyerson, *Les Fonctions psychologiques*, p. 134.
49. Adeline Daumard, "Données économiques et histoire sociale," pp. 62–85.

continuous phenomena[50] all seem ultimately to have entered into Daumard's frame of reference. The idea of discontinuity, stressed so much by Cournot, Febvre,[51] and Braudel, has not, however, been uppermost in her mind. Unlike Cournot, but in keeping with one of the main interpretations of third-generation *Annales* scholarship, she maintains that the French Revolution did not represent a major discontinuity between the eighteenth and nineteenth centuries.[52]

Daumard's recommendation to defer long duration to generational studies may have led her, in fact, to neglect the search for possible discontinuities and thus unintentionally expose herself to being thought—merely because she was not concerned with the long term—an advocate of the doubtful view that long duration is the sum of certain short durations, that long-term phenomena can be understood simply by piling up and organizing short-term or middle-term data.[53] But if one rejects the concept of historical

50. A.-A. Cournot, *Considérations sur la marche des idées et des événements dans les temps modernes,* 2 vols. (1872; reprint, New York: Burt Franklin, 1972), I, 119–35, Chap. VIII, significantly entitled "De l'ère des temps modernes et de leur coupure par espaces séculaires."

51. Febvre, "Vivre l'histoire," pp. 18–33.

52. Adeline Daumard, "Une référence pour l'étude des sociétés urbaines en France aux XVIIIe et XIXe siècles, projet de code socio-professionnel," *Revue d'histoire moderne et contemporaine,* X (July–September 1963), 185–210. See also the exchange of views between Adeline Daumard, Albert Soboul, and C.-E. (or Ernest) Labrousse, in *L'Histoire sociale,* pp. 168–72, 175–76, with Soboul as a protagonist of discontinuity, Daumard favoring continuity, and Labrousse taking a middle position.

53. For a rejection of the additive conception of long duration, see Witold Kula, *Théorie économique du système féodal: Pour un modèle de l'économie polonaise 16e–18e siècle,* trans. rev. and enlarged ed., Ecole Pratique des Hautes Etudes (VIe Section), "Civilisations et sociétés," 15 (Paris, The Hague: Mouton, 1970), p. 84; "Etat des recherches sur l'histoire économique quantitative de la Belgique," December 1971, statement of the research objectives of a group of Belgian scholars at the Law Faculty of the University of Liège who aspire to achieve a quantitative economic history of Belgium considered as a whole society, joined to a letter from P. Lebrun, May 12, 1972.

discontinuities, it is perfectly logical to focus on generational and other short-term and conjunctural studies on the basis of which a general history presumably can be written later.

Professor Daumard considers herself indeed a partisan of total history despite her call for the postponement of studies of the "longue durée." Her conception of total history falls short of our definition not only in this respect, but also because she has steadfastly refused to recognize an historical fact as a construct. She thus distinguishes sharply between the "facts," or givens, of history and the "symbols" of economics, even though she herself has constructed new historical facts by codifying and classifying data for computer analysis. Another deviation from total history results from her isolation of the total social facts (economics, politics, religion, collective psychology, and the others) into separate—almost impenetrable—compartments, instead of interrogating them in terms of their relationships to one another and to the whole society. She thus defines the Parisian bourgeoisie of 1815–1848 largely in terms of their own attitudes—especially their conviction in their own bourgeois reason and capacity and their conception of wealth as a means rather than an end—instead of probing into the interrelationships between material life, social organization, and bourgeois psychology and conceptions of power.[54]

54. Adeline Daumard, *La Bourgeoisie parisienne de 1815 à 1848*, Ecole Pratique des Hautes Etudes (VIe Section), "Démographie et sociétés," 8 (Paris: S.E.V.P.E.N., 1963). For criticisms of Daumard's work and of work that she has done jointly with François Furet, see Jean-Yves Tirat, "Problèmes de méthode en histoire sociale," *Revue d'histoire moderne et contemporaine*, X (July–September 1963), 211–18; Roland Mousnier, "Problèmes de méthode dans l'étude des structures sociales des seizième, dix-septième, dix-huitième siècles," in Konrad Repgen and Stephan Skalweit, eds., *Spiegel der Geschichte: Festgabe für Max Braubach zum 10. April 1964* (Münster: Verlag Aschendorff, 1964), pp. 550–64. Mousnier regards Daumard and Furet as "the Labrousse group" because their joint *Structures et relations sociales à Paris au XVIIIe siècle*, "Cahiers des Annales," 18 (Paris: Armand Colin, 1961), grew out of Labrousse's exhortation to historians, at the 10th International Congress of History in Rome (1955), to

Properly total, or global, on the other hand, is Braudel's methodology. According to his own analysis, it requires at an early stage the translation of the facts, or constructs, of social reality of simultaneous diversity and successive variation into an overall model or ideal type, after which the historian must return from the model to the realities, only to return again to the model, making revisions and corrections at every step. To explain a whole society, or some other whole system, the historian should supplement this method with the comparative approach, seeking similar realities and models in other long periods and other geo-historical systems. The various models would serve both as temporary explanations and as instruments of control, comparison, and verification.[55]

Frédéric Mauro recommends a similar methodology. After his initial observations, the historian should engage in a static

pursue new methods in investigating the problem of the bourgeoisie. See C.-E. Labrousse, "Voies nouvelles vers une histoire de la bourgeoisie occidentale aux XVIIIe et XIXe siècles (1700–1850)," in Tenth International Congress of History (Rome), *Relazioni*, 7 vols. (Florence, 1955), VI, 367–96; Edward R. Tannenbaum, "French Scholarship in Modern European History: New Developments since 1945," *Journal of Modern History*, XXIX (September 1957), 251 (246–52). For a reply to Tirat, see Adeline Daumard and François Furet, " 'Problèmes de méthode en histoire sociale': Réflexions sur une note critique," *Revue d'histoire moderne et contemporaine*, XI (October–December 1964), 291–98. See also the earlier study by Daumard and Furet, "Méthodes de l'histoire sociale: Les Archives notariales et la mécanographie," *Annales ESC*, XIV (October–December 1959), 676–93.

55. Braudel, "La Longue durée," p. 746. Recommended by Marc Bloch and questioned by Claude Lévi-Strauss, comparative history has been pursued little in France except in Braudel's way. For an excellent brief analysis of the problems of comparative history, see William H. Sewell, Jr., "Marc Bloch and the Logic of Comparative History," *History and Theory*, VI, 2 (1967), 208–18. For Marc Bloch's own view of the subject, see his "Pour une histoire comparée des sociétés européennes," *Revue de Synthèse historique*, XLVI (1928), 15–50, translated by Jelle C. Riemersma as "Toward a Comparative History of European Societies," in Frederic C. Lane and J. C. Riemersma, eds., *Enterprise and Secular Change: Readings in Economic History* (Homewood, Ill.: R. D. Irwin, 1953), pp. 494–521, with explanatory notes but without Bloch's own footnotes.

macroanalysis or definition of the whole system's conditions of general equilibrium. He should proceed subsequently to a micro-analysis of the functioning of the parts. The final step would entail a dynamic macroanalysis of the whole system in the process of its renewal, transformation, and deformation.[56]

Histoire globale may be justified on the assumption that it is an error to consider a small group the microcosm of a whole society and to apply to complex whole societies a model applicable to simple whole societies of the type dealt with by Lévi-Strauss and other anthropologists—that is, to regard a society with a high division of labor, and with a high degree of indirectness in the exchange or distribution of awards as the simple continuation of a society with a low division of labor.[57] There are, of course, resemblances between the small group and the macrocosm and between elementary and complex forms of social action and organization. Labor, for example, may be an economic, political, and religious act in both a highly developed and in a less highly developed society,[58] but the degree to which and how each of these constituent elements will be stressed in the two societies (and two types of society) are likely to be different. The function of labor thus will vary from society to society.

For reasons of this kind Braudel recommends the elaboration of models of many different types of whole society, civilization, or economy and the specification of their temporal and spatial limits. He consequently welcomed the formulation by the Polish Marxist economic historian Witold Kula of a well-defined model of

56. Frédéric Mauro, "Théorie économique et histoire économique," *Recherches et dialogues philosophiques et économiques*, "Cahiers de l'Institut de Science Economique Appliquée," 79 (Series M, No. 4) (Paris: I.S.E.A., April 1959), pp. 45–75.

57. George Caspar Homans, *Social Behavior: Its Elementary Forms* (New York: Harcourt, Brace and World, 1961), pp. 378–79, 385–86.

58. Witold Kula, "On the Typology of Economic Systems," in *The Social Sciences, Problems and Orientations; les Sciences sociales, problèmes et orientations* (The Hague, Paris: Mouton/UNESCO, 1968), p. 111 (108–44).

Polish feudalism between the sixteenth century and the close of the eighteenth century.[59]

Many intellectually inquisitive French Marxist historians have greeted total history with enthusiasm. If some of them have been less enraptured with the concept of long duration, that is so, not because of their rejection of, but because of their commitment to the idea of historical discontinuities, based on their firm conviction that in critical periods certain new events and conjunctures will usurp the role of the old or conventional structures. Citing the French Revolution as an example of a period in which the short term should take precedence over the long, Albert Soboul holds that the historian who aspires to a total history of the French Revolution must shift his emphasis from structure, tradition, repetition, and long duration to contradiction, struggle, change, and short duration.[60]

Braudel observed in "La Longue durée" that the new narrative history of conjunctures—that is, of short economic (and conceivably social and cultural) cycles, intercycles, and Kondratieff cycles—should have culminated logically in a history of long duration. It may have hindered that trend, however, since "the sewing together of 'cyclical' history and traditional history of the narrative type" appeared to many scholars to be of greater urgency than "going ahead toward the unknown." The preference for cyclical and short-term history was the product, however, not only of a fear of the unknown, and of the fact that the historian is "by inclination a *metteur en scène*," reluctant to "disown the drama of the brief time," but of the firm conviction of Marxist historians that a short-term orientation is the correct one for revolutionary periods. Thus after focusing on the secular trend of price movements in eighteenth-century France, La-

59. Fernand Braudel, "Préface" to Kula, *Théorie économique du système féodal*, p. vi (v–viii).

60. Albert Soboul, "Avant-propos" to Claude Mazauric, *Sur la Révolution française: Contributions à l'histoire de la révolution bourgeoise* (Paris: Editions Sociales, 1970), p. 6; Soboul, *La Civilisation et la Révolution française*, I, 23, 28, 34–36.

brousse shifted to "the very hollow of the depression of 1774–
1791" to identify, as Braudel puts it, "one of the powerful well-
springs, one of the launching ramps," of the French Revolution.
In his communication to the 1948 International Congress of
History (Paris) on the mechanisms of revolution, "1848–1830–
1789: How Revolutions Are Born," he shifted to a still briefer
span of events and of the links between "an economic motivation
of short duration (but of a new style) and a political motivation
(of very old style), that of the revolutionary days."[61]

Annales historians François Furet and Denis Richet, on the
other hand, maintain that a proper evaluation of the French
Revolution requires study of the structures of the preindustrial
commercial economy, already in place by the middle of the
sixteenth century and not undone until the middle of the nineteenth. They argue, in effect, that neither the explanation of a
short aristocratic prerevolution nor Labrousse's explanation of an
"intercyclical depression" allows a sufficient length of time to
embrace the origins of the French Revolution. Unlike Marxist
historians, they interpret it less as a bourgeois revolution than as
an "Enlightenment Revolution," hence a product of the transformation of the communications system (printing press, growth of
literacy, option for modernity) in conjunction with a crisis of
political absolutism, a crisis in the society of traditional statuses,
a struggle for power between competing elites, and the constant
extension of seignorial property to the bourgeoisie.[62]

61. Braudel, "La Longue durée," pp. 730–31 (or in Braudel, *Ecrits sur
l'histoire*, pp. 49–50). For the studies in question, see C.-E. Labrousse,
Esquisse du mouvement des prix et des revenus en France au XVIIIe siècle,
2 vols. (Paris: Dalloz, 1933); C.-E. Labrousse, *La Crise de l'économie
française à la fin de l'Ancien Régime et au début de la Révolution*, I,
Aperçus généraux, sources, méthode, objectifs; la crise de la viticulture
(Paris: Presses Universitaires de France, 1944); C.-E. Labrousse, "1848–
1830–1789: Comment naissent les révolutions," in Comité Français des
Sciences Historiques, *Actes du Congrès historique du centenaire de la
Révolution française* (Paris: Presses Universitaires de France, 1948), pp. 1–
20, followed by a discussion, pp. 20–29.
62. François Furet, "Le Catéchisme révolutionnaire," *Annales ESC*, XXVI

In the heat of argument, the two groups have not realized that part of the truth may lie in both camps or that both constructs may be useful. As "repeated" in 1789 (and the immediately subsequent years, perhaps even to the end of the Napoleonic regime), 1830, and 1848, the French Revolution did institutionalize new rites of passage. The old structures persisted, however, precisely because the effective creation of new rites of passage (and thus of new structures) was an achievement only of the long term. The Furet-Richet model thus takes insufficient notice of the elements of disruption or discontinuity, the Soboul model takes insufficient account of the elements of conservation. Both models therefore fall short of total, or "global," history, albeit not as a matter of choice but for the more fundamental reason that the individual scholar can understand the historical process in its totality only by means of certain fragments of the totality. In fact, however, the part can be comprehended only within the framework of the whole and the whole only through the mediation of the parts. Interpretations consequently will always be imperfect. The renewal of interpretation by the use of new methods and constructs is intellectually enriching, since the latter serve to transform our very conceptions of history.[63]

(March–April 1971), 255–89; Denis Richet, "Autour des origines idéologiques lointaines de la Révolution française," *Annales ESC*, XXIV (January–February 1969), 1–23; Denis Richet, "Croissance et blocages en France du XVe au XVIIIe siècle," *Annales ESC*, XXIII (July–August 1968), 759–87; François Furet, "Pour une définition des classes inférieures à l'époque moderne," *Annales ESC*, XVIII (May–June 1963), 459–74. For Richet's accusations of Soboul's carelessness and failure to make proper acknowledgments, see the exchange of letters between Denis Richet and Albert Soboul in "Correspondance," *Annales ESC*, XXV (September–October 1970), 1494–96. Richet also objects to the application to non-Marxist historians of such epithets as "publicists" and "renegades" in Soboul's "Avant-propos" to Mazauric, *Sur la Révolution française*, p. 5. For a general critique of François Furet, Denis Richet, Robert R. Palmer, Alfred Cobban, Elizabeth L. Eisenstein, and George V. Taylor, see Albert Soboul, "L'Historiographie classique de la Révolution française: Sur des controverses récentes," *Historical Reflections, Réflexions historiques*, I (Winter/hiver 1974), 141–67.

63. Adam Schaff, *Histoire et vérité: Essai sur l'objectivité de la connais-*

Marxist scholars who have maintained a dialogue with the *Annales* have achieved a partial clarification of the relationship between structures and longue durée. Anthropologist Maurice Godelier, a scholar under the triple inspiration of Marxism, Lévi-Strauss, and *Annales* scholarship, thus underlines that every social system and structure is characterized by longevity. There are limits, however, to the invariance of relationships among the traits that comprise a structure, since a modification of the variables ultimately provokes a change in functional relationships. The system or structure then evolves toward another form. It is in this sense that Godelier can perceive an objective relationship between structure and event: "A structure has the property of tolerating and 'digesting' certain types of events until a point and time at which the event digests the structure."[64]

Emphasizing the instability of structures, their internal inconsistencies, and the general tendency toward the periodic affirmation of a new dialectical equilibrium, Soboul has reached a similar conclusion.[65] He has also drawn attention to the limited ability of "great men" (Charlemagne and Napoleon, for example) to transform structures, and he elucidates this imperfection by reference to François Guizot's two aspects of the great man. On the one hand, the great man comprehends the mental and other structures of his own time better than anyone else and acts accordingly to accomplish his purpose. On the other, he ultimately acts at cross-purposes with those structures, expressing personal views and seeking personal goals, without consulting the requirements of his time and society, and fails.[66]

Since great men rarely can impose new enduring structures

sance historique, translated from the Polish by Anna Kaminska and Claire Brendel (Paris: Editions Anthropos, 1971), pp. 337–39; Adam Schaff, "Why History Is Constantly Rewritten," *Diogenes,* No. 30 (Summer 1960), pp. 62–74.

64. Maurice Godelier, "Rationalité des systèmes économiques," *Rationalité et irrationalité en économie,* 2 vols. (Paris: François Maspero, 1971), II, 199, translated by Brian Pearce as *Rationality and Irrationality in Economics* (London: NLB, 1972; New York: Monthly Review Press, 1973).

65. Soboul, *La Civilisation et la Révolution française,* I, 33–34.

66. Albert Soboul, "Le Héros et l'histoire," *Revue d'histoire moderne et*

unless these correspond to an existing demand, it is all the more imperative that the historian explain how structures are altered.[67] It is incumbent on the historian, according to Marxist thought, to articulate "*a general theory of societies in movement*," for in the final analysis "history is the change of rhythms, the change of structures, and the quest to clarify and interpret these changes."[68]

Lucien Goldmann even defined the Marxist historical method as one of "genetic structuralism," governed on the one hand by totality and on the other by development or change. Between two distinct moments of historical genesis, some particular structure or group of structures will prevail. At the same time, internal contradictions are an integral aspect of each structure and system of structures.[69] Each structure performs "*a function* within a larger social structure. And when the situation changes, [it ceases] to fulfill this function and thus loses [its] rational character, which leads men to abandon [it] and to replace [it] with [a] new and different [structure]."[70] Characterized at once by stability,

---

contemporaine, XVII (July–September 1970), 333–38. See also the eloquent François Guizot, *Histoire de la civilisation en France depuis la chute de l'Empire Romain*, 4 vols. (new ed.; Paris: Didier, 1846), II, 110–13 (20th lesson of the course of 1828–1829).

67. Jean Bouvier, "L'Appareil conceptuel dans l'histoire économique contemporaine," *Revue économique*, No. 1 (January 1965), pp. 8–9, 12 (1–17).

68. Pierre Vilar, "Histoire sociale et philosophie de l'histoire," *La Pensée*, No. 118 (November–December 1964), p. 66 (64–77), address at a colloquium under the auspices of the Centre Catholique des Intellectuels Français, Feb. 22–24, 1964. See also Vilar, "Histoire marxiste," p. 181.

69. Lucien Goldmann, "Genèse et structure," *Marxisme et sciences humaines* (Paris: Gallimard, 1970), pp. 17–30; Goldmann, "Le Sujet de la création culturelle," *ibid.*, pp. 94–120; Goldmann, "Le Structuralisme génétique en sociologie de la littérature," in Colloque International de Sociologie de la Littérature, *Littérature et société: Problèmes de méthodologie en sociologie de la littérature, Colloque organisé conjointement par l'Institut de Sociologie de l'Université Libre de Bruxelles et l'Ecole Pratique des Hautes Etudes (6e Section) de Paris du 21 au 23 mai 1964* (Brussels: Editions de l'Institut de Sociologie, Université Libre de Bruxelles, 1967), pp. 195–211; Goldmann, "Pour une approche marxiste des études sur le marxisme," *Annales ESC*, XVIII (January–February 1963), 114 (114–18).

70. Goldmann, *The Human Sciences and Philosophy*, pp. 14–15.

movement, and ambivalence,[71] a functioning structure can become dysfunctional.

Similar conceptions but with a different stress are held by non-Marxist structuralists, who perceive the bipolar character of structure, simultaneously inhibitive and creative of new forms of action.[72] Georges Gurvitch, for example, was unable to explain structure without reference to structuring (or structuration), destructuring, and restructuring. The Genevan psychologist Jean Piaget defines a structure as a self-regulating total system of transformations. Being a system, it is endowed with the property of being "structured" (*structurée*), or inhibiting new forms of action along contradictory lines. Being a system of transformations, it possesses the quality of "structuring" (*structurante*), or reaffirming, transforming, and discarding old forms and forming new forms. In the language of Pierre Bourdieu, Director of the Paris Centre de Sociologie, a symbolic system expresses itself simultaneously as a *structured structure* and as a *structuring structure*.[73]

In the final analysis, histoire globale sympathizes more fully with these last nuances than with the views of those Marxists who are too exclusively under the fascination of the processes of destructuring and incipient restructuring. Georges Duby thus assigns structural characteristics to ideology, which he defines as a complete, globalizing system that seeks to imbue a given society with a unifying representation of its past, present, and future. As

71. Ernest Labrousse, at the session "Structure et mouvement en histoire," in *Structuralisme et marxisme*, p. 152.

72. Tulio Halperin Donghi, "Histoire et longue durée: Examen d'un problème," *Cahiers Vilfredo Pareto*, No. 15 (1968), pp. 130–32 (109–33), first published in the Argentine review *Cuestiones de filosofía*, I, 2–3 (1962), 74–96.

73. Gilles Granger, "Evénement et structure," in J. Lacroix, ed., *Recherches et dialogues philosophiques et économiques*, "Cahiers de l'Institut de Science Economique Appliquée," No. 96 (Series M, No. 6) (Paris: I.S.E.A., December 1959), p. 165 (149–86); Viet, *Les Méthodes structuralistes*, p. 210; Jean Piaget, *Le Structuralisme*, "Que sais-je?" No. 1311 (Paris: Presses Universitaires de France, 1968), pp. 6–7, 10–11; Pierre Bourdieu, "The Thinkable and the Unthinkable," *Times Literary Supplement*, Oct. 15, 1971, pp. 1255–56.

such, ideology aspires to stability but since it is in rivalry virtually always with other ideologies it strives simultaneously to alter existing social and ideological forms. *Annales* scholarship is alert also to the continuing process of structuration or *progrès neutre*, as Braudel has identified tentatively the kind of change that reinforces, perfects, and prolongs a particular structure.[74]

In other words, *Annales* scholars are on the lookout for what Roland Barthes calls "diachronic change": change that has "no history" since it is purely endogenous and maintains a more or less constant rhythm. Most changes in fashion, for example, are of diachronic character. Once in a great while, however, there is an "historical change," involving the transformation of one or more structures. The innovation among the cultures of Western Europe of the very idea of fashion as part of a general predisposition toward neomania represents a change of that kind.[75] Histoire globale is concerned with both types of change.

Histoire globale is thus "une impossible science globale de l'homme." It is "impossible" because it simultaneously embraces (or may embrace) a Hermaean or communications approach and requires a framework of totality. But it is impossible only in the sense of being very difficult, not in the sense that it cannot be done or that it has not been done. Its practice is still hesitant and imperfect, and some of the younger scholars (third and fourth generations) of the *Annales* community are not wholly committed to it. Their arguments are weak and unconvincing, however, and histoire globale, in some of its aspects at least, has been incorporated into the general matrix of the historical discipline as practiced in France.

74. Georges Duby, "Histoire sociale et idéologie des sociétés," in Le Goff and Nora, eds., *Faire de l'histoire*, I, *Nouveaux problèmes*, 147–68; Fernand Braudel, seminar, Collège de France, spring 1971, for the term "progrès neutre," which may have been introduced at a scholarly meeting in Italy.

75. Roland Barthes, *Système de la mode* (Paris: Editions du Seuil, 1967), pp. 298, 302. For an earlier version by Barthes on fashion, see his "Histoire et sociologie du vêtement: Quelques observations méthodologiques," *Annales ESC*, XII (July–September 1957), 430–41.

5 Culture Areas and Modes of Production

Although not always easy, the confrontation between *Annales* and Marxist scholars has probably been mutually beneficial. Partly as a result of their dialogue, *Annales* historians have learned to put greater stress on the role of production, while Marxists have been persuaded to re-examine their initially hostile attitude toward a geohistory of long duration and to revise their conceptions of modes of production. Both groups of scholars have modified their Europocentrism. Both, in effect, have decided to approach the problem of civilizations not simply as one of degrees of development and of the possibility of imitation by "backward" societies of more "progressive" models of social organization, but mainly as a problem of distinctive civilizational choices—of justifiably separate, even if chronologically coexistent, modes of cultural organization. In the process, however, there has been a curious divergence, as some Marxists were attracted to the *Annales* bailiwick of culture areas and civilizations, and as some *Annales* and other non-Marxist scholars became disenchanted with these concepts, at least as a frame of analysis for the technologically advanced societies of the contemporary era.

Marxists were long disinclined to deal with the problem of civilization beyond the terms of Marx's own contribution to the subject. In the late 1940s and early 1950s, at the height of the Cold War, Charles Parain and other Marxist scholars harshly criticized anthropologist André Varagnac for his attachment to the concept of "traditional civilization" and to the notion of *genres de vie*, praised by Febvre and Braudel but regarded by orthodox Marxists as an underpinning for the myth of historical immobility and as an obstacle to the myth (in the Sorelian sense) of the class struggle. They took no note of Varagnac's emphasis on the dual function of folklore: that folklore was not just repetition but also a means of innovation, of relating the past to some new need or aspiration.[1]

Not unlike Marcel Mauss, who perceived civilization in terms of its "qualities of movement" rather than of permanence,[2] Parain defined civilization as "life, movement, a quest for progress," and he insisted—somewhat as Varagnac—that peasants are prompted not only by conservative motives but by a "faculty for adaptation" and "a spirit of initiative."[3] Although Marxists and non-Marxists vaguely agree that societies function simultaneously in terms of the principles of conservation and change, Marxists (like Saint-Simonians, although unlike Comtians) are afraid that too much weight may be given to conservation.

The development in continental Europe between 1750 and 1850 of integrated national markets and the quick self-assertion of new nation-states and propagation of the principle of nationality may have contributed to the confusion of the ideas of nation and civilization. In addition, Marxists may have been diverted from the concept of civilization as a distinctive cultural entity—with definite if fluctuating temporal and spatial dimensions—following the widespread diffusion of Augustin Thierry's and

1. Lucien Febvre, "Folklore et folkloristes," *Pour une histoire à part entière*, p. 611 (607–19), first published in *Annales d'histoire sociale*, XI (1939), 152–60.

2. Braudel, *La Méditerranée*, II, 95, citing Marcel Mauss, "Civilisation: Eléments et formes," in Centre International de Synthèse, *Civilisation*, Ière Semaine Internationale de Synthèse (Paris, 1929), pp. 81–108.

3. Charles Parain, "Un nouveau mythe: La Civilisation traditionnelle," *La Pensée*, No. 23 (March–April 1949), pp. 93–98; "Une falsification: L'Archéo-civilisation," *La Pensée*, No. 51 (November 1953), pp. 129–32, part of the program (pp. 109–43) "Le Marxisme et l'histoire de France," University Colloquium, May 25, 1953, in commemoration of the seventieth anniversary of Marx's death; Blot, "Le Révisionnisme," pp. 55–56.

François Guizot's definition of civilization as a general expression of "progress" (hence, of the lack of need for revolution) and of the rise and growth of a bourgeoisie.

Guizot even set up a hierarchy of civilizations, with the most advanced types being situated in Western Europe—in the societies with the greatest diversity of ideas and social arrangements. France, however, was the only "pure type of civilization," or civilization in which society and individuals had improved virtually abreast of each other and in which ideas had assumed a clear precedence over social organization.[4] Civilizations without an autonomous bourgeoisie were inferior types. Consequently, all the superior civilizations were situated in Europe and in Europe's overseas projections.

Despite his preference for the concept of national market, Marx himself, under Hegel's pervading influence and under the inspiration of the general trend of European thought during the first half of the nineteenth century, espoused a similar image of civilization. According to Marx's model, the world was fragmented into three basic cultural types, each linked to a different geographic base, exhibiting a different degree of cultural mobility, and developing a corresponding type of city. The oldest cultural type comprised an Eastern—also identified as Asiatic and Slavic—group of cultures, characterized by very little basic change over long periods of time. Extending over a smaller area, a second and later type of culture comprised the classical and, inferentially, postclassical Mediterranean way of life, in which a greater degree of formal mobility prevailed. The third type was at first territorially the least extensive and most peripheral, being confined to Western and Central Europe. The last to be formed, it developed into the most plastic of the three. It was so mobile indeed that it acquired three successive cultural forms—Germanic, feudal,

---

4. Robert Mandrou, "Avant-propos" to Boris Porchnev, *Les Soulèvements populaires en France de 1623 à 1648*, Ecole Pratique des Hautes Etudes (VIe Section), "Oeuvres étrangères," 4 (Paris: S.E.V.P.E.N., 1963), pp. 32–37; Guizot, *Histoire de la civilisation en France*, I, 1–27.

and bourgeois-modern—in the same core area and then spread both westward and eastward in its third cultural manifestation to occupy an area ultimately more extensive than that of the Eastern cultural type.[5]

Interest in the correspondences between cultural forms and modes of communication and production languished after Guizot's and Marx's time partly because the difficulty of elaborating a suitable methodology for a history of civilization(s) was so great —that is, of going beyond a discussion of technology, economics, religion, politics, science, art, and literature as separate categories of experience to a meaningful analysis of their interactions.[6] Two Marxist exceptions to this generality during the first half of the twentieth century were Louis Aragon and Antonio Gramsci.[7]

Aware of the role of the principle of rationality—Montesquieu's law of totality and unity, or of the adequate and contradictory reason of a society—in consequence of which a society can effect a partial resolution of the contradictions between its several subsystems, Gramsci named it *egemonia* (hegemony). One of Gramsci's interpreters subsequently defined *egemonia* as "an order in which a certain way of life and thought is dominant, in

5. My interpretation here is of Karl Marx, *Pre-capitalist Economic Formations*, trans. Jack Cohen, edited and with an introduction by Eric J. Hobsbawm (New York: International Publishers, 1964), originally *Formen die der Kapitalistischen Produktion vorhergehen*, which was not published until 1939; and of Daniel Thorner, "Marx on India and the Asian Mode of Production," *Contributions to Indian Sociology*, IX (December 1969), translated into French as "Marx et l'Inde: Le Mode de production asiatique," *Annales ESC*, XXIV (March–April 1969), 337–69.

6. Georges Lefebvre, "Quelques réflexions sur l'histoire des civilisations," *Annales historiques de la Révolution française*, XXVII (1955), 97–109. Lefebvre is critical of the multivolume *Histoire générale des civilisations*, edited by Maurice Crouzet, for its lack of an integrated analysis, at least in the fifth volume by Roland Mousnier and Ernest Labrousse, with the collaboration of Marc Bouloiseau, *Le XVIIIe siècle: Révolution intellectuelle, technique et politique, 1715–1815* (Paris: Presses Universitaires de France, 1953).

7. Louis Aragon, *La Culture et les hommes* (Paris: Editions Sociales, 1947).

which one concept of reality is diffused throughout society in all its institutional and private manifestations, informing with its spirit all taste, morality, customs, religious and political principles, and all social relations, particularly in their intellectual and moral connotations."[8]

The notions of culture offered by Aragon and by Gramsci especially helped to divert European Marxist historians from a history conceived in terms of separate categories to one that seeks linkages between the various subsystems and the general culture. They did so, however, only after (and in consequence of) the triumph of communism in China and the maturation of the concepts of civilization and culture areas under the impact of Braudel's leadership and scholarship.

Turning first to Braudel and the *Annales,* let us note that the President of the Conseil Supérieur de la Recherche Scientifique et du Progrès Technique, Henri Longchambon, submitted a report to the French government in June 1957 urging changes in the approach to higher education. Calling the report a "remarkable monument" deserving "reflection and prompt realization," the *Annales* published the sections relating to the social and human sciences. Sounding almost as if it had come from the pen of Braudel himself, who had been on an official tour of American universities to inspect their area studies programs, the report recommended the regrouping of the social and human sciences and the integration of their research centers in a common Maison des Sciences Sociales. It also strongly advocated the development of area studies programs of contemporary cultures and societies

8. Gwyn A. Williams, "The Concept of 'Egemonia' in the Thought of Antonio Gramsci: Some Notes on Interpretation," *Journal of the History of Ideas,* XXI (October–December 1960), 587 (586–99). See also John M. Cammett, *Antonio Gramsci and the Origins of Italian Communism* (Stanford: Stanford University Press, 1967), p. 204; Eugene D. Genovese, "On Antonio Gramsci," *In Red and Black: Marxian Explorations in Southern and Afro-American History* (New York: Pantheon, 1971), pp. 391–422, article published originally in *Studies on the Left,* No. 7 (March–April 1967), pp. 83–108.

under the aegis of the Sixième Section and political science, and with an emphasis on three factors generally neglected in the United States: to give area studies and political science a geographical basis, to include philosophy in such programs in order to provide them with a logical structure, and to incorporate in this general endeavor and in history teaching in particular the idea of long duration.[9]

The recommendation for the proper study of contemporary societies was extended in 1959 from higher education to secondary education; a provision specified that the *classes terminales* of the French *lycées* give depth to the study of contemporary civilizations by devoting some attention to geographical history and to the durational aspects of culture. In less than a decade, however, non-Marxist interest in long duration, culture areas, and whole cultures began to wane, undermined in part by the very concern for the study of contemporary societies and cultures. The latter can provide an inspiring introduction to the past. But the preoccupation with contemporary societies reflects also—as it camouflages—the bias of our time that history is of slight relevance for the scientifically and technologically advanced cultures of the world.

Lucien Febvre asked in 1922: "Is the action of natural conditions on man weakening?" He replied with an oracular ambivalence: yes and no, since there is no ready-made nature but only one subject to various natural agents, including man, whose nature it is to have a changing culture—that is, with both old and new works, including old and new engineering works.[10] An American scholar maintains, on the other hand, that a nonvoluntarist, even "post-voluntarist," vision informs Braudel's and the Sixième Section's labors, whose "philosophical assumptions" require rejection

9. Henri Longchambon, "Les Sciences sociales en France: Un bilan, un programme," *Annales ESC*, XIII (January–March 1958), 94–109.

10. Febvre, in collaboration with Bataillon, *La Terre et l'évolution humaine*, pp. 428–34; Febvre, in collaboration with Bataillon, *A Geographical Introduction to History*, p. 352, for the quotation.

of "the notion that human will, moral and pragmatic, determines social and political realities."[11] A superficial reading of Braudel may permit this conclusion, for Braudel holds indeed that man's struggle against space and the multiple fields of force (geology, geography, biology, demography, agriculture, industry, and other geohistorical phenomena identifiable in terms of volume, structure, layers, or "longue durée") is an unequal contest even for the mightiest states and most obstinate societies. He also posits, however, an ever evolving dialectic between the factors of relative immobility (fields of force) and the variables of movement (circulation, oscillation, fluctuation), between the prevailing milieu and, in a sixteenth-century ambience, the conflicting wills and decisions of plowmen, graziers, merchants, and states.[12]

Moreover, the trend among at least a segment of *Annales* historians and geographers is unambivalently "voluntarist." Writing in *Hommage à Lucien Febvre*, for example, Maurice-François Rouge contends that it is imperative to prevent the chaos threatened by the disorderly spread of the tentacular webs of contemporary communications technology, thus manifesting a greater preoccupation with space as a product of (human) technology than as a product of geography unaffected by man (natural technology).[13] Since the end of World War II, under the fascina-

11. Andrews, review of *The Mediterranean*, in *New York Times Book Review*, May 18, 1975, pp. 1–3, 42–45.

12. Traian Stoianovich, "With and Without the Accidents," comment at the session "The Mediterranean in Economic History: Braudel's Synthesis Twenty-Five Years Later," 89th annual meeting of the American Historical Association, Chicago, Dec. 29, 1974. A similar concern for the dialectic between "fields of force" and variables of mobility is evident throughout Le Roy Ladurie's *Les Paysans de Languedoc*. Indeed, Le Roy Ladurie entitles Part One of his book "Champs de Force" (climate and Mediterranean plants and techniques), even though one of the chapters in this part focuses on variables of mobility—the relatively new migration of goods and ideas from the north southward.

13. Maurice-François Rouge, "L'Organisation de l'espace et les réseaux," in *Eventail de l'histoire vivante: Hommage à Lucien Febvre offert par l'amitié d'historiens, géographes, économistes, sociologues, ethnologues*, 2 vols. (Paris: Armand Colin, 1953), I, 401–5.

tion of the Faustian spirit of logical order and in a conscious effort to overcome French economic backwardness and what the geographer Jean Labasse has called the failure of "the geography of laissez-faire," French geographers have sought, yet more unequivocally, to make geography an action-oriented discipline, concerned with questions of spatial, or geographical, economic planning. At the same time, they have tried to compensate for the shortcomings of "géographie volontaire" or "géographie prospective," their two names for the revised discipline, by consciously incorporating in their work Braudel's complementary concepts of longue durée and discontinuity. In an article published in the 1960s, Guy Arbellot thus focuses on the Hermaean problem of road-building and the improvement—*la grande mutation*—of routes and vehicles in eighteenth-century France, that is, of the transformation of man's geographical environment through an alliance of human will and human technology. By means of two excellent isochronal charts of travel time for different types of vehicles along France's land and water routes, he has been able to demonstrate a probable general reduction in travel time between 1765 and 1785 of about one-third.[14]

The development of a geography simultaneously "volontaire" and "prospective" was in part a response to widespread criticism of the inadequacies of the discipline in its currently prevailing form. Roger Bastide, for example, saw a widening gap between the low-energy and the high-energy cultures and societies. In folk and peasant cultures, as well as in other low-energy cultures,

14. Etienne Juillard, "La Géographie volontaire: Une recherche interdisciplinaire," *Annales ESC*, XV (September–October 1960), 927–35; Jean Labasse, *L'Organisation de l'espace: Eléments de géographie volontaire* (Paris: Hermann, 1966), pp. 15, 593, 596; Paul Claval, *Essai sur l'évolution de la géographie humaine*, "Cahiers de Géographie de Besançon," 12, Annales Littéraires de l'Université de Besançon, LXVII (Paris: Les Belles Lettres, 1964), p. 9, for the use of the term "géographie prospective." On routes and space in the eighteenth century, see Guy Arbellot, "La Grande mutation des routes de France au milieu du XVIIIe siècle," *Annales ESC*, XXVIII (May–June 1973), 765–91.

the impress of the geographical milieu continues to be very great. The high-energy cultures, on the other hand, are a product of the amplification of science, technology, and of the human consciousness. They possess not only an unprecedented number of artifacts per capita but such a large group of well-trained and intelligent social and human scientists that they can solve the problems created by technology almost without reference to the old-style geographical history. In countries such as the United States, with a dense and varied transportation system despite its weak public sector) and a plethora of communications media, contended Bastide, differences between geographic areas are diluted and yield in significance to the differences between social or cultural levels—that is, to the differences between groups with separate networks of communication. If contemporary societies need history, the sociologist suggested further, they are more likely to need psychosocial history than geohistory.[15]

Despite their longevity and identification with a particular space, cultures are essentially plastic in form and spatially fluid. With an increased intensity of communication flow, they acquire more plasticity and fluidity. One may therefore ask, do regional or geographic variations produce fewer cultural differences today than they once did? Or, on the contrary, do variations in the application of media and media themes in different geographic milieus in fact reinforce old and create new forms of areal differentiation?[16]

The reaction against the culture concept is also the product of a political mood of reaction against the idea of a total system

15. Roger Bastide, "Y a-t-il une crise de la psychologie des peuples?" *Revue de psychologie des peuples*, XXI, 1 (1966), 8–20; Paul Claval, "Géographie et profondeur sociale," *Annales ESC*, XXII (September–October 1967), 1012 (1005–46).

16. For a statement of this problem in American geography and geohistoriography, see David E. Sopher, "Place and Location: Notes on the Spatial Patterning of Culture," *Social Science Quarterly*, LIII (September 1972), 321–37. This issue is devoted to the subject "Idea of Culture in the Social Sciences."

or system of systems—an underlying coherence or "consensus." This political mood draws intellectual sustenance from two main trends in social history: functionalism and a growing interest in marginal and nonconsensual groups, subjects to which we shall have occasion to return.[17]

Somewhat later in France than in the United States, these trends were joined by another: the appeal of Max Weber, who interpreted history as part of the movement from the irrational to the rational (rationalization) and had a greater esteem for sociology —history become science—than for geography.[18] Weber's ideas have given succor to persons seeking a way out of geohistory. By the opening of the 1970s, a French historian was able to write an entire book on historiography without once mentioning geohistorian Braudel. Instead, he evaluated Max Weber's as "the most exemplary historical work of our century."[19] For some *Annales* scholars, indeed, Weber has become the "father of us all."[20]

As interest in geohistory and long duration slackened among

17. For the turning away from "consensus history" in the United States, see John Higham, "The Cult of the 'American Consensus': Homogenizing Our History," *Commentary*, XXVII (February 1959), 93–100; John Higham, "Beyond Consensus: The Historian as Moral Critic," *American Historical Review*, LXVII (April 1962), 609–25; Robert F. Berkhofer, Jr., "Clio and the Culture Concept: Some Impressions of a Changing Relationship in American Historiography," *Social Science Quarterly*, LIII (September 1972), 297–320.

18. Bastide, "Y a-t-il une crise de la psychologie des peuples?" p. 12.

19. Paul Veyne, *Comment on écrit l'histoire: Essai d'épistémologie* (Paris: Editions du Seuil, 1971), p. 340.

20. Pierre Vidal-Naquet referred to Max Weber as "notre père à tous" in Braudel's seminar, according to a 1972 letter (otherwise undated) from Jean-Jacques Hémardinquer. In a letter of Sept. 18, 1975, Vidal-Naquet agrees that his conception of Max Weber as "notre père à tous" may be given a wider context, but explains that he originally used the phrase with the aim of emphasizing Weber's role in obliging historians to take note of the fact that the economy of the city of antiquity, unlike that of the medieval city, could be understood only in terms of its political framework, since it was in the main an association of warriors and consumers rather than of producers.

non-Marxist *Annales* scholars during the 1960s, it began to find a raison d'être among Marxists. The latter were lured to this *Annales* domain through the realization that large portions of that one-third of the world that turned to communism between 1917 and 1950 differed from European and other Western societies in a fundamental way: they comprised a group of low-energy societies with a different type of civilization.

Under the impact of interest in the type of civilization common to the areas in which communism had triumphed or hoped to prevail, European Marxist scholars ceased to subscribe to the Stalinist Marxism of the 1930s that had explained human evolution in terms of five socioeconomic stages—primitive communalism, slave societies, feudalism, capitalism, and socialism-communism. Instead, from the late 1950s on, there was a revival of interest in Marx's concept of the "Asiatic mode of production." Especially illuminating was the debate initiated in 1962 under the auspices of the Paris Centre de Recherches Marxistes, published in successive issues of the Marxist review *La Pensée* and, in 1969, republished in part as a separate volume.

Marxists were thus compelled to examine a type of civilization that did not reflect the rise and growth of a bourgeoisie. Rather than simply focusing on the organization of production, the discussion was broadened to include the relationships between the so-called Asiatic mode of production and the corresponding general culture.

We may conclude on the basis of these Marxist contributions that the term "Asiatic mode of production" and its political counterpart—"Oriental despotism"—embrace not only a hydraulic society of the type analyzed by Max Weber and Karl A. Wittfogel[21] but, in Wittfogel's own words, "a nonhydraulic subtype

21. Otto Berkelbach Van der Sprenkel, "Max Weber on China," in Nadel, ed., *Studies in the Philosophy of History*, pp. 198–220, first published in *History and Theory*, III (1964), 348–70; Karl August Wittfogel, *Oriental Despotism: A Comparative Study of Total Power* (New Haven: Yale University Press, 1957), reviewed by S. N. Eisenstadt in the *Journal of*

of agromanagerial society" with several variants.[22] They identify a society with two basic forms of authority: a precarious balance between an infrastructure of customary authority, in which the right to the ownership of land resides primarily in small communities, and a unitary political superstructure sometimes called "despotism" or "Oriental despotism." This second authority often originates in conquest. Whatever its origins, however, it acquires the right of eminent domain and governs by means of bureaucracy and "liturgy," creating above the "customary economy" of the small communities of local lineages, villages, and craft organizations what Sir John Hicks has called a "command economy" by protecting trade routes, promoting public works, and performing other political-economic functions.

According to the Rumanian Marxist Ion Banu, the superstructure fosters a cosmic image that represents the "despot" as the repository of cosmic powers and virtues that assure fertility and abundance. The despot is a priest-king. His administrators are ritual figures who perform the agrobiological functions of guaranteeing production and reproduction. In return, they obtain a share in the society's production, while the king enjoys a share in reproduction in the form of slaves, public servants, and concubines (Marx's "generalized slavery").

The relationship between the superstructure (despot) and the little communities (villages), maintains Banu, was thus of a "tributary" character, and we may refer to the economy of such

Asian Studies, XVII (May 1958), 435–46, and by Pierre Vidal-Naquet, "Histoire et idéologie: Karl Wittfogel et le concept de 'Mode de production asiatique,'" *Annales ESC*, XIX (May–June 1964), 531–49. For the eighteenth-century debate over Oriental despotism, see Franco Venturi, "Oriental Despotism," *Journal of the History of Ideas*, XXIV (January–March 1963), 133–42, translated by Lotte F. Jacoby and Ian M. Taylor from Venturi's "Despotismo Orientale," *Rivista Storica Italiana*, LXXII, 1 (1960), 117–26.

22. Karl A. Wittfogel, "Russia and the East: A Comparison and Contrast," *Slavic Review*, XXII (December 1963), 627–43, with comments by Nicholas V. Riasanovsky and Bertold Spuler and a reply by Wittfogel, pp. 644–62.

a society as a tributary economy. Sir John Hicks's alternative designation—in place of command economy—for the mode of production and distribution "in which a 'surplus' of food and other necessaries is extracted from cultivators, and used to provide sustenance for public servants," is Revenue Economy.[23] The advantage of any one of these three names—command, revenue, or tributary economy—is that it allows a shift of focus from Asia to other parts of the world, where a similar type of economy may have prevailed.

Whether identified as a tributary, revenue, or Asiatic form of economy, however, this mode of production and distribution does not favor the existence of a powerful merchant class or any other economic authority able to function independently of the superstructure. Similarly, it cannot sanction a separate and powerful aristocratic order.

As a result, merchants and aristocrats usually present a less formidable threat to the superstructure of the Asiatic mode of production than do little communities, some of whose members preserve a sense of separateness by organizing themselves into "anti-communities" of secret and cult societies or by rising in rebellion or singing "songs of flight" and joining long "marches" to lands of salvation—that is, by engaging in ritually correct peasant rebellions and in antitheistic and millenarian movements.

Generally, however, it is of slight advantage to the little communities to pull down the superstructure, for its removal or weakening ends almost invariably in a significant regression of production and productivity alike. Its duality as a customary authority and as a superstructure, maintains Jean Chesneaux, gives such a society the dual economic character of a highly evolved and a primitive precapitalist type of economic formation. Since the impairment of an existing superstructure provokes economic primitivization, staunch support develops in favor of a viable new superstructure. In general, according to Maurice Godelier, the Asiatic, or trib-

23. Sir John Hicks, *A Theory of Economic History* (London: Oxford University Press, 1969), pp. 9–24, "Custom and Command Economy."

utary, mode of production encourages a more highly productive economy than do the other types of precapitalist economic formations. It yields in this respect only to the bourgeois-modern economy of the last phase of commercial capitalism, to industrial capitalism, and to contemporary (twentieth-century) forms of command economy.[24]

Marxist scholars have emerged from these debates with a clearer awareness that neither feudalism nor slave societies, neither a bourgeois-modern economy nor an Asiatic mode of production, has ever prevailed throughout the world at any one time. Indeed, each may have been or may now be peculiar to some very specific part of the earth's surface. Each is a way of managing scarce resources in a particular milieu. This does not mean that the geographic frontiers of a given mode of production have not varied in the course of time. Thus, according to some Marxist speculations, the Asiatic mode of production may have been practiced in pre-Columbian America. In the eastern Mediterranean, it was supposedly undermined by the Dorian invasions only to be restored 2,500 years later for two centuries through the incorporation of certain Seljukid customs into the Ottoman tributary system.[25] Between 1500 and 1800 or shortly thereafter, it seems to have receded from three major areas of the world—America, Southeast Asia, and the two extremities (Moorish and Ottoman) of the Mediterranean.

The Asiatic mode of production thus may have reached its

24. Centre d'Etudes et de Recherches Marxistes, Sur le "mode de production asiatique" (Paris: Editions Sociales, 1969). See in particular Jean Chesneaux, "Le Mode de production asiatique: Quelques perspectives de recherche," pp. 13–45; Maurice Godelier, "La Notion de 'mode de production asiatique' et les schémas marxistes d'évolution des sociétés," pp. 47–100; Ion Banu, "La Formation sociale 'asiatique' dans la perspective de la philosophie orientale antique," pp. 285–307; Léonid Sédov, "La Société angkorienne et le problème du mode de production asiatique," pp. 327–43. Banu's concept of state and kingship in the Orient is similar to that of the Viennese scholar Robert Heine-Geldern.

25. Sencer Divitçioglu, "Modèle économique de la société ottomane (les XIVe et XVe siècles)," La Pensée, No. 144 (April 1969), pp. 41–60.

greatest territorial extent around 1500. But it would be an error, according to Jean Chesneaux, to regard it as a "residual" category in which to put a society that fits nowhere else. Catherine Coquery-Vidrovitch, an anthropologist who contributes to the *Annales* and *La Pensée* alike, has found little evidence to suggest an Asiatic mode of production, feudalism, or slave societies in black Africa. She proposes instead the model of an "African mode of production," characterized by an infrastructure of controlling elites who obtain surpluses not through the development of agriculture and public works but by war and long-distance trade.[26]

Apart from re-examining the problem of modes of production and correcting misconceptions about Asiatic and other modes, Marxist scholars have turned to the general problem of civilization—that is, to the *Annales* focus of interest. In 1964, for example, the Centre de Recherches Marxistes started a debate on the applicability of the notion of civilization to the history and philosophy programs of the *classes terminales*. One of the participants, Antoine Pelletier, was uneasy with the new practice of dissociating the concepts of society (a term with which Marxists are at ease) and civilization, in other words, with Braudel's definition of a civilization as a system of realities that exceeds the life span of a specific society. He was still more critical of the reluctance of *Annales* and other non-Marxist historians to recognize a hierarchy of historical elements. He censured the "contemporary civilizations" texts and courses of the *classes terminales* for their undue stress on "collective representations" and the "collective unconscious," insisting that assigning so much value to the durable or to what is least subject to dialectic must be at the expense of the current, so much of which will lapse because of its highly dialectical nature. But his fundamental objection to applying the civilizational approach to contemporary societies was a practical one: the failure of textbook authors to explain "the

26. Catherine Coquery-Vidrovitch, "Recherches sur un mode de production africain," *La Pensée*, No. 144 (April 1969), pp. 61–78.

objective dialectic of change and permanence," or how the passage is made from the things of long duration (civilization) to the quickly changing contemporary things.[27] An indirect *Annales* response was that it would be difficult to convey an understanding of the "pulsations of civilizations on the grand scale" so long as educational programs continued to be oriented to "the mini-rhythm of a European and French pattern: Orient and Greece-Rome; 987–1492–1610–1715–1789–1848–1914."[28]

A second participant in the Marxist debate, Jean-Jacques Goblot, was more sympathetic to the concept of civilization as a theoretical and historical construct. Proposing a return to Marx's own idea that there are no absolutely necessary steps or stages in history, Goblot affirmed that tradition itself is a mode of development and that old cultural traits and structures are never discarded in exactly the same manner or to the same degree in every society, that they sometimes even undergo a change in form without suffering a change in quality or fundamental meaning. Civilizations and modes of production, he further reasoned, are usually transformed when a change occurs in the nature or degree of contact or confrontation between two cultures or types of culture—unless, indeed, the confrontation provokes a refusal or loss of power to innovate. Goblot's logic suggests that "Asiatic" forms of social and economic organization did not engender the "ancient classical" and that the latter did not produce the "feudal," but that every new form of civilization, like every new mode of production, requires some form of geographic displacement or a new system of communication. He maintains, indeed, that new forms of civilization tend to arise at the frontiers of two different cultural types, for that is where

27. Antoine Pelletier, "La Notion de civilisation," in Antoine Pelletier and Jean-Jacques Goblot, *Matérialisme historique et histoire des civilisations* (Paris: Editions Sociales, 1969), pp. 9–56, article published originally in *La Pensée*, No. 125 (January–February 1966), pp. 21–46.

28. Suzanne Citron, "Dans l'enseignement secondaire: Pour *l'aggiornamento* de l'histoire géographie," *Annales ESC*, XXIII (January–February 1968), 136–43.

simplifications—including the simplification of alphabets and other changes in the forms and styles of communication—are made.[29]

Goblot's basic source of reference was Braudel, who regards a civilization as a network and mode of communication and affirms that each civilization has its own special "grammar."[30] Anouar Abdel-Malek similarly stresses the communicational aspects of civilizations but acknowledges a spiritual indebtedness to Antonio Gramsci, who defined the problem of the *Mezzogiorno* and of his native Sardinia, to use Abdel-Malek's words, in terms of the "dialectic of civilization, the incompatibility of the North, industrialized and cultivated, with the South, which has its roots in the human landscape of the non-European Mediterranean."[31]

Like Braudel, Abdel-Malek envisages the problem of the relationships between countries at different levels of economic organization and equipment as essentially one of "civilization" rather

29. Jean-Jacques Goblot, "L'Histoire des 'civilisations' et la conception marxiste de l'évolution sociale," in Pelletier and Goblot, *Matérialisme historique*, pp. 57–197.

30. On the subject of civilization one should go not only to Braudel's *Méditerranée* and *Civilisation matérielle*, but also to his "L'Apport de l'histoire des civilisations," in *Encyclopédie Française*, XX, *Le Monde en devenir* (*histoire, évolution, prospective*) (Paris, 1959), pp. 20.10–11 to 20.12–14, reprinted in Braudel, *Ecrits sur l'histoire*, pp. 255–314, under the title "L'Histoire des civilisations: Le Passé explique le présent." See also "Grammaire des civilisations," in Suzanne Baille, Fernand Braudel, and Robert Philippe, *Le Monde actuel: Histoire et civilisations* (Paris: Librairie Classique Eugène Belin, 1963), one of the texts for the *classes terminales*. An augmented version of Fernand Braudel's contribution to this last study has been translated into Italian by Gamma Miani as *Il Mondo Attuale*, 2 vols. (Turin: Einaudi, 1966). Vol. I focuses on *Le Civiltà Extraeuropee*, Vol. II on *Le Civiltà Europee*.

31. Anouar Abdel-Malek, "Marxism and the Sociology of Civilizations," trans. Nicolas Slater, *Diogenes*, No. 64 (Winter 1968), p. 97 (91–117). The entire issue is devoted to the subject "Marxism Today." In another article, "L'Avenir de la théorie sociale," *Cahiers internationaux de sociologie*, L, n.s., 18e année (January–June 1971), 23–40, Abdel-Malek notes the difficulty of working with concepts and theories that have been developed in the context of the old *culture hégémonique* (a Gramscian idea) if one aspires to a generally valid science of man.

than of "development." He further regards explanations of cultural diversity in terms of "development," "cultural lag," or "modernization" as expressions of Europocentrism and Western subjectivity. Before uncritically adopting such explanations, Marxist and non-Western scholars should join in a common endeavor to carry out a systematic study of civilizations, as a result of which they may obtain answers that deviate substantially from the Western and Europocentric conclusions.[32]

Ignacy Sachs, a development economist who, after having been accused of Zionism and revisionism, left the University of Warsaw to teach in the Sixième Section, treads more cautiously between the developmental and civilizational explanations. Critical of the Europocentrism, or Westernism, that hinders a proper appreciation of non-Western cultures and peoples, he is equally censorious of other ethnocentrisms and of Europophobias. But he concurs with Abdel-Malek that economic, geographical, sociological, and historical concepts that have evolved out of a European or Western experience should be tested and modified as necessary by means of investigations of other "human societies as totalities," other "types of economy," other geographic and political realities.[33] He thus accepts the injunction of the non-Marxist specialist in the economic history of India, Daniel Thorner, that European history be re-examined on the basis of categories drawn from universal history and that historians stop trying to make world history fit the model of Western categories.[34]

32. Abdel-Malek, "Marxism and the Sociology of Civilizations," pp. 91–117.

33. Ignacy Sachs, "Du Moyen-âge à nos jours: Européo-centrisme et découverte du Tiers Monde," *Annales ESC*, XXI (May–June 1966), 465–87; Ignacy Sachs, "Overall and Prospective History of the Third World," *Diogenes*, No. 73 (Spring 1971), pp. 116–25.

34. Daniel Thorner, "Peasant Economy as a Category in Economic History," in *Deuxième Conférence Internationale d'Histoire Economique, Second International Conference of Economic History: Aix-en-Provence, 1962*, Ecole Pratique des Hautes Etudes (VIe Section), "Congrès et colloques," 8 (Paris, The Hague: Mouton, 1965), pp. 287–300.

Catherine Coquery-Vidrovitch contends, however, that the historical method itself, despite its European origins, is essentially untainted by Europocentrism and can be applied advantageously to societies very different from the European, including those of Africa.[35]

As late as 1958 Braudel was highly critical of the abusive way in which Marxists had handled Marx's model:

> The genius of Marx, the secret of his enduring power, derives from his having been the first to manufacture true social models with a basis in the long term of history. But these models have been congealed in their simplicity and given the value of law, of a priori and automatic explanations, applicable in all places and to all societies. If only the changing rivers of time were restored, their solid and expert woof would acquire a new prominence. Reappearing time and again, it would be toned down or made more vivid to cope with the demands of other structures, definable by other rules and consequently by other models. As things stand, the creative power of the previous century's most powerful method of social analysis has been stifled. It can recover its force and youthful vigor only in the long run. Should I add that the current vogue of Marxism seems to me the very image of the peril that stalks every social science that is in love with the model in the pure state, with the model for the model's sake?[36]

Some Marxist scholars, as we have seen, have given heed to such criticisms. They also have begun to distinguish between the assumptions and conclusions of scholars—both of which may be Europocentric—and their methods—which may be free of ethnocentrism except in the sense that they have grown out of a European context. Above all, they have developed an interest in civilizations as totalities of long duration and have sought to understand the non-Western civilizations in whose territories communism has triumphed or in which it seeks victory.

In 1973, however, a young *Annales* scholar was still pungently

35. Catherine Coquery-Vidrovitch, "Anthropologie politique et histoire de l'Afrique Noire," *Annales ESC,* XXIV (January–February 1969), 150–53 (142–63).

36. Braudel, "La Longue durée," p. 752.

critical of "militant" Marxist conceptions of historical laws and modes of production.[37] Because of basic differences between the two groups and because, in the meantime, *Annales* scholars have moved in directions that remain to be discussed, there has been no convergence. It is clear, nevertheless, that the continuing dialogue has enriched both *Annales* and Marxist scholarship.

37. Joseph Goy, "A propos du discours historique 'militant,' " in *Mélanges en l'honneur de Fernand Braudel*, II, 259–66.

6 Historyless and Nonconsensual

The difficult interchange between *Annales* scholars and Marxism has been accompanied by a much easier dialogue with Freudianism and with the analogous idea of Lévi-Strauss that the visible often is incomprehensible without an exploration of the hidden (Hestia). Like Marcel Mauss and Lévi-Strauss,[1] many persons associated with the *Annales* and Sixième Section insist that an intimate link exists between social facts (constructs) and mental structures and would agree with Paul Lacombe that "history is psychology realized and deployed in space and time."[2] A senior editor of the *Annales*, Charles Morazé, has counseled not only the application of a professionally sound psychology to history but also the formation of a history that embraces linguistics, epistemology, logic, and psychophysiology. Morazé aspires to give the discipline of history firmer foundations by making men conscious of the unity or common destiny of the "sciences of man."[3]

1. Claude Lévi-Strauss, "Introduction à l'oeuvre de Marcel Mauss," in Mauss, *Sociologie et anthropologie*, pp. xxv–xxvi (ix–liii).
2. Paul Lacombe, *La Psychologie des individus et des sociétés chez Taine, historien des littératures* (Paris: Félix Alcan, 1906), p. 369. On the desirability of linking empiricism to Gestalt psychology, see Abbott Payson Usher, "The Significance of Modern Empiricism for History and Economics," *Journal of Economic History*, IX (November 1949), 149–52 (137–55).
3. Charles Morazé, "The Application of the Social Sciences to History," *Journal of Contemporary History*, III, 2 (1968), 207–15, or the original version, "L'Histoire et l'unité des sciences de l'homme," *Annales ESC*,

Many *Annales* and Sixième Section scholars believe that the general and systematic introduction of psychology into history should aid the cause of transforming history into a true differential science. It should result, in particular, according to François Furet and Alphonse Dupront, in the weakening of Europocentric historiography and of the notion that "the most essential" psychohistorical fact of all time has been "the inversion of the sense of time."

A slow trend toward this inversion, manifest in Western Europe in the thirteenth century, gained momentum between 1500 and 1900. The conceptions of salvation and "eternal return" yielded to rationalism and to the idea of "progress." But through Freud's contributions to an understanding of the unconscious and Jung's concept of the collective unconscious, historians were made increasingly aware, especially after World War II, of the fragmentary nature of histories that are based wholly on the written word or take the written word at face value (as signification) without relating it to an entire sequence of words, without attention to form, without consideration for the meanings behind and beyond words. As a result, they have shown a growing interest in oral documents, and in myths, functions, forms, and symbols.[4] *Annales* scholarship responds, indeed, both to Freud's view that civilized men and women are no less irrational than primitive peoples and to Lévi-Strauss's emphasis that all thought (myth) has a hidden logical or problem-solving basis.

Certain scholars polemically described by François Furet as "an intellectual left deceived and demoralized by history" have

---

XXIII (March–April 1968), 233–40; Morazé, *Trois essais sur histoire et culture*; Morazé, *La Logique de l'histoire* (Paris: Gallimard, 1967); and a review of the last by Charles Grappin, "La Logique de l'histoire," *Annales ESC*, XXIII (July–August 1968), 869–79.

4. Alphonse Dupront, "L'Histoire après Freud," *Revue de l'enseignement supérieur*, No. 44–45 (1969), pp. 27–63. For Dupront's analysis of the need for systematic study of national psychologies and other manifestations of collective irrationality, see his "Problèmes et méthodes d'une histoire de la psychologie collective," *Annales ESC*, XVI (January–February 1961), 3–11.

even turned for solace to primitive man and to nonhistory, transhistory, and antihistory. They reject history as a mode of explanation and propose the creation in its place of a Kantian "reign of ends" or a Nietzschean civilization that transcends history.[5] This evolution reflects the contemporaneous trend toward nonart, the antinovel, and the theater of the absurd, all of which may corroborate the loss by Western societies of part of their former self-confidence.

François Furet, on the other hand, envisions the expulsion not of history but of the idea of progress, on the functionalist premise that every society works, or solves its problems, and hence is no better than any other society.[6] He is clearly right in his assertion that the notion of progress is in need of verification. Against Eric J. Hobsbawm's defense of progress on the ground that social, economic, and technological phenomena are related hierarchically—that some facts or types of facts cannot exist without the prior existence of others—and that a higher step in the hierarchy represents a step closer to man's emancipation from nature, one may argue that certain transformations of ecosystems may in fact ultimately provoke the loss of man's capacity to control nature.[7]

Lucien Febvre and other historians have noted the decline of the idea of progress since the turn of the century and especially

5. François Furet, "Les Intellectuels français et le structuralisme," *Preuves*, No. 192 (February 1967), pp. 3–12. This article was intended as a paper for an international colloquium, "End of Ideologies," which had been scheduled to meet in Barcelona on Dec. 5–10, 1966. As if to demonstrate unequivocally that it was premature to speak of the "end of ideology" in Spain, the Spanish government called off the meeting. From a short-term contemporary point of view the idea is probably untenable. For a vision of a "reign of ends," see Henri Lefebvre, *La Fin de l'histoire: Epilégomènes* (Paris: Editions de Minuit, 1970).

6. François Furet, "Sur quelques problèmes posés par le développement de l'histoire quantitative," *Social Science Information*, VII (February 1968), 81–82 (71–82).

7. Hobsbawm, "Karl Marx's Contribution to Historiography," pp. 37–56.

since the 1930s.[8] But if one questions progress and still more the notion of its irreversibility, one should not overlook the arguments in its behalf. The economist François Perroux, for example, readily accepts the notion of *economic progress,* which he distinguishes from quantitatively perceived economic growth and consequently defines as the (normally quick) diffusion of the effects of innovation "at the least social cost in a network of economic institutions" that tend to be generalized throughout human space.[9] Charles Morazé defends even the general notion of progress, which he defines as the amplification of the human consciousness through verbal abstraction and mathematical conceptualization. The advent in the twentieth century of an *humanité réfléchie,* individuals and societies that not only invent but also reflect on their inventions and innovations, has enabled people at last to improve their understanding of long duration and to abbreviate the lag between fast economic action, somewhat slower social organization, and very slow mind sets.[10] It may be this near-synchronization of the rates of economic, social, and psychological change that creates the illusion in highly advanced contemporary societies of the absence of progress, just as the initial acceleration of social and psychological change in early modern societies may have stimulated the sense of progress itself.

8. Lucien Febvre, "L'Effort scientifique de la Renaissance" (1937), *Pour une histoire à part entière,* p. 733 (730–35), reprinted from *Les Cahiers de Radio-Paris,* VIII (1937), 1208–13; Febvre, "Le Progrès: Puissance et déclin d'une croyance," *Pour une histoire à part entière,* pp. 844–48, originally published in *Annales d'histoire économique et sociale,* IX (1937), 89–91, review of Georges Friedmann, *La Crise du progrès* (Paris: N.R.F., 1936).
9. François Perroux, "Théorie générale du progrès économique," *Cahiers de l'Institut de Science Economique Appliquée* (1956–1958), cited by René Fruit, *La Croissance économique du pays de Saint-Amand (Nord), 1668–1914,* Ecole Pratique des Hautes Etudes (VIe Section), Centre d'Etudes Economiques, "Etudes et mémoires," 55 (Paris: Armand Colin, 1963), p. 9.
10. Morazé, *La Logique de l'histoire;* Grappin, "La Logique de l'histoire," pp. 869–79; Marcel Cohen, "La Linguistique et l'histoire," in Samaran, ed., *L'Histoire et ses méthodes,* p. 833 (823–46).

While the *Annales* School is divided over the notion of progress, its members have opted in the main not for the abolition of history but rather for the construction of a history that includes everything hitherto regarded as *ungeschichtlich* and encompasses all groups previously considered historyless. The "new history" consequently embraces "material civilization" and mass phenomena.[11] It also necessitates a search for Marcel Mauss's "unconscious categories" in magic, religion, and language,[12] and an elaboration of a history of the private, secret and unconscious.[13] It seeks in addition, in the words of Chaunu, "to quantify the past in order to relate it to the present and to lay the foundations for a study of the future [*fournir les bases d'une prospective*]," a future founded not only in a science of action but in a science of action that subsumes the longue durée, the past with all its varying rhythms, degrees of oscillation, continuities, convergences, divergences, breakdowns, and discontinuities.[14]

The object of *Annales* work is to construct a history of every group and subject whose investigation has been suppressed or neglected. It thus aspires to bring ancient, contemporary, and future history (but a *prospective* future, not a projective or futurological history deprived of foundations in the past or with a basis in the recent past only) into its focus of concern instead of limiting itself to the years 1000–1800. It aims similarly at the "demasculinization of history"[15] and at the development of a his-

11. Jeannin, "Une histoire planétaire de la civilisation matérielle," p. 72.

12. Claude Lévi-Strauss, "L'Anthropologie sociale devant l'histoire," *Annales ESC*, XV (July–August 1960), 626 (625–37).

13. Braudel, "La Longue durée," p. 739.

14. Chaunu, "Les Entraves au changement," p. 59; Chaunu, "Histoire et prospective: L'Exemple démographique," *Revue historique*, CCL (July–September 1973), 131–48. For a similar outlook toward prospective history, see Alphonse Dupront, "Présent, passé, histoire," in *Recherches et débats du Centre Catholique des Intellectuels Français*, No. 47 (June 1964), 13 (13–27).

15. Jacques Le Goff, "Histoire et ethnologie: L'Histoire et 'l'homme quotidien,' " in *Mélanges en l'honneur de Fernand Braudel*, II, 237–38 (233–43), published in English as "The Historian and the Common Man," in

tory of women, of youth, of childhood, of oral cultures, of voluntary associations, of non-Western civilizations, of nonconsensual cultures, and of Lévi-Strauss's "cold societies," which are made to last, and Braudel's "inert" societies, which offer constant resistance to the triumph of change and progress but ultimately lose.[16] Conscious of the multidimensional role of film—aesthetic, psychological, pedagogical, and acculturating (notably, the role of universalizing custom, according to Edgar Morin, "on the American model")—its proponents hope to apply cinema and television resources to devising a more complete and precise history of the techniques, collective states of mind, and mass functions of contemporary society.[17]

To achieve their exalted goal of penetrating the arcana, they are ready to use linguistics, demography, folklore, psychology, and psychoanalysis. They will look at a text not only for what it says but for its silence as well, which may relate to the said or the written as the unconscious relates to the con-

Dumoulin and Moïsi, eds., *The Historian Between the Ethnologist and the Futurologist*, pp. 204–15. On the close connection between the "demasculinization of history" and the use of unwritten sources, see Maurice Agulhon, "Esquisse pour une archéologie de la République: L'Allégorie civique féminine," *Annales ESC*, XXVIII (January–February 1973), 5–34. Half of this issue of the *Annales* is devoted to this subject, "Histoire non écrite."

16. Fernand Braudel, "Pour une économie historique," *Revue économique*, I (May 1950), 37–44, reprinted in Braudel, *Ecrits sur l'histoire*, pp. 123–33. Lévi-Strauss finds three obstacles to developmental change: a high preference for social unity or cohesion, a high respect for natural forces, and a repugnance for historical becoming. Western societies, however, have accepted change as the principle of their structure and organization: Claude Lévi-Strauss, "Les Discontinuités culturelles et le développement économique et social," *Anthropologie structurale deux*, pp. 365–76, first published in *Social Sciences Information, Information sur les Sciences Sociales*, II (June 1963), 7–15.

17. Edgar Morin, "Le Cinéma sous l'angle sociologique," in *Hommage à Lucien Febvre*, I, 391–99; Marc Ferro, "Société du XXe siècle et histoire cinématographique," *Annales ESC*, XXIII (May–June 1968), 581–85; Marc Ferro, "Le Film, une contre-analyse de la société?" *Annales ESC*, XXVIII (January–February 1973), 109–24.

scious. The application of psychology and psychoanalytic principles has had the effect of turning attention to one of the hitherto neglected components of historiography, *repetition* (as against *evolution*). This has served to shift the focus from oriented change as the basic stuff of history to the conception of history as a body of arrangements by means of which people enact but also conceal "again and again their monotonous conflicts." Psychoanalysis has made possible a probing of the document behind the document, of the unsaid behind the said, of the secret behind the secret, of the relationships between words, works, and other signs (external, public), and their significations (internal, hidden, Hestian). Applied to history, its object is to make visible and verbalize the historically invisible and the ineffable.[18]

Following in Lucien Febvre's footsteps, several *Annales*-oriented historians—chiefly Robert Mandrou, Alberto Tenenti, Gaby and Michel Vovelle, François Lebrun, and Philippe Ariès—have shown much interest in attitudes toward life and death and in the maintenance and transformation of tradition and of the "collective *sensibilité*."[19] Georges Duby has called attention to linguistic and

18. Alain Besançon, "Psychoanalysis: Auxiliary Science or Historical Method?" *Journal of Contemporary History*, III, 2 (1968), 149–62; Alain Besançon, "Vers une histoire psychanalytique," *Annales ESC*, XXIV (May–June 1969), 594–616; XXIV (July–August 1969), 1011–33.

19. Lucien Febvre, "La Sensibilité et l'histoire: Comment reconstituer la vie affective d'autrefois?" *Combats pour l'histoire* (Paris: Armand Colin, 1953), pp. 221–38, published originally as *Annales d'histoire sociale*, III (1941), 5–20; Robert Mandrou, "Pour une histoire de la sensibilité," *Annales ESC*, XIV (July–September 1959), 581–88, review of Louis Trénard, *Histoire sociale des idées: Lyon, de l'Encyclopédie au pré-romantisme*, 2 vols. (Paris: Presses Universitaires de France, 1958); Robert Mandrou, *Introduction à la France moderne: Essai de psychologie historique* (Paris: Plon, 1968); Alberto Tenenti, *La Vie et la mort à travers l'art du XVe siècle*, "Cahiers des Annales," 8 (Paris: Armand Colin, 1952), revised and enlarged as *Il Senso della Morte e l'Amore della Vita nel Rinascimento (Francia e Italia)* (Turin: Einaudi, 1957); Alberto Tenenti, "Ars moriendi: Quelques notes sur le problème de la mort à la fin du XVe siècle," *Annales ESC*, VI (October–December 1951), 433–46; Gaby and Michel Vovelle,

iconographic, or symbolic, "mutations" as a reflection of the social as well as the mental state of the groups among which they occur.[20] José-Gentil Da Silva, a Mediterranean specialist and third-generation *Annales* scholar, has probed into a special network of message systems: the relationship between the "centralization" of the means of power, the concentration of the means of production, and the maturation of exchange mechanisms and banking techniques as a means of shifting labor in stored form (as money or credit) from places where it is in low demand to those where it is in low supply or high demand. The modification of these systems in Portugal, Spain, and England toward the end of the sixteenth century and in the course of the seventeenth, observes Da Silva, was attended by lexical change—the introduction, for example, of the terms "political conjuncture" and "economic conjuncture" to denote the cyclical passage from an upward to a downward curve of political or economic life (and perhaps the reverse). A more satisfactory definition of the general interrelational phenomenon, however, will require a methodological study of the points of contact between the lexical system

Vision de la mort et de l'au-delà en Provence d'après les autels des âmes du purgatoire, XVe–XXe siècles, "Cahiers des Annales," 29 (Paris: Armand Colin, 1970); Michel Vovelle, *Piété baroque et déchristianisation en Provence au dix-huitième siècle: Les Attitudes devant la mort d'après les clauses des testaments* (Paris: Plon, 1973); Michel Vovelle, *Mourir autrefois: Attitudes collectives devant la mort aux XVIIe et XVIIIe siècles* (Paris: Gallimard, 1974); François Lebrun, *Les Hommes et la mort en Anjou aux XVIIe et XVIIIe siècles: Essai de démographie et de psychologie historiques,* Ecole Pratique des Hautes Etudes (VIe Section), "Civilisations et sociétés," 25 (Paris: Mouton, 1971); Philippe Ariès, *Histoire des populations françaises et de leurs attitudes devant la vie depuis le XVIIIe siècle* (Paris: Editions Self, 1948); Philippe Ariès, *Western Attitudes toward Death: From the Middle Ages to the Present,* The Johns Hopkins University lectures, trans. Patricia M. Ranum (Baltimore: The Johns Hopkins University Press, 1974); Philippe Ariès, "La Mort inversée: Le Changement des attitudes devant la mort dans les sociétés occidentales," *Archives européennes de sociologie,* VIII, 2 (1967), 169-95.

20. Georges Duby, "Histoire des mentalités," in Samaran, ed., *L'Histoire et ses méthodes,* pp. 952-57, 962-64 (937-66).

and the other "languages" of culture.[21] Another scholar, Jean-Pierre Vernant, has shown that the passage in archaic Greece from mythopoeic thought to logic and philosophy was advanced by the transmission of the magic of hereditary magicians to a corps of disciples and, more largely, by the creation of a collegial society and the adoption of a system of political organization and administration with a geographic instead of kinship basis. Yet another thinker of the *Annales* persuasion, Nathan Wachtel, has made use of Marc Bloch's notion of a "prudently retrogressive method," going from the readily observable present to the occasionally and unsystematically recorded past, in order to capture the logic of the differential convergence and divergence of memories of the past as preserved in various Indian folklores.[22]

Lucien Febvre's concerted efforts to provide *l'ouï-dire*, or folklore, and collective psychology with an historical framework,[23] furthermore, have spurred on *Annales*-oriented scholars

21. José-Gentil Da Silva, *Banque et crédit en Italie au XVIIe siècle*, 2 vols. (Paris: Editions Klincksieck, 1969), I, 12–13, 15, 23, 313–14, 407, 413, 464, 676–77, 731, 734–36; Da Silva, "L'Histoire: Une biologie de l'événement politique," *Annales ESC*, XXVI (May–August 1971), 854–72. Da Silva expects to publish eventually a book on the subject "Lexique, temps, histoire."

22. Jean-Pierre Vernant, "Du Mythe à la raison: La Formation de la pensée positive dans la Grèce archaïque," *Annales ESC*, XII (April–June 1957), 183–206. For a discussion of myth, work, war, and the lack of a high appreciation of technique in ancient Greece, as expounded in the publications of Jean-Pierre Vernant, Pierre Lévêque, Pierre Vidal-Naquet, and Marcel Detienne, see Jean-Pierre Darmon, "Un cours nouveau dans les études grecques," *Critique*, XXVI (March 1970), 265–86; Jean-Pierre Darmon, "Problèmes de la guerre en Grèce ancienne," *Annales ESC*, XXV (September–October 1970), 1298–1308. On the retrogressive method, see Bloch, *The Historian's Craft*, pp. 45–46; Nathan Wachtel, "La Vision des vaincus: La Conquête espagnole dans le folklore indigène," *Annales ESC*, XXII (May–June 1967), 554–85, translated by M. Ross as "The Vision of the Vanquished: The Spanish Conquest of America Presented in Folklore," in Marc Ferro, ed., *Social Historians in Contemporary France* (New York, 1972), pp. 230–60, 318–27; Nathan Wachtel, *La Vision des vaincus: Les Indiens du Pérou devant la conquête espagnole* (Paris: Gallimard, 1972).

23. Lucien Febvre, *Le Problème de l'incroyance au XVIe siècle: La*

to study popular cultures and the interactions between high literary culture and popular culture.[24] Partly as a result of the authority of *Annales* tendencies, folklore, or oral literature, has been given both structural and historico-geographic foundations instead of being confined to a structural or to a structural and geographic basis.[25] Folklorists have not only added a temporal dimension; they have shown a desire to adjust the methods of literary history, linguistics, philology, sociology, anthropology, psychology, and psychoanalysis to the study of oral literature.[26]

Interest in the hidden and historyless, moreover, has encouraged folklorists and anthropologists to examine the culture or subculture of rituals of social reversal and of the carnival vision and style of expression, which, according to the Soviet historian Mikhail Bakhtin, disdains distinctions between actors and spectators and is governed by laws of liberty, by the "suspension of all hierarchical rank, privileges, norms, and prohibitions."[27] These

---

Religion de Rabelais, in series "L'Evolution de l'Humanité" (Paris: Albin Michel, 1942), pp. 418–20.

24. Examples of such studies include Robert Mandrou, *De la culture populaire aux XVIIe et XVIIIe siècles: La Bibliothèque Bleue de Troyes* (Paris: Stock, 1964); Geneviève Bollème, *Les Almanachs populaires aux XVIIe et XVIIIe siècles: Essai d'histoire sociale* (Paris, The Hague: Mouton, 1969); Geneviève Bollème, *La Bibliothèque Bleue: La Littérature populaire en France du XVIe au XIXe siècle* (Paris: Julliard, 1971); Jean-Jacques Darmon, *Le Colportage de librairie en France sous le Second Empire: Grands colporteurs et culture populaire,* in series "Civilisations et mentalités" (dir.: Philippe Ariès and Robert Mandrou) (Paris: Plon, 1972).

25. Marie-Louise Tenèze, "Introduction à l'étude de la littérature orale: Le Conte," *Annales ESC,* XXIV (September–October 1969), 1104–20.

26. Marc Soriano, *Les Contes de Perrault: Culture savante et traditions populaires* (Paris: Gallimard, 1968). For a discussion of this book with Soriano by Jacques Le Goff, Emmanuel Le Roy Ladurie, and André Burguière, see "Débats et combats: Les Contes de Perrault," *Annales ESC,* XXV (May–June 1970), 633–53.

27. Mikhaïl Bakhtine, *L'Oeuvre de François Rabelais et la culture populaire au Moyen âge et sous la Renaissance,* trans. Andrée Robel (Paris: Gallimard, 1970). Originally published in Moscow in 1965, the book is available in English: Mikhail Bakhtin, *Rabelais and His World,* trans. Helene Iswolsky (Cambridge, Mass.: M.I.T. Press, 1968), p. 10. For similar studies

rituals, spectacles, and carnivals act simultaneously to reinforce the existing social order and to undermine it further if it is unable to fulfill the objectives for which it was set up.

Both a continuation and a sharp critique of Febvre's great work, Bakhtin's study was welcomed in France for its choice of theme, late medieval and Rabelaisian popular culture. The work itself, however, has been criticized for identifying popular culture too closely with the ambivalent—at once joyous and sarcastic —fête and hardly at all with the work habits, work techniques, and labor organizations of the people.[28]

Bakhtin provides, nevertheless, a brilliant analysis of the fête as an act of repetition and renewal, whose form and content were devitalized as "the state encroached upon festive life and turned it into a parade," restricting the privileges of the marketplace and thus forcing the former festivities into the private life of the home.[29] Pierre Chaunu has dealt further with the problem of the existence of three types of fête, or three levels of festive expression and appreciation, in sixteenth-century Spain: the fête of the popular cultures, the religious liturgical fête, and the political liturgical fête, based on a Burgundian model, which was crucial to the affirmation of the Spanish state. Around 1550, however, the political fête was still much less influential, and much more poorly formulated, than the religious fête.[30]

Another *Annales* historian, Mona Ozouf, more specifically

---

by scholars in other countries, see Natalie Zemon Davis, "The Reasons of Misrule: Youth Groups and Charivaris in Sixteenth-Century France," *Past and Present*, No. 50 (February 1971), pp. 41–75; E. P. Thompson, " 'Rough Music': Le Charivari anglais," *Annales ESC*, XXVII (March–April 1972), 285–312; Claude Gaignebet, "Le Combat de Carnaval et de Carême de P. Bruegel (1559)," *ibid.*, pp. 313–45; Leo Košuta, "Il Mondo Vero e il Mondo Rovescio in 'Dundo Maroje' di Marino Darsa (Marin Držić)," *Ricerche Slavistiche*, XII (1964), 65–122.

28. Marc Soriano, "Quelques travaux récents sur la littérature populaire," *Annales ESC*, XXVI (May–August 1971), 781 (771–81).

29. Bakhtin, *Rabelais and His World*, p. 33.

30. Pierre Chaunu, *L'Espagne et Charles Quint*, 2 vols. (Paris: Société d'Edition d'Enseignement Supérieur, 1973), II, 564–68.

directs her attention to the creation of a new system of festivals—secular, popular, and of urban inspiration, with reminders of an older rural society—in revolutionary France as a reaction against the ancien régime's vision of the world as pageant, parade, and garden theater, and its expression of fête, in Pierre Francastel's words, as *fête galante, fête parée*.[31] To herald the advent to power, in and after 1789 or 1792, of new men and new rites of passage, and to celebrate the general reassignment of space (the formation of juridically equal and geographically nearly equal *départements* to replace the geographic and juridical inequalities of the former provincial administration; the sale of *biens nationaux*) and time (a new calendar, a new work week, the beginning of a new era), Parisians and other French urban citizens created new fêtes, to which they gave spatial as well as temporal dimension. The new sacred space was generally more open and more extensive, more luminous, and essentially horizontal (unlike the vertical cathedral)—a plain, a heath, a moor, or a *champ de mars*, in preference to the confining space of the garden and of the village or city square. Like the old holidays, the new ones were commemorated by processions. Their celebration was fixed on a specific day, and each city and village designated the itinerary to be followed and the duration of each processional manifestation. The new fêtes like the old were acts of mythical repetition and renewal, but the frame of reference of the repetition was temporally and spatially different.[32]

Annales historians have been nourished in the tradition of Jules

31. Pierre Francastel, "L'Esthétique des Lumières," in Pierre Francastel, ed., *Utopie et institutions au XVIIIe siècle: Le Pragmatisme des Lumières*, Ecole Pratique des Hautes Etudes (VIe Section), "Congrès et colloques," 4 (Paris, The Hague: Mouton, 1963), pp. 331–57.

32. Mona Ozouf, "Le Cortège et la ville: Les Itinéraires parisiens des fêtes révolutionnaires," *Annales ESC*, XXVI (September–October 1971), 889–916; Mona Ozouf, "La Fête sous la Révolution française," in Le Goff and Nora, eds., *Faire de l'histoire*, III, *Nouveaux objets*, 256–77; Mona Ozouf, "Space and Time in the Festivals of the French Revolution," *Comparative Studies in Society and History*, XVII (July 1975), 372–84.

Michelet, the model historian even for Marxist Albert Soboul.[33] Overtly, at least, they aspire to a history of the people like Michelet's—not of a hero without blemish but of one who exhibits faults of sluggishness and impatience even as he pursues his quest for social justice.[34] More particularly, they aspire to a history like Paul Bois's study of the rural folk of western France; it opens with a tableau of the twentieth century—thus with the contemporary knowns—and proceeds to the unknowns of the French Revolution and eighteenth century in order to ascertain why for two centuries there have been in the Sarthe, in addition to townsmen, "two *bocage* peoples," two cultural and social anthropologies: an occupationally relatively homogeneous, self-sufficient, and assertive rebel (*chouan*) people in the west, with a strong dislike for the city; and an occupationally more heterogeneous and culturally more docile or receptive (*bleu*) people in the east or southeast, more prone to follow the example of the French capital.[35] A similar but more extensive model for a history of the people is offered by Le Roy Ladurie, who distinguishes between two main ethnocultural, historical, and economic organizations of the space occupied by the political entity known as France: a Languedocian and western continental space and culture, and a French, Franco-Provençal, and eastern continental space and culture. In the first, writes Le Roy Ladurie, there was little

33. Soboul, *La Civilisation et la Révolution française*, I, 32.

34. Paul Viallaneix, *La Voie royale: Essai sur l'idée du Peuple dans l'oeuvre de Michelet* (Paris: Librairie Delagrave, 1959), pp. 332–33.

35. Paul Bois, *Paysans de l'Ouest: Des structures économiques et sociales aux options politiques depuis l'époque révolutionnaire dans la Sarthe*, Ecole Pratique des Hautes Etudes (VIe Section) (Paris, The Hague: Mouton, 1960). In 1971 Flammarion published a shortened version of this work. For Bois's failure to use a rank-order correlation coefficient in comparing peasant property-holding with bourgeois, ecclesiastical, and noble property-holding, which leads him to the possibly erroneous conclusion that "peasant property is in opposition above all to that of the bourgeoisie," see Charles Tilly, "Quantification in History as Seen from France," in Lorwin and Price, eds., *The Dimensions of the Past*, pp. 114–16 (93–125).

modernity even in the second half of the eighteenth ⸺
the second, two different conceptions of modernity clas⸺
each other. One was the modernity (or modernizatio.
peasants, derived from the development of literacy and the
tensification of contacts with towns and markets and culminatii.
in "rising expectations" and a heightened distrust of market
forces. The other was the modernity (or modernization) of landlords—noble, nonnoble, and ecclesiastical—who sought to extend
and enclose their properties and who aspired to give their production a market orientation.[36]

The *Annales* masters have shown great skill, too, in handling
various aspects of associational life: Braudel on banditry, Le Roy
Ladurie on millenarian and peasant movements in Languedoc,
Georges Duby on the medieval peasantry and nobility in Western
Europe, Jacques Le Goff on the tripartite structure of medieval
life, Pierre Goubert on the agrobiological basis of the social
structure of the ancien régime. On the whole, however, *Annales*
scholars appear to have devoted less analytical effort to the
associational life than to economic change, *genres de vie*, and the
tangible realities (*vie matérielle*) of culture. In his revised *Méditerranée*, for example, Braudel devotes 291 pages to micropolitics, 231 to geographical history, 231 to economics, 89 to
macropolitics (empires and polemology), 69 to routes and
techniques of communication, 68 to civilizations, and only 46
pages to society (including banditry but excluding cities), and
22 to demography. In other words, he consecrates five times as

36. Emmanuel Le Roy Ladurie, "Révoltes et contestations rurales en
France de 1675 à 1788," *Annales ESC*, XXIX (January–February 1974), 8–
22. For an elaboration of the concept of "rising expectations," see James C.
Davies, "The J-Curve of Rising and Declining Satisfactions as a Cause of
Some Great Revolutions and a Contained Rebellion," in Hugh Davis
Graham and Ted Robert Gurr, eds., *Violence in America: Historical and
Comparative Perspectives*, a report submitted to the National Commission
on the Causes and Prevention of Violence (New York: Bantam Books,
1969), pp. 690–730.

much space to economic history as to social history, five times as much to geographical history, and more than six times as much to micropolitics.

Jack Hexter has remarked of Braudel that

in dealing with *structures*, he attends almost entirely to material structures—peninsulas, islands, mountains, plateaus and plains, seas and oceans, climate and seasons; routes, shipping, and towns. Routines imbedded in custom and law receive less attention or none. The Mediterranean world is the world of grain, the olive tree, the vine, and the sheep. . . . Of the daily, scarcely changing practices of the vineyard, the olive grove, and the wheat field we hear too little. Nor do we learn much about how small communities . . . or large ones . . . actually ordered their affairs or of what held them together in durable structures.

Another American critic, H. G. Koenigsberger, regards the *Mediterranean* as "original, protean, suggestive, compellingly readable." It is not, however, a model of "total history," since it contains very little about "sophisticated culture"—music, science, and other signs of genius—and hardly much more on "popular culture." It is, on the other hand, "a new kind of economic, social and political history," equal to the work of Burckhardt but unequal to the "great histories" of Gibbon and Macaulay.[37] Such subjective hierarchies, however, may tell the reader more about the critic than about the subject of his criticism.

In all fairness to Braudel, it must be noted that one of the chief subjects of the *Mediterranean*, as of his other studies, is civilization, a combination of Koenigsberger's "sophisticated culture" and "popular culture." Moreover, Braudel also deals with the problem of popular culture by his systematic treatment of "material culture." We are similarly able to get at popular culture and popular organizational forms through Le Roy Ladurie's studies of "rural civilization" and of Languedoc's peasants and small communities.[38] It is true, nevertheless, that social history

37. Hexter, "Fernand Braudel," p. 519; Koenigsberger, "Fernand Braudel," pp. 10–12.

38. Le Roy Ladurie, *Les Paysans de Languedoc*, pp. 160–68, in which he

began to come into its own in France only during the 1950s, despite the foundations laid earlier by Lucien Febvre, Marc Bloch, Georges Lefebvre, and Ernest Labrousse. Until then, indeed, the first of the three subcategories in the official title of the *Annales*—Economies, Sociétés, Civilisations—took a clear lead, while Sociétés held last place among the three orientations of chief interest to *Annales* scholars.

With the partial "emancipation" of social history in the 1950s, economic history lost ground among *Annales* historians, and the Sorbonne economic historian François Crouzet insists that the preoccupation with total history led to "amateurism" and an unnecessary "dispersion of efforts," resulting in harm for economic history. The "largely beneficial, but also sometimes stifling" personality cult of Braudel and Labrousse, he holds, had a similar effect.[39] But if the proportion of *Annales* scholars drawn to economic history has not kept pace, the quality of French economic history has improved since its exposure to Anglo-American methods and to long-term and total-economic analysis.[40]

Social history, however, is still poorly defined. Should it focus on elementary social groups, on social classes, or on whole societies, and how should each of these be defined? Are political groups, economic organizations, and friendly and intellectual associations all part of social history? What is the relationship among elementary social groups, fragmentary societies, and a whole society? How can one understand the parts of society without understanding the whole, and how can one know the

notes in Languedoc between 1350 and 1500 (or 1550) an effervescence of "brotherhood" associations and "a last awakening of the enlarged [or extended] family"; Emmanuel Le Roy Ladurie, "La Civilisation rurale," *Le Territoire de l'historien*, pp. 141–68, written originally as "Rurale (Civilisation)" for *Encyclopaedia Universalis*, XIV, 510–18.

39. François Crouzet, "The Economic History of Modern Europe," *Journal of Economic History*, XXXI (March 1971), 144, 147–48 (135–52).

40. Pierre Léon, "Histoire économique et histoire sociale en France: Problèmes et perspectives," in *Mélanges en l'honneur de Fernand Braudel*, II, 303–15.

whole without knowing the parts? How do whole and part societies (such as peasantries) differ from the whole and part cultures (such as popular cultures)?[41] How much weight should the historian give to social arithmetic and how much to the quality of life? Moreover, if every social organization is religious, political, or economic, can there be an autonomous social history at all?

Annales social history has been oriented primarily toward *genres de vie*, "the life of the mind," and the deep layers of history. More concerned with *socioeconomies* than with *societies*, it long left the study of social classes and of the social distribution of power to Marxists, sociologists, and political scientists.

Annales scholars similarly neglected the family despite their admiration for the late nineteenth-century historian, Paul Lacombe, who wrote a history of the Roman family.[42] Despite Febvre's long-standing interest in "family monographs" (noble, *robin*, and bourgeois) and family history in general, they tended to relegate family and childhood to anthropologists and sociol-

41. The last two questions have been raised by Robert Mandrou in his "Cultures ou niveaux culturels dans les sociétés d'Ancien Régime," *Revue des études Sud-Est européennes,* X, 3 (1972), 415–22. Mandrou inclines to the view that the French popular cultures of the seventeenth and eighteenth centuries constituted a separate category of culture, characterized by a literature of colportage portraying an unchanging wonderland of magic and miracle. Geneviève Bollème maintains, on the other hand, that there was a gradual shift in some of France's popular cultures during the eighteenth century from supernaturalism to a partial integration with the Enlightenment culture but at a lower level. Bollème thus distinguishes between different levels of one general culture, while Mandrou depicts the popular cultures as a distinct and separate group. On this subject, see also Robert Mandrou, "Littérature de colportage et mentalités paysannes, XVIIe–XVIIIe siècles," *Etudes rurales,* No. 15 (October–December 1964), pp. 72–85; Robert Darnton, "In Search of the Enlightenment: Recent Attempts to Create a Social History of Ideas," *Journal of Modern History,* XLIII (March 1971), 125–27 (113–32); Darnton, "The High Enlightenment and the Low-Life of Literature in Pre-revolutionary France," *Past and Present,* No. 51 (May 1971), pp. 81–115.

42. Paul Lacombe, *La Famille dans la société romaine* (Paris: Lecrosnier et Babé, 1889).

ogists.[43] They did this, moreover, despite the romantic portrayal of the child by the model historian Michelet as "the interpreter of the people"—indeed, as "the people themselves before they are deformed," because children are simple and the simple "seldom divide their thought. Not being armed with the machinery of analysis and abstraction, they see everything as one, entire and concrete, just as life presents it."[44]

The neglect of the family was the product of the old habit, developed when historians were concerned almost exclusively with events relating to the growing power of state and nation, of excluding the family—or all except ruling or governing families— from the scope of history because the family had lost part of its functional autonomy. Historians who conceived of history as the evolution of political events could not be interested in more than a few families, those that constituted a recognized political authority. Historians among whom political history became unfashionable, on the other hand, could not formulate new historical facts in regard to the family with ease until the assertion of a climate of opinion favorable to the study of nonconsensual and vanquished groups.

Under a multiple impact—the growing attraction of nonconsensual history; the affirmation of historical demography as an autonomous discipline and adoption of Louis Henry's "family reconstitution" approach to historical demography; the appear-

43. Febvre, *Philippe II et la Franche-Comté*, pp. 180–83, 208–11, 232–35, 237–41; Febvre, "Ce que peuvent nous apprendre les monographies familiales," *Pour une histoire à part entière*, pp. 404–9, published originally in *Mélanges d'histoire sociale*, I (1942), 31–34. See also Roger Aubenas, "La Famille dans l'ancienne Provence," *Annales d'histoire économique et sociale*, VIII (1936), 523–40. Other *Annales* family studies and reviews of works on the family are cited in Maurice-A. Arnould, in collaboration with Vital Chomel, Paul Leuilliot, and Andrée Scufflaire, *Vingt années d'histoire économique et sociale: Table analytique des "Annales" fondées par Marc Bloch et Lucien Febvre (1929–1948)* (Paris: Association Marc Bloch, 1953), items 756–90 and others listed under the rubric "Familles," p. 287.

44. Jules Michelet, *The People*, translated with an introduction by John P. McKay (Urbana: University of Illinois Press, 1973), pp. 119–20.

ance of Philippe Ariès's *L'Enfant et la vie familiale sous l'Ancien Régime* (1960); and the interest of the *Annales* historians Jean Meuvret and Pierre Goubert in parish records—the family became a primary *Annales* concern.[45] As early as 1946, Meuvret noted the regularity of a sharp fall in the number of births as well as a sharp rise in the death rate in the wake of famine, one of the ways by means of which family size was limited in the seventeenth and earlier centuries.[46] Pursuing an elementary form of "family reconstitution" for a few Beauvaisis villages, especially Auneuil, Goubert was able to demonstrate, among other things, that the Beauvaisis rural family was small and mononuclear. He

45. Etienne Gautier and Louis Henry, *La Population de Crulai, paroisse normande: Etude historique* (Paris: Presses Universitaires de France, 1958); Michel Fleury and Louis Henry, "Pour connaître la population de la France depuis Louis XIV: Plan de travaux par sondage," *Population*, XIII (October–December 1958), 663–86; Michel Fleury and Louis Henry, *Des registres paroissiaux à l'histoire de la population: Manuel de dépouillement et de l'exploitation de l'état civil ancien* (Paris: Editions de l'Institut National d'Etudes Démographiques, 1956); Michel Fleury and Louis Henry, *Nouveau manuel de dépouillement et de l'exploitation de l'état civil ancien* (Paris: Editions de l'Institut National d'Etudes Démographiques, 1965); Louis Henry, *Anciennes familles genevoises: Etude démographique, XVIe–XXe siècle* (Paris: Presses Universitaires de France, 1956); Louis Henry, "Une richesse démographique en friche: Les Registres paroissiaux," *Population*, VIII (April–June 1953), 281–90; Philippe Ariès, *L'Enfant et la vie familiale sous l'Ancien Régime* (Paris: Plon, 1960), translated by Robert Baldick as *Centuries of Childhood: A Social History of Family Life* (London: Cape; New York: Knopf, 1962). For a review of Ariès, *L'Enfant et la vie familiale*, see Jean-Louis Flandrin, "Enfance et société," *Annales ESC*, XIX (March–April 1964), 322–29.

46. Jean Meuvret, "Les Crises de subsistances et la démographie de la France d'Ancien Régime," in *Etudes d'histoire économique: Recueil d'articles* (Paris: Armand Colin, 1971), pp. 271–78, published originally in *Population*, I (October–December 1946), 643–50. See also Jean Meuvret, "Demographic Crisis in France from the Sixteenth to the Eighteenth Century," translated by Margaret Hilton, in D. V. Glass and D. E. C. Eversley, eds., *Population in History: Essays in Historical Demography* (London: Edward Arnold, 1965), pp. 507–22; Claude Gindin, "La Pensée historique de Jean Meuvret: Quelques-uns de ses enseignements," *La Pensée*, No. 169 (June 1973), pp. 92–102.

also discovered that the parish records of this region were fairly good after 1670 but poorly kept in earlier periods.[47] After 1960, the interest of French historians in family history quickly snowballed. Philippe Wolff drew attention to the relatively unexplored character of "the history of the family and its role in the economy, the passage from the patriarchal to the conjugal family, and the gradual loosening of familial solidarities."[48] Georges Duby called for a study not only of the family but—under the suggestion of Ariès's example—of the role of children in the family as well, of the work and play groups through which the socialization of children and youth was achieved, of a society's collective representations of its children and youth, and of the relationship between the flourishing legends in Western Europe of the child Jesus and the collective representations of children.[49] Duby was able to offer evidence supporting the view (construct) that the aristocratic family of the Rhineland

47. Pierre Goubert, *Beauvais et le Beauvaisis de 1600 à 1730: Contribution à l'histoire sociale de la France du XVIIe siècle*, 2 vols., Ecole Pratique des Hautes Etudes (VIe Section), Centre de Recherches Historiques, "Démographie et sociétés," 3 (Paris: S.E.V.P.E.N., 1960), Goubert's principal thesis, of which the first part has also been published under the title *Cent mille provinciaux au XVIIe siècle: Beauvais et le Beauvaisis de 1600 à 1730* (Paris: Flammarion, 1973); Goubert, "En Beauvaisis: Problèmes démographiques du XVIIe siècle," *Annales ESC*, VII (October–December 1952), 453–68; Goubert, "Une richesse historique en cours d'exploitation: Les Registres paroissiaux," *Annales ESC*, IX (January–March 1954), 83–93, reply to Louis Henry, "Une richesse démographique en friche"; Goubert, "Recent Theories and Research in French Population between 1500 and 1700," trans. Margaret Hilton, in Glass and Eversley, eds., *Population in History*, pp. 457–73; Goubert, "Historical Demography and the Reinterpretation of Early Modern French History: A Research Review," *Journal of Interdisciplinary History*, I (Autumn 1970), 37–48; Emmanuel Le Roy Ladurie, "Du Quantitatif en histoire: La VIe Section de l'Ecole Pratique des Hautes Etudes" (paper for the American Historical Association, Toronto, December 1967), in *Le Territoire de l'historien*, p. 27 (23–37).

48. Wolff, "L'Etude des économies et des sociétés," p. 865.

49. Georges Duby, "Histoire des mentalités," in Samaran, ed., *L'Histoire et ses méthodes*, pp. 957–58 (937–66).

and northern France was transformed radically between the tenth and twelfth centuries. Whereas the earlier family did not have large real properties—it did not need them so long as it was rewarded amply for its service to the ruling household—and recognized inheritance of real property by females as well as males, the later aristocratic family held extensive properties of land and admitted the principle of inheritance of real property by a single male member of the house only.[50] A third French medievalist, Jacques Heers, has projected the view of the aristocratic family of the cities of medieval Italy and Germany as a large family of relatives, clients, and domestic slave women—thus having members of diverse condition and fortune—which declined only with the growth of princely power.[51]

A Sorbonne critic of the *Annales*, Roland Mousnier, has moved on from his interest in social structure as a system of relationships between "fundamental social groups, or groups of existence," defined in terms of associations and oppositions, or intensity and regularity of positive and negative communication (social, biological, and intellectual), to an identification of the family as the main form of human association. On the basis of marriage patterns —who marries whom—one can distinguish effectively, he maintains, between the different "groups of existence" in every society.[52]

50. Georges Duby, "Dans la France du Nord-Ouest au XIIe siècle: Les 'Jeunes' dans la société aristocratique," *Annales ESC*, XIX (September–October 1964), 835–46, translated by M. Gwyer as "Northwest France: The 'Young' in Twelfth-Century Aristocratic Society," in Ferro, ed., *Social Historians in Contemporary France*, pp. 87–99, 276–79; Duby, "Structures familiales dans le Moyen âge occidental," XIIIe Congrès International des Sciences Historiques, 16–23 août 1970; Duby, "Lignage, noblesse et chevalerie au XIIe siècle dans la région mâconnaise: Une révision," *Annales ESC*, XXVII (July–October 1972), 803–23.

51. Jacques Heers, *Le Clan familial au Moyen âge: Etude sur les structures politiques et sociales des milieux urbains* (Paris: Presses Universitaires de France, 1974).

52. Roland Mousnier, "Préface" to Marcel Couturier, *Recherches sur les structures sociales de Chateaudun 1525–1789*, Ecole Pratique des Hautes

Given their own orientations, *Annales* scholars have had no compunction in defining a fundamental social group in Mousnier's terms of degree and nature of communication. Their interest in the family has also led them, however, to attempt a distinction between family types and to define the spatial and temporal limits of each. Le Roy Ladurie thus emphasizes that the nuclear, or mononuclear, family prevailed increasingly in rural northwestern Europe between the thirteenth and eighteenth centuries, whereas "diverse forms of large families" coexisted with the nuclear family in the rural regions of southern (one should add nonmaritime, hence continental) Europe. In times of crisis, such as the greater part of the fourteenth and fifteenth centuries, various large family types were preferred to the nuclear type. Large families continued to be an important phenomenon in southern France, he contends, as late as the seventeenth and eighteenth centuries, constituting in some regions as much as 30 or 40 per cent of the total population.[53] Other research indicates that the large family made up of parents and married children was more common in rural Haute Provence as late as the first half of the eighteenth century.[54] Many of these findings,

Etudes (VIe Section), Centre de Recherches Historiques, "Démographie et sociétés," 10 (Paris: S.E.V.P.E.N., 1969), pp. 7–9.

53. Le Roy Ladurie, "La Civilisation rurale," pp. 150–51; Le Roy Ladurie, "Systèmes de la coutume: Structures familiales et coutume d'héritage en France au XVIe siècle," *Annales ESC*, XXVII (July–October 1972), 825–46 (part of the special number "Famille et société"), reprinted in Le Roy Ladurie, *Le Territoire de l'historien*, pp. 222–51. This last article is a review of Jean Yver, *Egalité entre héritiers et exclusion des enfants dotés: Essai de géographie coutumière* (Paris: Sirey, 1966); Jean Yver, "Les Caractères originaux du groupe de coutumes de l'Ouest de la France," *Revue historique de droit français et étranger*, 4th ser., XXX, 1 (1952), 18–79; Jean Yver, "Les Deux groupes de coutumes du Nord," *Revue du Nord*, XXXV (October–December 1953), 197–220; XXXVI (January–March 1954), 5–36.

54. Alain Collomp, "Famille nucléaire et famille élargie en Haute Provence au XVIIIe siècle (1703–1734)," *Annales ESC*, XXVII (July–October 1972), 969–75.

along with the contributions of other scholars, were incorporated in an *Annales* issue entitled "Famille et société."[55]

Le Roy Ladurie's perception of large family types in southern France has received support from the earlier research of Robert-Henri Bautier, whose study of the demography of Carpentras shows that town to have numbered, in 1473, 520 Christian families (*feux*) comprising a total Christian population of 2,706 (excluding the clergy, who added to the Christian element about 150 persons more) and 69 Jewish families comprising a total Jewish population of 298. An average Christian family thus numbered 5.2 persons, compared to an average Jewish family of 4.3 persons. Of still greater importance, 50 per cent of the town's inhabitants lived in families of 5 to 9 persons, 21.2 per cent in family groups of 10 to 25 persons, and only 28.8 per cent in small families of 1 to 4 persons. In 1478, on the other hand, only 8.6 per cent of the population lived in families of 10 persons or more, while more than 32 per cent lived in families of fewer than 4 persons and about 59 per cent in families of 4 to 9 persons.[56]

Differences in the size and function of families were accompanied in general, according to the research of *Annales* and other (non-French) scholars, by differences in the age at marriage, with three main patterns discernible in the eighteenth century: a puberty-age pattern for both males and females in the Balkan interior, a delayed-marriage pattern for males and a transitional pattern for females in some portions of the Mediterranean and Baltic, and a delayed-marriage pattern for males and females alike (with a somewhat later age for males) in northwestern Europe and the more densely settled parts of Italy. In England, the Low Countries, northern France, Bavaria, Venice, and Tuscany, the average age at marriage rose between 1300 and the mid-eighteenth

55. André Burguière introduces the volume with a penetrating analysis, "Famille et société," *Annales ESC*, XXVII (July–October 1972), 799–802.

56. Robert-Henri Bautier, "Feux, population et structure sociale au milieu du XVe siècle: L'Exemple de Carpentras," *Annales ESC*, XIV (April–June 1959), 255–68.

century to close to 24 or 25 (even 28) for women and to 27 or
even more than 30 for men, attaining in many places the foregoing figures even before 1550 or 1650.[57] A transitional pattern
prevailed in England before 1377, when 67–70 percent of all
women 15 years of age or over were married, whereas a puberty-
age pattern would have given 90 per cent (as in Serbia as late
as 1846) and a delayed-marriage pattern of the mid-eighteenth-
century type would have yielded only 50 per cent. In Castile
proper, the average age at marriage for females was 20–21; in
Granada it was 19–20; in Catalonia (and perhaps Valencia) it was
higher, thus in greater conformity with the northwestern European (and Italian) pattern, which Pierre Chaunu identifies as the
model of "modernity" and of a commercial "system of civilization."

The system of modernity first grew—if one disregards precocious Italy—in that part of Europe where there was an early
development of the nuclear family, delayed marriage for men and
women alike, and a technological transformation capable of supporting the aforementioned changes. The technological innovations included the heavy wheeled plow and iron plowshare, an
improved horse collar and harness that would permit the use of
the horse as a draft animal, and windmills with a horizontal axle.
This new ecotechnological system was concentrated at first in
an area of 150,000–200,000 square kilometers stretching from the

57. John Hajnal, "European Marriage Patterns in Perspective," in Glass
and Eversley, eds., *Population in History*, pp. 101–43; Peter Laslett, *The
World We Have Lost* (New York: Scribner's, 1965), p. 82; *Household
and Family in Past Time: Comparative Studies in the Size and Structure
of the Domestic Group over the Last Three Centuries in England, France,
Serbia, Japan, and Colonial North America, with Further Materials from
Western Europe*, edited, with an analytic introduction on the history of
the family, by Peter Laslett, with the assistance of Richard Wall (Cambridge: Cambridge University Press, 1972); André Burguière, "De Malthus
à Max Weber: Le Mariage et l'esprit d'entreprise," *Annales ESC*, XXVII
(July–October 1972), 1128–38; Andrejs Plakans, "Peasant Farmsteads and
Households in the Baltic Littoral, 1797," *Comparative Studies in Society
and History*, XVII (January 1975), 2–35.

central Loire to the Scheldt (Escaut) basin. Soon, however, in concentric rings (customarily called von Thünen rings, after the early nineteenth-century German economist Johann Heinrich von Thünen), it was diffused to the broad Rhine corridor, to northern Italy, and to England. In France, it did not spread to any significant degree beyond the northern approaches to the Massif Central, partly for ecological reasons—mountainous terrain, shallower soil, less influential westerlies—and partly for ethnocultural reasons.

Wherever the new technology was adopted and wherever commercial activity played a similar role in giving the economy a boost, it became possible for a small nuclear family to do the work that previously had required a greater number of adults. When an enlarged family was no longer necessary, the age of marriage could be delayed. The delay for women, indeed, increased their life expectancy by several years, through the reduction of the risks of child-bearing at an early age and, in many cases, the reduction of the period of child-bearing itself by five to ten years. This in turn tended to increase the total work period of each woman. At the same time, because man and wife had fewer children they could divert investments—however small— to education or, at least, to the encouragement of literacy. Finally, the new type of family and marriage pattern may have reduced— without eliminating—some of the most glaring inequalities between the sexes.

Just as there is a close connection between the new mode of production and the nuclear family and delayed-marriage pattern, there is a close connection between the older mode of production—which was, in effect, also a concurrent mode but in a different space—and the preference for various forms of enlarged families and for the puberty-age marriage pattern. The older patterns were indeed rooted in the need of an agricultural and stockraising society, with a fairly low level of productivity and a relatively high level of insecurity and disease, for the kind of family that would be able to furnish protection against marauders, serve as an insurance policy against disease, and assure the production needs of a society that was spatially denser than the societies of food-gatherers but that had a lower density than the societies of the new ecotechnological system. (Hunting and food-gathering societies had very different requirements.)[58] In view of the prevalence of a high death rate, the self-perpetuation of this type of society required a high birth rate. But because the simple addition of children or consuming nonproducers made for a family that was unable to produce as much as it had to consume the nuclear family tended to become dysfunctional. Doubtless through a process of trial and error, many societies of a similar type discovered the utility of a household with a sufficiently large number of children to assure the family's perpetuation and with enough adults to guarantee protection and production. Varying needs and different power associations made, however, for many variations of the enlarged family. In Poland, where lords were powerful, limits were set on the growth of peasant families through the practice of shifting children and young adults from family units with a large number of growing children and adults to those with few children and few adults. Such shifts had two objects: to maintain the weak family as a producing unit and to prevent the strong family from becoming too powerful.[59]

The critical threshold of passage from the enlarged family and puberty-marriage pattern to the pattern of "modernity" normally is reached, according to Chaunu, when a society's technology allows it to achieve a density of 35–40 persons per square kilometer.[60] It therefore may be of interest to note that,

58. Maurice Godelier, "Modes de production, rapports de parenté et structures démographiques," *La Pensée*, No. 172 (December 1973), pp. 7–31.

60. Chaunu, *L'Espagne et Charles Quint*, I, 73, 132–49; Chaunu, "Les Seigneurie et la famille paysanne dans la Pologne du XVIIIe siècle," *Annales ESC*, XXVII (July–October 1972), 949–58.

60. Chaunu, *L'Espagne de Charles Quint*, I, 73, 132–49; Chaunu, "Les Entraves au changement," pp. 54–68. Except where otherwise indicated, the arguments developed in the preceding paragraphs are based to a large extent on Chaunu. In his *Histoire, science sociale*, pp. 316–23, 354–62, on the

as late as the end of the sixteenth century, such a density existed in none of Castile's provinces. In 1541, for example, six provinces (Murcia, Granada, Madrid, Cuenca, Guadalajara, and Zamora) had a density of less than 10 persons, eight provinces (León, Toledo, Salamanca, Córdoba, Seville, Burgos, Jaén, and Soria) had a density of 10–15 persons, and four provinces (Avila, Segovia, Palencia, and Valladolid) had a density, of 15–25 persons. In 1591, there were only two provinces (Murcia and Granada) with a density of less than 10 persons, two other provinces (Guadalajara and Salamanca) with a density of 10–15 persons, eleven provinces (Córdoba, León, Seville, Zamora, Soria, Cuenca, Burgos, Madrid, Jaén, Toledo, and Avila) with a density of 15–25 persons, two provinces (Segovia and Palencia) with 25–30 persons per square kilometer, and one province (Valladolid) with a density of 31.6 persons.[61] In terms of Chaunu's quantification of the demographic threshold, Castile could not have started on the delayed-marriage pattern (he does not discuss the nuclear and enlarged family types) until after the sixteenth century. On the other hand, my own research on the Balkans suggests that the passage from the enlarged family to the nuclear family and from the puberty-marriage to the delayed-marriage pattern (for women) starts after the attainment of a population density of 15 but before one of 30. If this hypothesis is correct, the transition should have begun in Castile during the second half of the sixteenth century, whereas it did not start in the Balkan interior until the middle of the nineteenth.[62]

Through its attention to the family, *Annales* scholarship has strengthened its links with social history. And to clarify the pre-

---

other hand, Chaunu seems to accept more unreservedly Peter Laslett's thesis of the universal preponderance of the nuclear family.

61. Alvaro Castillo, "Population et richesse en Castille durant la seconde moitié du XVIe siècle," *Annales ESC*, XX (July–August 1965), 719-33.

62. Traian Stoianovich, "The Balkan *Domestic* Family: Geography, Commerce, Demography," IIIe Congrès International d'Etudes du Sud-Est Européen, Bucharest, Sept. 4–10, 1974. The arguments that were not used by Chaunu in the preceding paragraphs are developed here.

vailing *Annales* conception of social history, we may refer with profit to the inaugural address, at the Collège de France, of Georges Duby. Respecting the repeated injunctions of Lucien Febvre, Duby defined "man in society" as "the final object" and "the first principle" of historical research. But a basic aim for Duby, as for a good many in the *Annales* movement, is to analyze society on the basis of its functions—the tripartite functions of war, prayer, and work; age categories and generations; family types; and the functions of such groups as lepers and the poor— or in terms of the statics and dynamics of cities, popular discontents and revolts, millenarian movements, and other large aspects of life, such as demography, collective states of mind, varying levels of culture, and different cultures. More precisely, Duby aspires to the "simultaneous and equally rigorous analysis of the material, ecological, and economic infrastructures, of the political structure, and finally of the ideological superstructures." Above all, the social history of *Annales* historians shows concern for the ambiguous frontiers at which social life converges on material culture and collective psychology, for "l'histoire des mentalités," which Jacques Le Goff situates "at the point of meeting between the individual and the collective, between the long time span and everyday experience, between the unconscious and the intentional, between the structural and the conjunctural, between the marginal and the general."[63]

63. Georges Duby, "Les Sociétés médiévales: Une approche d'ensemble," *Annales ESC*, XXVI (January–February 1971), 1–13, Collège de France inaugural lecture, translated as "History of Medieval Societies: Inaugural Lecture Delivered at the Collège de France," *Social Science Information*, X (June 1971), 7–21; Jacques Le Goff, "Les Mentalités: Une histoire ambiguë," in Le Goff and Nora, eds., *Faire de l'histoire*, III, *Nouveaux objets*, 80 (76–94). A main *Annales* concern has been with social history as total history. For an exception to this rule, that is, for a view of social history as a study of segmentary groups and especially volunteer associations as ends in themselves rather than as the microcosms of a whole unit, see Maurice Agulhon (a graduate of the Ecole Normale Supérieure), *La Sociabilité méridionale*, 2 vols., Publications de la Faculté des Lettres Aix-en-Provence, "Travaux et mémoires," 36 (Aix-en-Provence: La Pensée Uni-

Complementing their call for a history of the ignored, down-trodden, proscript, vanquished, and nonconsensual, the "demo-cratic" goal of a history of the people is not unattractive to *Annales* historians. Taking precedence over the aim of a history of the people *as* people or of the social *as* social, on the other hand, is their objective of a history of the social as it impinges on, and is impinged on by, the material and the mental. They seek to comprehend a society not by one means alone, nor by isolating the social from the economic and affective, but by identifying its communicant groups and analyzing its modes of communication, its global configurations, and—not least—its functional modes.[64]

versitaire, 1966). But see Agulhon, *La République au village* (Paris: Plon, 1970), for a partial rehabilitation of the notion of social history as total history.

64. François Furet, "Histoire et ethnologie: L'Histoire et l'homme sauvage,'" in *Mélanges en l'honneur de Fernand Braudel*, II, 232 (227–33), translated as "History and Primitive Man," in Dumoulin and Moïsi, eds., *The Historian Between the Ethnologist and the Futurologist*, pp. 197–203.

7 Series and Functions

It is not at all easy to define a whole society, a whole economy, or a whole civilization. Partly for this reason, most *Annales* scholars have set themselves a more modest and immediate task— to explain one of the systems in the system of systems. One *Annales* group has thus sought to apprehend a system as it is externalized in some kind of series. It uses numbers as signs, accepting the supposition—to quote Ernst Cassirer, although Cassirer did not have the *Annales* work in mind—that "number stands at the threshold of a series of relationships which, further pursued and conceived more concretely, should lead finally to the determination of 'reality' and be included in it."[1] "Serial history" was the result: the analysis of a system in terms of price, wage, demographic, and other determinable variables. Another group has been more interested in how a system functions. Accepting the premise that every system functions differently, a few persons concluded that histoire globale is senseless. Others more unassumingly noted the impropriety of analyzing the system of systems (whole society) before the subsidiary systems are known.

The terms "function" and "functionalism" have not entered this study fortuitously. They are here by design and possess a more or less formal (or technical) signification. The methods, if not the goals, of functionalism are quite different, for example, from those of an historian's structuralism, which is genetic and historical by definition.

1. Cassirer, *The Problem of Knowledge*, pp. 65–66.

One form of functionalism, known as formalism, strives toward an absolute distinction between form and content, attributing intelligibility only to form and regarding content as a residue without a signifying function. One of the best examples of formalist functionalism is offered by the early work of the Soviet philologist and folklorist Vladimir Propp, whose theory of the Russian folktale, developed in the 1920s, subsequently exerted a worldwide impact on scholars with interdisciplinary orientations. After examining more than a hundred Russian tales, Propp concluded that the Russian folktale form possesses thirty-one elementary units, or character "functions": seven introductory, or preparatory, and twenty-four central acts. While one or more functions are absent from some of the tales, the order (pattern) of appearance or succession of functions is the same in every story; many of the functions occur in pairs (interdiction/transgression, flight from danger/quest of danger, interrogation/information); and each tale contains seven necessary roles: aggressor, donor, ally, king or princess, messenger, hero, and false hero. As a formalist, Propp was concerned not with uncovering or determining the conditions under which the folktale structure appears, is upheld, and vanishes, but simply—although not unimportantly —with explaining how the folktale functions, how it *is* over and over again.[2]

As a half-admiring critic, Claude Lévi-Strauss suggests that some duplication may occur in Propp's functions. His chief criticism, however, is of Propp's analysis of functions at a purely empirical level (his analysis of form *as* visible form), that is, of his treatment of vocabulary as if it were subject to structural

2. Vladimir [Iakovlevich] Propp, *Morphologie du conte* (with "Les Transformations des contes merveilleux," and E. Mélétinski, "L'Etude structurale et typologique du conte"), trans. Marguerite Derrida, Tzvetan Todorov, and Claude Kahn (Paris: Editions du Seuil, 1970). This translation of Propp's *Morfologiia skazki* is based on the revised edition of 1969, whereas the Gallimard translation (1970), like the Italian (1966) and American (1958, 1968) translations, is based on the original edition of 1928.

analysis like language at the phonological level and perhaps at the level of grammar—thus for failing to recognize the principle of the complementarity between the sign and its signification and between form and content.[3]

If not functionalist in a purely formalist sense, much of the research of *Annales* scholars during the past two decades has been, consciously or unconsciously, functionalist in Lévi-Strauss's sense, generally with the additional criterion of an historical dimension. An early impetus to this orientation may have come from Marcel Mauss's analysis of the psychological function of exchange. Functionalist research made little headway among historians, however, until Mauss's work was reinforced by Ignace Meyerson's *Les Fonctions psychologiques et les oeuvres* (1948), which Fernand Braudel extolled in his seminars during 1950–1952.[4]

Meyerson was convinced that "the analysis of the separate functions" may ward off the difficulties of comparing whole units, *le comparatisme global*. But which separate functions should the psychologist or historian study? Those, he replied, that resemble as much as possible the functions that are of interest to the more exact sciences, that is, the hidden functions that lie "behind or within the content." Moreover, observed Meyerson, such functions can be uncovered best perhaps by "historical analysis, through which it should be possible to verify the degree to which the notions underlying today's psychology are sufficiently fundamental to continue playing this role."[5]

3. Claude Lévi-Strauss, "La Structure et la forme: Réflexions sur un ouvrage de Vladimir Propp," *Anthropologie structurale deux*, pp. 139–73, first published in *Cahiers de l'Institut de Science Economique Appliquée*, No. 9 (Series M, No. 7) (March 1960), pp. 3–36. This article refers to the first English edition of Propp's book, with an introduction by Svatava Pirkova-Jakobson, *Mythology of the Folktale* (Bloomington, Ind.: Indiana University Press, 1958). Greatly offended, Propp replied to Lévi-Strauss's criticisms in the Italian edition of his book, *Morfologia della fiaba: Con un intervento di Claude Lévi-Strauss e una replica dell' autore*, ed. Gian Luigi Brivo (Turin: Einaudi, 1966).
4. Struck by this, I immediately bought the book. I return to it often.
5. Meyerson, *Les Fonctions psychologiques*, pp. 135, 137.

Functionalism, however, assumes several different forms among *Annales* scholars. Georges Friedmann, a sociologist and philosopher who is a member of the *Annales* editorial board, for example, informally defines a function as an "aspect" or "factor." Among the functions of work he includes the following: work techniques, the representation of work as a thing, labor law, and the physiology, history, geography, ethnology, demography, sociology, and economics of work. His analysis of the special function of technical change deviates from Propp's conception of a function as a constant or stable elementary unit and from Meyerson's conception of it as something hidden. Friedmann concludes that the unprecedented transformation of the function of technological change since 1850 has provoked so much and such rapid change in the other functions that there is no longer much point to studying any of these functions in the framework of Fernand Braudel's longue durée. What is required, rather, is a study of the relationships of the various functions to one another.[6]

A similar form of functionalism is manifest in the work of the Soviet historian Aron Iakovlevich Gurevich, whose book *Problemy genezisa feodalizma v Zapadnoi Evrope* was hailed by the *Annales* as "a remarkable feat" by "one of the most brilliant Soviet medievalists . . . to renovate the conceptual apparatus of the highly interesting problem of the origins of feudal society."[7] But in July 1970, half a year before the above words were published, with the comment that the appearance of the book—which made extensive use of the work of Western and especially *Annales* medievalists, sixteenth-century specialists, and anthropologists— was "a good sign and promise," the Publishing Ministry of the USSR withdrew its imprimatur from the book. It did so on the ground (as established by the medievalists of Moscow Univer-

6. Georges Friedmann (with the aid of F.-I. Isambert), "Sciences sociales et sociologie du travail," *Annales ESC*, XVI (May–June 1961), 477–96; XVI (September–October 1961), 908–21.

7. In the unnumbered blue pages, "Le Choix des *Annales*," *Annales ESC*, XXV (November–December 1970).

sity's Department of History) of the book's unsuitability as a textbook. The work was criticized in particular for placing too much stress on noneconomic factors, for implying that there are no laws of historical development by its explanation of change in terms of the intensity of relations between neighboring societies and in terms of the specific character of each individual society, for its excessive borrowings from Western anthropology, and for polemicizing against Soviet historiography.[8]

What Gurevich had done was to study the functional basis of Western feudalism. In an article later published in the *Annales*, he emphasized that the stable system of relationships between the early medieval macrocosm and its microcosmic expression required a functional approach in preference to a dynamic one. He identified this relational system as "the signifying function of wealth in a situation of ceremonial exchange,"[9] which presumably grew out of the magical function of wealth in prefeudal barbarian societies. The amount and nature of a person's wealth and ability to give determined his position in society. Giving gave prestige to the giver. It also authorized him to take. There was thus a complex and detailed ritual for the redistribution of wealth. In Scandinavian and Germanic societies, for example, there was a close association between religion, the *Thing* or judicial assembly, the place where fairs were held, and the occasions for play, banqueting, and drinking. In other words, donation was

8. S. L. Pleshkova, "Ob uchebnom posobii [The Promotion as a Textbook of] 'Problemy genezisa feodalizma v Zapadnoi Evrope,'" *Voprosy istorii*, No. 9 (1970), pp. 154–67. Gurevich's book had been published as a textbook for the historical faculties (Moscow: "Vysshaia Shkola," 1970). If it had been published as a monograph it might have escaped some of the more hostile criticism. For an American review of the book, see David B. Miller, in *American Historical Review*, LXXVI (June 1971), 756–57.

9. A. Gurevič, "Représentations et attitudes à l'égard de la propriété pendant le Haut Moyen âge," trans. Bernard Kreise, *Annales ESC*, XXVII (May–June 1972), 523–47. The article strives to cope with Soviet criticism by examining more fully how the extra-economic problem was transformed into an economic one. It tries to answer the *Annales* criticism that it is too schematic by giving more attention to medieval literature.

less a way of managing capital and other scarce resources, as in contemporary capitalist societies,[10] than an overt process of managing egocentric and altruistic impulses. Only at a semiconscious level was it a system of economic management. The function of "give and take" operated through the whole sociocultural system and gave it meaning.

We return thus by another route—functionalism—to Hermes: "Empfangen und Geben: das ist das Leben." But we may go forward also to the equally brilliant Maussian formulation of the Middle Ages made by Georges Duby: The essence of the Middle Ages was "to take, to give, to consecrate" what had been ravished, by redistributing a portion to the invisible forces of the world, to the dead, to one's companions and friends, to the poor, and to guests, and to constitute another portion as a treasure (Hestia) to be consumed sensually (ravished) with the eyes.[11]

Another type of functionalism comprises a thematic analysis of the elementary sets, or functions, of a particular mode of social thought. Marc Ferro (a member of the *Annales* board of editors since 1969) embraced this type in his work on the Russian Revolution by devising a "retrospective public opinion survey"—Eric J. Hobsbawm's name for the practice—on the basis of sample letters and telegrams addressed to newspapers (such as *Izvestiia*), the Petrograd Soviet, and the Provisional Government in the weeks and months following February 1917.[12] Ferro engages in a

10. François Perroux, "The Gift: Its Economic Meaning in Contemporary Capitalism," translated from the French, *Diogenes*, No. 6 (Spring 1954), pp. 1–21.

11. Georges Duby, *Guerriers et paysans VIIe-XIIe siècle: Premier essor de l'économie européenne* (Paris: Gallimard, 1973), pp. 60–69, translated by Howard B. Clarke as *The Early Growth of the European Economy: Warriors and Peasants from the Seventh to the Twelfth Century* (Ithaca, N. Y.: Cornell University Press; London: Weidenfeld and Nicolson, 1974).

12. Marc Ferro, *La Révolution de 1917*, I, *La Chute du tsarisme et les origines d'Octobre* (Paris: Aubier, Editions Montaigne, 1967), translated by John Lamb Richards as *The Russian Revolution of February 1917* (Englewood Cliffs, N.J.: Prentice-Hall, 1972); Ferro, "The Aspirations of Russian Society," in Richard Pipes, ed., *Revolutionary Russia* (Cambridge,

skillful analysis of the pattern of elementary functions of "revolutionary" public opinion, but Hobsbawm is basically correct in his contention that "a concentrated study of brief periods of crisis, however dramatic and significant," and even with the most original and highly developed techniques, is not likely to produce an entirely satisfying answer to how structural change occurs.[13]

The most clearly innovative functionalist approach has been to treat a particular form of communication as a psychological process and to analyze the products of (mass) communication as much in terms of the container as of the content, as a function of their circulation through the systems of production, consumption, exchange, and perhaps even distribution. Like other functionalists, this method's practitioners desire to avoid aesthetic, ethical, political, and utilitarian criteria in order to create an "objective" science—in their case, a value-free science of communication. They consequently prefer the "literary fact" to the "literary work"—hence, one of the elementary units, or functions, of communication. In the case of literary communication, one might call this unit a *liteme*, by analogy with the phoneme of linguistic analysis and with the *mytheme* and *gusteme* of Lévi-Strauss's cultural anthropology.

One of the initiators of this approach was the sociologist Robert Escarpit, who defined the elements of a sociology of the book and proceeded to elaborate a more general sociology of literature.[14]

Mass.: Harvard University Press, 1968; Garden City, N.Y.: Doubleday-Anchor Books, 1969), pp. 183–208, with comments by John M. Thompson and a general discussion; Ferro, "Le Soldat russe en 1917: Indiscipline, patriotisme, pacifisme et révolution," *Annales ESC*, XXVI (January–February 1971), 14–39, and an English version, "The Russian Soldier in 1917: Undisciplined, Patriotic, and Revolutionary," *Slavic Review*, XXX (September 1971), 483–512.

13. Eric J. Hobsbawm, "From Social History to the History of Society," *Daedalus*, C (Winter 1971), 40, 44 (20–45).

14. Robert Escarpit, "Le Littéraire et le social," in Robert Escarpit, ed., *Le Littéraire et le social: Eléments pour une sociologie de la littérature* (Paris: Flammarion, 1970), pp. 9–41; Robert Darnton, "Reading, Writing

190 French Historical Method

The propagation of an improved form of this method among historians, however, has been largely the accomplishment of a Sixième Section research team under the direction of François Furet.

The Furet project was initially conceived as "Literature and Society" but quickly was made more precise: *Livre et société dans la France du XVIIIe siècle* became a volume prepared for the 1965 International Congress of History. The stated aim of this volume was to amend the "quantitative tradition" of Daniel Mornet's history of ideas and so escape his highly criticized "literary eventism."[15] The Furet team's "common unit" of functional analysis consequently became the bound publication of unspecified length known as a *"book*, not the object sacralized by literary tradition and romantic individualism but the merchandise the printing of which flooded Europe and popularized a corpus of both ancient and new knowledge. Our preoccupation with quantity was thus not a simple precaution of erudition. For only quantity allows an appreciation of the whole weight of the social [fact] and of the past in the reading and writing of a society. The history of ideas should embrace the factors of inertia even if for no reason other than to measure the relative share of innovation in the social process."[16]

and Publishing in Eighteenth-Century France: A Case Study in the Sociology of Literature," *Daedalus*, C (Winter 1971), 216 (214–56).

15. For a devastating critique of Daniel Mornet's *Histoire de la littérature classique, 1600–1700: Ses caractères véritables et ses aspects inconnus* (Paris: Armand Colin, 1940), see Lucien Febvre, "Littérature et vie sociale: De Lanson à Daniel Mornet, un renoncement?" *Combats pour l'histoire*, pp. 263–68, originally published in *Annales d'histoire sociale*, III (1941), 113–17.

16. François Furet, "Avertissement," in François Furet, ed., *Livre et société dans la France du XVIIIe siècle*, 2 vols., Ecole Pratique des Hautes Etudes (VIe Section), "Civilisations et sociétés," 1 and 16 (Paris, The Hague: Mouton, 1965–1970), I, 1–2. Volume I includes an article by Furet on book authorizations and publications, a quantitative study of the *Journal des savants* and of the *Mémoires de Trévoux* by Jean Ehrard and Jacques Roger, an illuminating study of popular reading and of the

Sixième Section scholars, moreover, intend to treat Rousseau's correspondence in the way the Furet team has treated the book. In an effort to develop a social psychology of communication, one of these scholars points out that exchange of letters was so important in Enlightenment society that the epistolary novel became one of its typical formal expressions. Since such real and fictional letters may reflect a psychosocial dimension intermediate between the written and oral cultures of the period, they may be an effective means of bridging the gap between the two.[17]

An Enlightenment scholar at Princeton, Robert Darnton, who led a Sixième Section seminar in 1971 on publishing and bookselling (la librairie) in eighteenth-century France, concludes that the functionalist approach may have allowed "the social history of ideas" to break out of "the old categories of Marxist sociology."[18] Perhaps, but one should note Talcott Parsons's observation that a "heavy emphasis on 'empiricism' tends to fragment the world of knowledge, because each class of concrete phenomena is in some respects always unique—whichever of many levels may be selected for emphasis—if no attempt is made to understand other aspects."[19] Since functionalists tend to regard every system of signs—including books, work, opinions, paintings, symbols and

---

littérature de colportage by Geneviève Bollème, an article on the Enlightenment and the provincial academies by Daniel Roche, and some general observations on culture by Alphonse Dupront, published in part in Annales ESC, XX (September–October 1965), 867–98.

17. Daniel Roche, "Les Primitifs du Rousseauisme: Une analyse sociologique et quantitative de la correspondance de J.-J. Rousseau," Annales ESC, XXVI (January–February 1971), 151–72.

18. Darnton, "In Search of the Enlightenment," p. 130. For a further review and sympathetic critique of French quantitative studies of eighteenth-century culture, see Darnton, "Reading, Writing and Publishing in Eighteenth-Century France," pp. 214–56. In "Le Livre français à la fin de l'Ancien Régime," Annales ESC, XXVIII (May–June 1973), 735–44, Darnton offers a résumé of his 1971 Sixième Section seminar.

19. Talcott Parsons, "Theory in the Humanities and Sociology," Daedalus, IC (Spring 1970), 504 (495–523). The entire issue is devoted to the subject "Theory in Humanistic Studies."

images, tools, clothing, architecture, gestures—as a language, however, they should have no objection to establishing the correlations and discordances among the different systems of signs once the various languages of discourse are understood.[20]

The second volume of *Livre et société* thus contains a section on historical semantics, with an article by Furet on the frequency of use and the meaning of the term "history" in eighteenth-century French book titles and two highly technical articles by Alessandro Fontana on the semantic method and its application to history.[21] Members of the Centre de Recherches de Lexicologie Politique of the Ecole Normale Supérieure at Saint-Cloud and of the Groupe d'Etudes sur le Vocabulaire de la Révolution, however, have been critical of the focus on book titles as a semantic field without reference to the complete texts. They suggest instead that the items to the left and right of each polar item and the items between which there is a constant relationship throughout a given text be specified. They further recommend that the rules of association *and* opposition or co-occurrence between individual words (items) and groups of words be ascertained. In effect, they propose to treat words as phonologists treat phonemes, determining connections and significations by a rigorous analysis of the lexical patterns.[22]

One scholar's defense of the hypothesis that the frequency of

20. Louis Trénard, "Histoire et sémantique," *Revue des études Sud-Est européennes*, X, 3 (1972), 428–29 (423–48).

21. Articles by Julien Brancolini and Marie-Thérèse Bouyssy, Jean-Louis and Maria Flandrin, and Daniel Roche complete the second volume, continuing along the lines marked out by the first.

22. Maurice Tournier (of the Centre de Recherches de Lexicologie Politique) and R. Arnault, L. Cavaciuti, Annie Geffroy, and F. Theuriot (all of the Groupe d'Etudes sur le Vocabulaire de la Révolution), "Le Vocabulaire de la Révolution: Pour un inventaire systématique des textes," *Annales historiques de la Révolution française*, No. 195 (January–March 1969), pp. 109–24. See also Annie Geffroy, Pierre Lafon, and Maurice Tournier, "Lexicometrical Analysis of Co-occurrences," Centre de Recherches de Lexicologie Politique (Ecole Normale Supérieure de Saint-Cloud), E.R.A. 56, CNRS, March 1972; Alphonse Dupront, "Sémantique historique et histoire," *Cahiers de lexicologie*, XIV (1969), 15–25.

words "at the title level is a surer sign of value and power than the frequency of a word at any other level" indicates, indeed, why book titles may not provide an equally satisfactory approach to every period of history. They may constitute a means of apprehending sixteenth-century culture that is subtly different from their use in perceiving eighteenth-century culture. In the sixteenth century, titles were long and served as the table of contents, from which they were indistinguishable. Two centuries later, and thereafter, the separation between titles and tables of contents was much more general and titles became shorter.[23] Unless appropriate mathematical controls (normalization) are applied, comparison between sixteenth- and eighteenth-century cultures on the basis of a semantic analysis of book titles may distort as much as it reveals.

Alphonse Dupront of the Sixième Section therefore counsels that organic studies of the whole system of signs of the printed language of particular thinkers and social groups be made, as also of medicine, of "preciousness" (*la préciosité*), and of other social and mental phenomena, including preferences among suffixes. He believes that semantics can be made especially amenable to the historical understanding through the examination of signs and functions in historicosemantic studies that group their data in series of consecutive, and perhaps overlapping, intervals of ten years.[24]

23. Jean-Louis Flandrin, "Sentiments et civilisation: Sondage au niveau des titres d'ouvrages," *Annales ESC*, XX (September–October 1965), 939–40 (939–66).

24. Dupront, "Sémantique historique et histoire," pp. 15–25; A. Prost, "Vocabulaire et typologie des familles politiques," *Cahiers de lexicologie*, XIV (1969), 115–26. With a less ambitious and only partly similar goal, Marxist historian Claude Mazauric examines the question of the associative use in 1789 of such value-laden words as "régime féodal," "féodalité," and "régime tyrannique," in opposition to the equally value-laden cluster "liberté," "propriété," and "vertu": Claude Mazauric, "Note sur l'emploi de 'régime féodal' et de 'féodalité' pendant la Révolution française," *Sur la Révolution française*, pp. 119–34. Other valuable studies on this subject are Guy Lemarchand, "Le Féodalisme dans la France rurale des temps

Concerned primarily with the analysis of collective states of mind, Dupront agrees with the functionalists that it may be too soon to attempt to analyze a complex "whole" society. Scholars should first take inventory and establish many different series of homogeneous data. Only after this has been done can the coherences and correlations among the several groups of serialized phenomena be determined.[25]

Serial history is functionalist history that concentrates on a quantifiable function—such as prices, wages, demography, trade cycles—in terms of its serial organization. Its origins go back to the practices of nineteenth-century statisticians, to the conceptualizations of Antoine-Augustin Cournot, Henri Berr, and Lucien Febvre, and to the practical achievements of François Simiand and Ernest Labrousse.

Cournot, for example, mentions his belief that events can be grouped into a "regular series" in his *Considérations sur la marche des idées* (1872).[26] Febvre's predecessor, associate, and later rival in the fight for a "new history," Henri Berr, emphasizes in *La Synthèse en histoire* (1911) that history should not restrict itself to the study of change as a succession of singular events. It should also embrace change in relationship to duration—change as *développement*,[27] which presumably exhibits a serial character. And we have already noted Febvre's view that a fact or construct may acquire a greater significance by being set in a series.

Serial history at a high professional level—but not clearly distinguishable yet from what later came to be known as quantita-

---

modernes: Essai de caractérisation," *Annales historiques de la Révolution française*, No. 195 (January–March 1969), pp. 77–108; Albert Soboul, "Survivances 'féodales' dans la société rurale française au XIXe siècle," *Annales ESC*, XXIII (September–October 1968), 965–86.

25. Dupront, "Problèmes et méthodes d'une histoire de la psychologie collective," pp. 8–10.

26. Cournot, *Considérations sur la marche des idées*, I, 123.

27. Henri Berr, *La Synthèse en histoire, son rapport avec la synthèse en général*, new rev. ed. (Paris: Albin Michel, 1953), p. 26.

tive economic history—started with Labrousse's *Esquisse du mouvement des prix et des revenus en France au XVIIIe siècle* (1933) but found few adherents until after World War II. Under the postwar guidance and inspiration of the *Annales* and of Labrousse himself, who, pursuing an independent course, was sympathetic to many *Annales* aims, serial history became the primary form of professional historical scholarship in France.

The reality of the practice existed prior to the name. In 1960, Pierre Chaunu, co-author with Huguette Chaunu of an impressive multivolume serial study of the commerce between Seville and the West Indies during the sixteenth and first half of the seventeenth centuries, confirmed that reality by christening it "serial history."[28]

Serial historians then became increasingly conscious of how it differed from quantitative history—that is, from history concerned mainly with production and consumption functions, or the application of input-output analysis to large social aggregates, as practiced in particular by the American general-equilibrium economist Simon Kuznets and later by a distinguished group of French economic historians that included François Perroux and Jean Marczewski.[29] The main thrust of the serial historians of

28. Huguette and Pierre Chaunu, *Séville et l'Atlantique, 1504–1650;* Pierre Chaunu, "Dynamique conjoncturelle et histoire sérielle," *Industrie* (Brussels), June 6, 1960.

29. Jean Marczewski, "Buts et méthodes de l'histoire quantitative," *Cahiers Vilfredo Pareto*, No. 3 (1964), pp. 125–64; Jean Marczewski, *Introduction à l'histoire quantitative* (Geneva: Droz, 1965); Louise A. Tilly, "Materials of the Quantitative History of France since 1789," in Lorwin and Price, eds., *The Dimensions of the Past*, pp. 138–39 (127–55); Henri Lefebvre, "Réflexions sur le structuralisme et l'histoire," *Cahiers internationaux de sociologie*, n.s., X (July–December 1963), 8 (3–24); Furet, "Sur quelques problèmes posés par le développement de l'histoire quantitative," p. 75. For the use of the term "production function" and "consumption function," see Wassily Leontief, "The Problem of Quality and Quantity in Economics," in Daniel Lerner, ed., *Quantity and Quality: The Hayden Colloquium on Scientific Method and Concept* (New York: Free Press of Glencoe, 1961; copyright 1959 by the American Academy of Arts and Sciences), p. 118 (117–28).

Annales persuasion against quantitative (aggregative) history was aimed against the latter's view of the whole economic process as a coherent function susceptible of historical analysis. One might even say that it was a sideswipe at histoire globale—at least as an immediate objective.

According to François Furet, for example, a necessary prelude to the specification of an historical model of the process of production (or consumption) is the construction of numerous macro-economic series that can be used to specify the constants and variables and so raise history to the rank of "a science of man." At one with Chaunu, Le Roy Ladurie, and the Marxist historian Pierre Vilar in his fear of an abusive application of quantitative data to social aggregates,[30] Furet warns that total quantification cannot be extended with ease to any period that precedes "the introduction of the statistical or proto-statistical recording of data, which corresponds with the centralization of the great European monarchies." Much more credible than a fragile total quantification of discontinuous data is the pursuit of serial history, the espousal of François Simiand's predilection for the study of each social fact as a separate entity ordered in a homogeneous series.[31]

---

30. Emmanuel Le Roy Ladurie, "Les Comptes fantastiques de Gregory King," *Annales ESC*, XXIII (September–October 1968), 1086–1102, reprinted in Le Roy Ladurie, *Le Territoire de l'historien*, pp. 252–70, translated by Peter Wexler as "The Fantastical Accounts of Gregory King," in Ferro, ed., *Social Historians in Contemporary France*, pp. 141–56, 306–8; Pierre Vilar, "Pour une meilleure compréhension entre économistes et historiens: 'Histoire quantitative' ou économie rétrospective?" *Revue historique*, CCXXXIII (April–June 1965), 293–312.

31. François Simiand, "Méthode historique et science sociale," *Annales ESC*, XV (January–February 1960), 105, 109 (83–119), published originally in Henri Berr's *Revue de Synthèse historique*, VI (1903), 1–22, 129–57, under the longer title "Méthode historique et science sociale: Etude critique à propos des ouvrages récents de M. Lacombe et de M. Seignobos." The article was reprinted by the *Annales* in order to give perspective to France's "young historians," allow them to measure the progress made in historical method since the beginning of the century, and to appreciate the importance of the dialogues between history and the social sciences.

However wary quantitative historians may be of serial history, or *histoire ponctuelle*[32]—history as a series of points distributed with precision in space and time—they, too, in the words of Simon Kuznets, aspire to the organization of "historical fact into temporal series of homogeneous and comparable units, so that their evolution can be measured in terms of fixed intervals." They similarly admit that the supply of continuous, comparable, and comprehensive statistical data is limited to a few forms of social organization and a few periods of history. They therefore urge that statistical analysis be employed pertinently in "universal history" and that it be combined with, or subordinated to, "a wider view of social change that would use all types of data and more than one type of analysis."[33] They even acknowledge the existence of "independent variables," which are subject to forces external to the system and by means of which the general equilibrium sometimes is transformed.[34] Quantitative history does not aim to discard serial history. But knowing its limitations, it seeks to surpass it.

It would be an error to assume that all *Annales* historians are wedded irrevocably to serial history in any exclusive sense, or that quantitative historians are all economists or economic historians under the unique impress of prestigious Anglo-American economic history. Braudel, for example, is a serial historian or quantitative historian, as the occasion demands. The error of such categorizing, nevertheless, contains a kernal of truth.

The *Annales* collaborator who has stated most succinctly the

32. The term "histoire ponctuelle" is Marczewski's. It is well to note, however, that he applies it only to spatially and temporally limited serial history and that he regards vertical chronological series as the indispensable condition for a good quantitative or aggregate analysis of a succession of horizontal layers of quantitative history. See Marczewski, *Introduction à l'histoire quantitative*, pp. 48–49.

33. Simon Kuznets, "Statistical Trends and Historical Changes," *Economic History Review*, 2d ser., III, 3 (1951), 277–78 (265–78).

34. Jean Marczewski, "Les Variables historiques," *Revue économique*, No. 1 (January 1965), pp. 86–104.

shortcomings of serial history—a typically, if in no sense exclusively, French institution—is thus not a French historian but a Polish Marxist open to the insights of Anglo-American economic history, the economic historian Witold Kula. Inspired also by Henri Hauser's price history (1936), Kula notes a possible contradiction between the goal of serial history and that of longue durée. The more a series is extended either temporally or spatially, he contends, the less homogeneous it tends to become. The comparability of its data, he observes in apparent agreement with Lévi-Strauss, diminishes as the material, social, or mental forms subject to scrutiny change their character—coal is not everywhere and at every time the same coal nor bread the same bread, nor is all iron of the same hardness, nor a given tool everywhere of the same design and craftsmanship—or as old material objects and significations of utility or consumption (and therefore of production) disappear and new things, signs, and significations acquire utility. Such differences are compounded, moreover, as one moves from one field of spatial or temporal action to another. Comparability is contingent, in effect, on shared experience. But during most of world history, despite constant or occasional contact with one another, people have lived in relatively confined spatial compartments. Within the same village, city, province, or state, for example—to paraphrase the Yugoslav novelist Miroslav Krleža—individuals live at different temporal rhythms, keeping their distance even as they rub shoulders. To be of the greatest possible use, however, serial history (Kula does not use the term but that is what he means) should be both temporally and spatially extensive. But if it is, it loses its homogeneity and comparability. Its primary utility derives from its applicability to relatively homogeneous cultural areas and periods.[35]

The serial data of different culture areas lack total comparability even today, and in the past they were still less comparable. They are useful, nevertheless, not only for the light they shed on

35. Witold Kula, "Histoire et économie: La Longue durée," *Annales ESC*, XV (March–April 1960), 294–313.

the operation of a given function (such as prices or wages) in an individual culture, but for drawing attention also to the varying degree of serial stability in different cultural systems and thus making impossible comparative history possible. On the basis, for example, of studies of price movements going back to the perceptions of the nineteenth-century Russian agrarian historian Georgii Emelianovich Afanasev and continuing with the admirably systematic analyses of Ernest Labrousse, Jean Meuvret, and Fernand Braudel and Frank Spooner, Europe of the period 1500–1800 may be divided into three major geohistorical areas: a Mediterranean region in which wheat and other grain prices were very high and fluctuations were relatively low, an Atlantic zone in which the prices were not so high but in which the fluctuations were of greater magnitude, and a continental zone extending from France's central regions deep into Russia with very low grain prices but immense fluctuations that became ever greater as one moved eastward and inland.[36] On the basis of Spooner's calculations and Braudel's observations, the differences between the three zones were not attenuated until the wider diffusion of market forces after 1740.[37] Serial history is not without weaknesses. Under proper control, however, it can be a useful tool of comparative history.

36. Georges Afanassev (Georgii Emelianovich Afanasev), *Le Commerce des céréales en France au dix-huitième siècle,* translated from the Russian under the direction of Paul Boyer (Paris: A. Picard et fils, 1894), pp. 177, 257–70; C.-E. Labrousse, "Prix et structure régionale: Le Froment dans les régions françaises, 1782–1790," *Annales d'histoire sociale,* I (October 1939), 382–400. Jean Meuvret's article, "La Géographie des prix des céréales et les anciennes économies européennes: Prix méditerranéens, prix continentaux, prix atlantiques à la fin du XVIIIe siècle," was first published in *Revista de Economia,* IV, 2 (1951), 63–69, and reprinted in Meuvret, *Etudes d'histoire économique,* pp. 97–104. Pierre Goubert discusses the article, "In memoriam: Jean Meuvret (1901–1971)," *Annales ESC,* XXVII (January–February 1972), 281–84.

37. Fernand Braudel and Frank Spooner, "Prices in Europe from 1450 to 1750," in Rich and Wilson, eds., *The Cambridge Economic History of Europe,* IV, 394–400, 472–73 (374–486).

Emboldened by the achievements of American economic history, several *Annales* historians have been tempted to raise serious objections to the serial-based analysis of the nineteenth century made by economist François Simiand. Charles Morazé, it is true, had leveled criticism at Simiand's method as early as 1942, but perhaps because of the restricted circulation in wartime his article seems to have escaped notice.[38] In 1969 and 1970, however, two *Annales* scholars initiated criticism that could not fail to draw attention. Le Roy Ladurie, for example, observed that the period 1820–1850 was characterized by a stagnation of prices, which, in terms of Simiand's analysis, should have stifled economic development.[39] Instead, the period was one of economic growth. Prices failed to rise, he emphasizes, because of the rapid growth of production (supply) and, let us add, because the depression of wages through obstacles to labor organization allowed only a slow rise in demand. The economic historian Maurice Lévy-Leboyer further dared to criticize Simiand for "dramatizing history" and explaining nineteenth-century economic growth in cyclical terms and in terms of such "external" factors as war, military demands, and even a rise in the consumption of alcohol—Simiand may have introduced the last factor only as an hypothesis—while neglecting economic growth as part of a long-term secular trend and as a function of technological change.[40] Although serial history was not the direct object of his attack, implicit in his argument is the

38. Charles Morazé, "Essai sur la méthode de François Simiand," *Mélanges d'histoire sociale*, I (1942), 5–24; II (1942), 22–44.

39. Emmanuel Le Roy Ladurie, "La Révolution quantitative et les historiens français: Bilan d'une génération (1932–1968)," *Le Monde*, Jan. 25, 1969, reprinted in Le Roy Ladurie, *Le Territoire de l'historien*, pp. 15–22.

40. Maurice Lévy-Leboyer, "L'Héritage de Simiand: Prix, profit et termes d'échange au XIXe siècle," *Revue historique*, CCXLIII (January–March 1970), 77–120. For a criticism of Lévy-Leboyer and a defense of Simiand and his present disciples, see Jean Bouvier, "Feu François Simiand?" *Annales ESC*, XXVIII (September–October 1973), 1173–92, also available in *Conjoncture économique, structures sociales: Hommage à Ernest Labrousse*, Ecole Pratique des Hautes Etudes (VIe Section), "Civilisations et sociétés," 47 (Paris, The Hague: Mouton, 1974), pp. 59–78.

view that a linear social history tends to inflate the importance of data that can be put in a homogeneous series while deflating that of data not easily subject to serialization.

François Furet notes, furthermore, that a ceiling has been imposed on the achievements of serial history by the very fact that archives have been organized on the basis of the political orientations and questions of the nineteenth century. These orientations include the conviction that events serve the general cause of "progress" even though they are unique and thus incapable of being integrated into a statistical order. But progress, maintains Furet, is a Europocentric model of social action and cultural change of late modernity. Its use as a measure may thwart the comprehension not only of world history but of pre-eighteenth-century European history as well.[41]

To answer the new questions of an anthropology that excludes the notion of progress, what is necessary is "a new kind of archive preserved on perforated tapes" and suited to treatment by computer. The source partly defines the problem, but the awareness of new questions summons a redefinition of sources. Furet thus adopts Lucien Febvre's view that the historian constructs his facts. How much better, then, that he should be conscious of what he is doing. Since the practitioners of serial history *are* conscious of this, their method constitutes "not only a transformation of the raw material of history," but also "a revolution in the historiographical consciousness." Under contemporary circumstances, historical objectivity is a function of "the use of correct methods" of coding, programming, and analyzing.

In its brief existence, serial history has already disputed the soundness of "the old postulate that all the elements of a society follow a homogeneous and identical evolution." General or comprehensive history, not to mention histoire globale, is thus not for the present. It may "be kept as a goal on the horizon" but, adds Furet, "if history wants to go forward it should abandon this am-

41. Furet, "Sur quelques problèmes posés par le développement de l'histoire quantitative," pp. 71–82.

bition as a point of departure." This does not mean that historiography "has to restrict itself to microscopic analyses of one
chronological series. It can group several series together and put
forward an interpretation of a system. But today, a comprehensive analysis [in French: *analyse globale*] of the 'system of systems' or 'société globale' is probably beyond its power."

Contemporary historiography should, rather, strive to revise
the "traditional periodizations, which are mainly an ideological
inheritance from the nineteenth century, and which presuppose
precisely what is still to be demonstrated." A second goal would
be to distinguish between the sectors of quick change and those
of slower transformation in order to determine how much the
dynamism of change is of economic inspiration and how much of
demographic, political, religious, or broadly cultural inspiration.
This objective would require in turn the application of serial history to demography, sociology, education, religion, ideology,
and politics.[42] Through such an analysis, for example, it may be
possible to determine to what extent French Protestantism was a
rural phenomenon that was deprived of its foundations when the
petite noblesse that was its agent reconverted, emigrated, or was
urbanized. It also should be possible to clarify the correlation between the zones in which Protestantism succumbed and the later
zones of de-Christianization.[43] According to Pierre Chaunu, an
adequate explanation of the dynamism of change would necessitate a refinement of the techniques of serial history in order to
enable the historian to effect the passage from the economic (the
first or best developed level of history) to the conjunctures of

42. François Furet, "Quantitative History," trans. Barbara Bray, *Daedalus*, C (Winter 1971), 151–67. A slightly modified version of this article
appeared in French under the title "L'Histoire quantitative et la construction du fait historique," *Annales ESC*, XXVI (January–February 1971),
63–75, reprinted in Le Goff and Nora, eds., *Faire de l'histoire*, I, 42–61,
as "Le Quantitatif en histoire."

43. Pierre Chaunu, "Une histoire religieuse sérielle: A propos du diocèse
de La Rochelle (1648–1724) et sur quelques exemples normands," *Revue
d'histoire moderne et contemporaine*, XII (January–March 1965), 5–34.

"social quantity" (the second level of history) and to a serialization of the mental and affective life (third level of history).[44] As for conjuncture, Le Roy Ladurie has defined it as a temporarily transformed interrelationship among a variety of signifying variables (functions) of the oscillatory type (such as, for example, prices, wages, population, production, public opinion).[45]

The functional and serial approaches shift the stress from structures to functions and conjunctures and from the wholeness or globality of a society to its multifunctionality. Their general conclusion is that apprehension of a whole society is unattainable until all or very many of the functions are understood, not simply the three (or even the hundred) dimensions of temporality. There is thus a conflict between the aims of histoire globale and those of functionalist and serial (conjuncturalist) history. Conflict is not inherent, however, in the relationship between these two general approaches to history, for the historian may move from one to the other, correcting at each step the errors of histoire globale on the basis of the contributions of functionalist and serial history and the errors of functionalist and serial history on the basis of the latest findings of histoire globale.

44. Pierre Chaunu, "Un nouveau champ pour l'histoire sérielle: Le Quantitatif au troisième niveau," in *Mélanges en l'honneur de Fernand Braudel*, II, 105–25. Chaunu attributes the terms "social quantity" and "third level" to C.-E. Labrousse. See also Chaunu, "Les Entraves au changement," pp. 57–60.
45. Le Roy Ladurie, "Du Quantitatif en histoire," p. 32.

8 Mass and Event:
"Une Histoire Autre"

The question how to relate serial and functional history to structural history and comprehensive histoire globale has led, through a succession of dialogues among historians and between historians and nonhistorians, to a consideration of "the event" (or certain events) as the unifying factor. For a time, especially during the 1960s, it seemed that an antihistorical current might prevail, especially hostile to histoire globale. But after an extended debate over its appropriateness, and through a re-examination of the notion of event, histoire globale has been able to consolidate its position.

As a friendly critic, Claude Lévi-Strauss accepted the notion of total social fact, which he defined in terms of a three-dimensional function (synchronic, developmental, and physiopsychological),[1] but rejected the likelihood of total history on the ground that the total input of factors of immobility would nullify the total output of volatile events. History, according to Lévi-Strauss, tends toward informing more and explaining less (a narrative history of volatile events), or explaining more but informing less (histoire totale). The only escape from this impasse is to forsake history. History is useful and even indispensable for preparing an inventory, but for intelligibility one must interrogate biology, psychology, anthropology, and the physical sciences. If there is an over-

1. Lévi-Strauss, "Introduction à l'oeuvre de Marcel Mauss," pp. xxiv-xxxii; Lévi-Strauss, *Anthropologie structurale deux,* pp. 14–15.

all conscious system, it must be the "dialectical mean" of a multiplicity of unconscious semiological infrasystems, each possessing its own logical but dynamic and disequilibrated structure.[2]

While concurring with Lévi-Strauss on the function of the conscious system as a "dialectical mean," the anthropology-oriented linguist Emile Benveniste thought there might be a hidden or unconscious general law by means of which one system of signs could be converted into another.[3] Benveniste's interpretation suggests that the functional approach need not result automatically in the expulsion of histoire globale. Indeed, it may require it.

But serialist and functionalist historians tended to sympathize with Lévi-Strauss's conclusion. Perceiving many different kinds of functions, each with its own rhythm of movement and autonomous organization, they were prompt to recommend that histoire globale be postponed until all or nearly all functions were analyzed and clarified. Moreover, several forms of functionalism, among them the epistemic and at first sight the *discursif*, or semantic, seemed to reject altogether the logic of a comprehensive history even as an ultimate goal.

Epistemic functionalism, like functionalism in general, is a product of the search by scholars to remove subjective factors from their field of vision, as a result of which a few highly gifted philosophizing nonhistorians have been persuaded to deny all need for investigating human societies *as* societies. Instead, they propose to summon man and society only to the extent necessary to identify the epistemes, or ordering codes, underlying the

2. Claude Lévi-Strauss, "L'Anthropologie sociale devant l'histoire," *Annales ESC*, XV (July-August 1960), 625–37; Lévi-Strauss, *La Pensée sauvage* (Paris: Plon, 1962), pp. 340–48; Jean-Marie Auzias, *Clefs pour le structuralisme* (Paris: Editions Seghers, 1971), pp. 102–3; Lawrence Rosen, "Language, History, and the Logic of Inquiry in Lévi-Strauss and Sartre," *History and Theory*, X, 3 (1971), 269–94.

3. Emile Benveniste's explanation of his current research and teaching, in *Annuaire du Collège de France*, XLV (Paris: Imprimerie Nationale, 1965), p. 325.

functions of human discourse and to define the ordering code of each particular discipline or body of systematized knowledge (and the ways of discovering it and avoiding forbidden methods and themes) at a given time in a given society. They are prone to define an episteme as an aleatory artifact "of semantic units and transformation rules."[4]

The chief guide to epistemic functionalism was Michel Foucault's *Les Mots et les choses: Une archéologie des sciences humaines* (1966). In this and in *L'Archéologie du savoir* (1969), Foucault proposed a model in terms of which words (and by implication things) were to be situated in a particular "archeological" stratum and scrutinized without undue reference to the people who made use of them. The object was to create a science of knowledge free of subjective phenomenology or *anthropologisme*—not a progress-free anthropology but a man-free science —by treating the artifacts of language (or technology) as if they possessed an existence independent of people. Thus one would create a science of the past that is neither a "doxology," or affirmation of prevalent attitudes and opinions, nor a history, but rather an "archeology."

Foucault posited, in *Les Mots et les choses*, not only an intimate association between the words (and, incidentally, between the things) of a given stratum but startling and disconcerting discontinuities between strata, or fields, of "artifactual" relationships. Within each epistemic field, on the other hand, there is a general correspondence between the various types of knowledge. He thus conceptualized the Renaissance, the so-called classical age (1640–1789), and the modern century and a half after 1770/1789/1820 as individually distinct and homogeneous "archeological" layers or epistemic fields, each governed by a different general episteme

4. "The Language-Field of Nazism," *Times Literary Supplement*, April 5, 1974, pp. 353–54, a review of Jean-Pierre Faye, *Théorie du récit: Introduction aux langages totalitaires; critique de la raison, critique de l'économie narrative* (Paris: Hermann, 1972); Jean-Pierre Faye, *Langages totalitaires* (Paris: Hermann, 1972).

and each separate from and without dialectical links to the others. Each of these epistemic fields was the product of mutation. But holding that each episteme is necessary and inescapable until replaced parthenogenetically by a new episteme, Foucault did not concern himself with the conditions under which an epistemic mutation occurs.

The Renaissance, he affirmed, was regulated by the laws of resemblance and association among signs, things, and meanings— by what he calls the system of signs. In this system words, power, money, and other generalized media of communication or inter- action function as signs for the signified things (*signifiés*) circulat- ing through the system, while the signified things function in turn as signifying signs, or significants (*signifiants*).

The classical age gave up this ternary form of communication for a binary form under the governance of the law of analysis and representation. Language and institutions were desacralized and deprived of their signifying functions in order to be endowed with an instrumental and representative character. Things, too, became instruments or representations, for the model of the new age was the machine—in radicalized form, La Mettrie's *L'Homme Machine* (1748). Even God came to be understood in terms of that model.

Now perhaps over, Foucault's modern age was sustained by the methods of analogy and history. It was recognizable by its "invention" of man and of the notions of progress and develop- ment, by its fascination with the idea that the negation is con- tained in the affirmation, and by the assertion of the human and historical sciences of philology, biology, and political economy.

The contemporary era questions the former preoccupation with origins and development, with causes and results. Instead of dealing with signs as products of evolution, it seeks to explain the relationships between signs and thus to create a value-free "archeology of knowledge."

On the basis of his general assumptions, Foucault was led to conclude that histoire globale is impossible. One may aspire, however, to an *histoire générale*. By "general history," he understood not a comprehensive history of a whole society during a particular epistemic age but simply an analysis of the general episteme of a particular "archaeological" stratum—that is, the system of relationships among the literary, political, economic, technological, scientific, and other forms of discourse in that stratum.[5]

In an apparent effort to dissociate himself from "structuralist" currents,[6] Foucault abandoned the notion of episteme in *L'Archéologie du savoir*, for the analogy between episteme and structure was too close for comfort, particularly since he had not made an absolute distinction between the episteme as a semantic unit from which men could be removed completely and the episteme as a more subjective ordering code from which the removal of human beings was less easy. He shifted his focus to "discourse," an old favorite, with the object of defining—as another writer has said[7] —the function of semantic units longer than a sentence, therefore a function from which human beings can be excluded. That the shift involved much more than a simple diversion from one word to another is amply demonstrated by his concurrent rejection of the notion of historical discontinuities and the reassertion of his earlier repudiation of historical continuity. He continued to

5. For a Marxist critique of Michel Foucault, *Les Mots et les choses*, see Olivier Revault d'Allonnes, "Michel Foucault: Les Mots et les choses," in *Structuralisme et marxisme*, pp. 13–37. For existentialist critiques, see Michel Amiot, "Le Relativisme culturaliste de Michel Foucault," *Les Temps Modernes*, XXII (January 1967), 1271–98; Sylvie Le Bon, "Un positiviste désespéré: Michel Foucault," *ibid.*, pp. 1299–1319. For a psychoanalytical critique, see Gérard Mendel, *La Révolte contre le père: Une introduction à la sociopsychanalyse* (Paris: Payot, 1968), pp. 283–336.

6. Dominique Lecourt, *Pour une critique de l'épistémologie (Bachelard, Canguilhem, Foucault)* (Paris: François Maspero, 1972), pp. 100–1.

7. Roland Barthes, "Historical Discourse," in Michael Lane, ed., *Introduction to Structuralism* (New York: Basic Books, 1970), pp. 145–55, translated by Peter Wexler from Barthes, "Le Discours de l'histoire," *Social Science Information*, VI (August 1967), 65–75.

embrace as much as ever the notion of functional continuities
and discontinuities, but in this first model of *discursif* functionalism there was no need for history (if there was for diach-
rony), as there was no need for structure. What was necessary
was simply the function of constantly erupting events of discourse.[8]

Foucault's conversion between 1966 and 1969 from historical
psychology and historical philosophy to antihistory is hardly
astonishing. These were years during which the questioning of
authority, and probably an even greater partly suppressed desire
to question it—including the authority of the notions long duration and history of *envelopes*—reached a high point, and Foucault
was able to formulate an able scientific justification for such
resistance. But within a year or so of the publication of *L'Archéologie du savoir*, he delivered an inaugural lecture—*L'Ordre du
discours*—at the Collège de France in the new Chair of History
and System of Thought—by means of which he restored to the
discipline of history its rights of discourse. Concentrating on the
problem of "the production of discourse," he could ignore neither
the producers nor the inhibitions and restraints imposed on the
production and diffusion of discourse. Returning to the idea of
society, which he previously had sought to exclude, he observed
that "in every society the production of discourse is simultaneously controlled, selected, organized, and redistributed through a
certain number of procedures that serve to exorcise its powers
and dangers, to obtain mastery over the contingent nature of its
eventfulness, to escape its profound and redoubtable materialness."
Every discipline, he further maintained, is a way of managing

8. Michel Foucault, *L'Archéologie du savoir* (Paris: Gallimard, 1969),
pp. 9–28, 177–83, 205–75, translated by A. M. Sheridan Smith as *The
Archaeology of Knowledge* (New York: Pantheon, 1972); Dominique
Lecourt, "Sur l'archéologie et le savoir (à propos de Michel Foucault),"
La Pensée, No. 152 (August 1970), pp. 69–87; Jean-Marc Pelorson, "Michel
Foucault et l'Espagne," *ibid.*, pp. 88–99. Both articles are Marxist critiques.

discourse and thus of exercising a "restrictive and constraining function."

Under the restraining intellectual influence of the inaugural "discourse" addressed respectfully to colleagues in other disciplines as well as to those in his own, Foucault recognized the legitimacy of history. He did this through his definition of a discourse as an event and through his recognition that the events of discourse are so combative and threatening, so disordered and discontinuous, and so numerous and noisy that they must be treated in two ways if they are to be understood—as "discontinuous practices" (events) and as practices to be put in a series. Current historical modes, he correctly affirmed, have not abandoned the event but have rather extended its field of action through their use of official lists of produce exchange prices (*mercuriales*), notarial acts, parish registers, and port records. But the revised history of events "does not consider an event without defining the series of which it is a part." Won over ostensibly to the idea that ordering events of discourse in a homogeneous series is desirable, Foucault warned that the diverse series are neither successive nor simultaneous but rather products of a systematic discontinuity, which similarly characterizes the events in each series. For if a series is distinguished by regularity, that regularity is the result of contingency and chance.

Foucault's statement that no contradiction exists between "the pinpointing of the event and the analysis of long duration" should not be misread, for he has not become enamored of total history. By his recognition of the filiation between a history of events and serial history, however, he probably succeeded in persuading some *Annales* historians of the need to re-examine the nature and function of the event—which he describes as material but incorporeal, "neither substance nor accident, neither quality nor process"—and especially of the crucial paradigmatic event (Febvre's *gros événement*).[9]

9. Michel Foucault, *L'Ordre du discours*, Collège de France inaugural

The Foucault trilogy (epistemic functionalism, *discursif* anti-historical functionalism, and *discursif* serial historical functionalism) was accompanied by other signs of hostility to histoire globale. Notable among them was the critique of the German historian Dieter Groh, who maintains that the effort of French historians to move on from idiographic history to structural and total history was encouraged by the manifestation of mass phenomena in all sectors and aspects of European society as well as of other Western societies. But in dealing with the period since 1750, he observes, total history has been totally unsuccessful precisely because mankind has since then moved from an era of relative stability to one of incessant change. Total history is thus least capable of coping with the very phenomenon that engendered it—massification.[10]

Groh fails to mention the instabilities of pre-nineteenth-century stability, and he neglects to note that the failure of total history to deal with massification may not be due to some inherent defect but only to the special suitability of the period since 1800 to treatment in terms of serial history and other empirical methods. Nor does he mention Marc Ferro's *La Grande Guerre 1914–1918*, lauded by the *Times Literary Supplement* for its "unusual perspective: more than half the book concerns the masses."[11] And he could not have known that Ferro's book would be followed by Maurice Crubellier's *Histoire culturelle de la France, XIXe–*

---

lecture, December 2, 1970 (Paris: Gallimard, 1971), pp. 10–11, 37, 52–61, translated by Rupert Swyer as "Orders of Discourse: Inaugural Lecture Delivered at the Collège de France," *Social Science Information*, X (April 1971), 7–30.

10. Dieter Groh, "L'Histoire structurale—histoire *totale?*" Michael Keul's preliminary translation of the German manuscript for use in Braudel's seminar at the Collège de France, Winter–Spring 1971. Published as "Strukturgeschichte als 'totale' Geschichte?" *Vierteljahrschrift für Sozial- und Wirtschaftsgeschichte*, LVIII, 3 (1971), 289–322.

11. "Why Didn't the Masses Revolt?" *Times Literary Supplement*, Nov. 12, 1971, p. 1426, review of Marc Ferro, *La Grande Guerre 1914–1918* (Paris: Gallimard, 1969), translated by Nicole Stone as *The Great War, 1914–1918* (London: Routledge and Kegan Paul, 1973).

XXe siècle. With folklore and anthropological and sociological data and theory at his command the author analyzes the de-structuring and restructuring in nineteenth-century France of many closed (compartmentalized) cultures and the structuring, mainly in the twentieth century, of mass culture, characterized by two simultaneous tendencies: integration and contestation of authority.[12]

Perhaps mindful of the words of Charles Péguy—"We are a sacrificed generation, not even a vanquished generation"[13]—Ferro deals in *La Grande Guerre* with the unwashed and forgotten and with the war combatants, or *"classes des sacrifiés,"*[14] and with what Raymond Aron calls the battle of materiel, "subject to the law of number, of coal, and of steel."[15] He is similarly engrossed with the problem of "the mounting army of functionaries," whose role as protector of property in secular states is equivalent to that of organized religion in theocratic states.[16] As a result, points out an American historian, the term "hierarchy," which diction-aries defined mainly "in terms of sacred values" as late as the 1930s, has come "to cover any orderly bureaucracy with lines of authority extending downward from the top."[17]

Another mass phenomenon to which Ferro directs his attention is public opinion. As Jacques Ozouf has made amply clear, public opinion may be partly an expression of local attitudes and traditions.

12. Maurice Crubellier, *Histoire culturelle de la France, XIXe-XXe siècle* (Paris: Armand Colin, 1974), and a short review of the book in "Le Choix des *Annales,*" *Annales ESC,* XXIX (March–April 1974).

13. Charles Péguy, "A nos amis, à nos abonnés" (1909), in *Oeuvres en prose 1909–1914,* avant-propos and notes by Marcel Péguy (Paris: Gallimard, copyright 1957), p. 16 (4–49).

14. Ferro, *La Grande Guerre,* pp. 254, 274.

15. Raymond Aron, "Thucydide et le récit des événements," *History and Theory,* I, 2 (1961), 122–23 (103–28).

16. Ferro, *La Grande Guerre,* p. 15.

17. Thomas C. Cochran, "History and Cultural Crisis," *American Historical Review,* LXXVIII (February 1973), 2 (1–10), presidential address to the meeting of the American Historical Association, New Orleans, Dec. 28, 1972.

It emphatically differs from these, however, in being a product of mobility (rather than stability), or of the circulation of information and values. Because of this shiftiness or fickleness, public opinion is difficult to identify and fix.[18] Since the seventeenth century and especially the eighteenth, as some historians—among them Marc Ferro, Jacques Ozouf, and André Burguière—know well, the understanding of a society requires a study of opinions as well as of attitudes and traditions—indeed, increasingly so as we move from the eighteenth century to the twentieth.[19] Ferro therefore notes the role of newspapers, posters, books, films, and patriotic songs in the waging of the Great War. But public opinion was also formed in other ways, by "official ceremonies, the commemoration of victories, the cult of the dead, the roar and tinkle of brasses and drums, and the jingle of medals."[20]

The simultaneous development of technology and of public opinion, however, ended in the creation of immobility by means of movement. One of the devices for achieving this was *mobilization*, which quickly led to "the immobilization of the fronts." The

18. Jacques Ozouf, "Mesure et démesure: L'Etude de l'opinion," *Annales ESC*, XXI (March–April 1966), 324–45; Jacques Ozouf, "L'Opinion publique: Apologie pour les sondages," in Le Goff and Nora, eds., *Faire de l'histoire*, III, *Nouveaux objets*, 220–35.

19. In addition to Ferro's and Ozouf's studies, see André Burguière, 'Société et culture à Reims à la fin du XVIIIe siècle: La Diffusion des 'Lumières' analysée à travers les cahiers de doléances," *Annales ESC*, XXII (March–April 1967), 303 (303–39), in which he alludes to Tocqueville's awareness of the notion of public opinion. For an excellent definition of public opinion by the young revolutionary orator, Joseph Barnave, see Fernand Rude, ed., *Barnave: Introduction à la Révolution française,* text established on the basis of the original manuscript, "Cahiers des Annales," 15 (Paris: Armand Colin, 1960), pp. 3, 23, and *Power, Property, and History: Barnave's 'Introduction to the French Revolution' and Other Writings,* translated, with an introductory essay, by Emmanuel Chill (New York: Harper & Row, 1971). For some confusion of public opinion and attitudes, see Alfred Lajusan, "La Carte des opinions françaises: Point de vue d'un historien," *Annales ESC*, IV (October–December 1949), 406–14.

20. Ferro, *La Grande Guerre*, p. 222.

object of the mobilization of opinions—*la mobilisation des esprits*
—was, similarly, their immobilization.[21] But since opinion could
not be entirely directed, there were simultaneously currents of
counteropinion.[22]

Public opinion is a function of a society with an advanced
communications technology. Limited to a privileged few before
the sixteenth century and to no more than a privileged many in
the nineteenth century, it has, with the spread of mass phenomena
since 1880, become active on virtually all levels of social action—
government and public administration, business anl labor organization, production, consumption, and exchange.

One aspect of social action at the level of exchange was the
development of mass media, which had a deleterious effect on
tradition (even though tradition was partly incorporated in the
new fluctuating public opinion). As tradition declined, the field
of action of the mass media was further widened, and their
concern with *actualités*, or current events, was transformed into
a concern for the standardization of current events—for im-
mobilizing by mobilizing them, for converting a current event's
network of relationships among space, time, and people into a
standardized object of rapid mass consumption by means of what
one French sociologist has called *informatisation*.[23] As a result,
affirms Pierre Nora, contemporary everyday experience is characterized simultaneously by "supereventism," or the transforma-

21. *Ibid.*, pp. 94–110, 215–19.
22. In his "Préface" to Ferro, *La Grande Guerre*, p. 6 (5–8), the historian of international relations Pierre Renouvin refers to "la formation de
grands mouvements d'opinion, en dépit de 'la mobilisation des esprits.'"
23. Paul-Henry Chombart de Lauwe, *Pour une sociologie des aspirations:
Eléments pour des perspectives nouvelles en sciences humaines* (Paris:
Editions Denoël, 1969), pp. 20–21. The foregoing interpretation is similar
to literary and social critic Dwight Macdonald's notion of the function
of "fact-fetishism" in a consumption-oriented society, ever prone to treat
facts (events) as objects of mass consumption rather than as parts of a
larger whole: Macdonald, *Against the American Grain* (New York:
Random House, 1962), p. 396.

)

tion of events into inflated monster events, and by the standardization of events conceived and organized as consumers' goods. Among the particular victims of the standardization of current events have been the specialists in contemporary history. Just as historians of earlier societies began to take pains to give the objects of their studies an anthropological dimension, and just as the technologically and economically underdeveloped countries and underprivileged groups in the advanced societies began to raise their historical consciousness, specialists in contemporary history (Crubellier is one of the few exceptions) fell under the stamp of the standardized event of twentieth-century mass-media journalism. At the same time, they lost other aspects of contemporary life as these were diverted to economics, sociology, and psychology. Contemporary history, according to Nora, is consequently almost "a history without historians."[24] While precontemporary history is a product of contemporary social science, of the interest of historians in the methods and questions of the neighboring disciplines,[25] contemporary history reflects contemporary mass society.

Historians of the contemporary era cannot play their role properly until they design a different history, *"une histoire autre."*[26] That they cannot do without stepping out of their own time into "another time," adopting a comparative stance, seeing the present through the prism and strangeness of the past, just as the historian of the past starts with some awareness and knowledge of the often strange present.[27]

24. Pierre Nora, "Pour une histoire contemporaine," in *Mélanges en l'honneur de Fernand Braudel*, II, 419–26; Nora, "Le Retour de l'événement," in Le Goff and Nora, eds., *Faire de l'histoire*, I, *Nouveaux problèmes*, 210–28, revised version of "L'Evénement monstre," *Communications*, No. 18 (1972).

25. "History as a Contemporary Social Science" was one of the two themes of the *enquêtes* undertaken by the *Annales* in 1961. See Braudel, "Retour aux enquêtes," pp. 421–24.

26. Nora, "Pour une histoire contemporaine," pp. 419, 421.

27. Ariès, *Le Temps de l'histoire*, pp. 309–10, 321–22.

But the discipline contemporary history needs to do more. It must rethink the problem of the event. The event examined by the contemporary historian—the cinematic, radio, TV, or newspaper event, or the event conceived of and standardized by persons who have been raised by means of such media—differs from the event of the past in its origin as an homogenized mass-media construct, by its destiny as an object of mass consumption. In Nora's words, "If the heart of contemporary history beats somewhere, it does so not in the silence of the archives but in the hubbub of an editorial room or in the ceremonious hurly-burly of a press conference."[28]

Mass-media events could not be such facile objects of mass consumption if they lacked a superficial quality. But since they are standardized or homogenized in different ways by the various groups that vie for the eye and ear of the media consumer, the culture of the technologically advanced countries of the world tends to become a mosaic culture, a *culture (en) mosaïque*.[29]

Mass-media events are produced and consumed, moreover, in massive quantities. Contemporary official records, of course, are less easily available—and much less so in France than in the United States—than other types of records. As they are released, however, a question that may have to be asked is how they correspond to the massive data of other origin. Since each opinion-making agency may have a special way of standardizing events, what may first have to be established is the nature of its bias. Only then can the historian gain access to the hidden, bring out the share of the past in giving a provisional meaning to the present, place the event in "a significative series," and seize it in its totality.[30]

One fruitful consequence of the confrontation between mass

28. Nora, "Pour une histoire contemporaine," p. 424.
29. Abraham A. Moles, "Philosophie et esthétique des méthodes," in Roland Caude and Abraham A. Moles, eds., *Méthodologie vers une science de l'action* (Paris: Gauthier-Villars, 1964), p. 23.
30. Nora, "Pour une histoire contemporaine," p. 424.

culture and events is that, since the late 1950s, historians and other scholars have given the event the kind of careful scrutiny that it had not received since Paul Lacombe's analysis more than half a century earlier, now largely forgotten. Even Braudel, who has felt the influence of Lacombe's thought, has made no studied reference to the finesse of Lacombe's views on the subject of events.

Despite his distinction between unique and institutionalized acts —between innovation and event on the one hand and repetition, reiteration, imitation, and institution on the other—Lacombe maintained that "scientific" or "institutional" history should make use of both types of acts. It should give heed to events to the extent that they "cause some new institution" or, as one might say today, to the extent that they are agents of restructuration. Unlike his equally renowned Rumanian contemporary, A. D. Xenopol, who held that "facts of succession" (Lacombe's events) are the basic stuff of history,[31] Lacombe affirmed that both events and facts of repetition are matters of concern to historians. Facts of repetition, indeed, are events capable of being represented as recurring in much the same way and normally affecting large groups of people. Events and innovations may serve as points of departure for the realization of facts of imitation. No absolute difference exists, however, between events or innovations and facts of imitation, for the latter vary in form, degree, spatial extension, demographic effect, and temporal duration; some facts of imitation are consequently more like events than others.

Events and innovations, moreover, are almost never the simple creation of particular individuals, for each individual, like each human act, is simultaneously singular or particular (*singulier, particulier*), time-bound (*temporaire*), and general (*général*). In

31. A. D. Xenopol, "Les Faits de répétition et les faits de succession," *Revue de Synthèse historique*, I (1900), 121-36. See also Xenopol, "Zur Logik der Geschichte," *Historische Zeitschrift*, CII (1909), 473-98, and "Natur und Geschichte," *Historische Zeitschrift*, CXIII (1914), 1-21.

addition to his singular traits, the individual possesses some characteristics common to his own time and society and to one or more collectivities of all or some particular previous time. Since the producers of events—individuals and societies alike—are not wholly particular, it is unlikely that the events of their production will be entirely idiosyncratic.[32]

Lacombe thus did not discount the event as an object of legitimate research in "scientific" or "institutional" history. Nor, in practice, has it been driven from history, sociology, psychology, or economics. The main thrust of the opponents of *histoire événementielle* between 1900 and 1950 was not to banish the event but to show that a history of events is insufficient for the explication of a society. And the most fervent exponent of histoire globale, Fernand Braudel, has shown a healthy respect for events, the drama of history.

For two decades after World War II the quarrel between the proponents of a history of events and those of an institutional, economic, social, structural, total, or global history subsided as the position of the second group became more firmly institutionalized. But since the late 1960s the dispute has taken another turn, marked in one major instance not so much by a defense of a history of events as by a strong critique—perhaps disparagement—of the conceptions of histoire globale.

The informal leader of this intellectual current is Paul Veyne, teacher of ancient history at the University of Aix-en-Provence. Veyne has been identified by Raymond Aron as a member of "the third generation of the *Annales* School, the generation of forty to fifty years."[33] A Genevan scholar identifies him as an "exceptionally gifted" author but a product of the generally "exhausting *Annales* School," and he takes the occasion of a book

32. Paul Lacombe, *De l'histoire considérée comme science* (Paris: Hachette, 1894), pp. xiii, 3–7, 9, 11; Lacombe, *La Psychologie*, pp. 303–5.
33. Raymond Aron, "Comment l'historien écrit l'épistémologie: A propos du livre de Paul Veyne," *Annales ESC*, XXVII (November–December 1971), 1319 (1319–54).

review to incriminate "the French historical tradition, the habit of joining geography to history, the inveterate desire to model history after the natural sciences, in one word: the unconscious positivism of the [French] university tradition."[34] On the other hand, one *Annales* critic does not even honor Paul Veyne as a renegade, but rather denounces his act as part of a senseless effort on the part of Provence (and other provincial?) scholars to achieve "decolonization" from structuralism and other Paris neomaniac fashions.[35]

Acknowledging the influence of Anglo-American analytical philosophy and German *Wissenschaftstheorie*, Veyne is "first and foremost against" one thing after another.[36] He is antagonistic, above all, to the directions taken by the *Annales* since the end of World War II. Rejecting histoire globale without once mentioning Fernand Braudel's name, he belittles the notions of longue durée, of collective mind sets or any kind of mind sets (*mentalités*)—which he reduces to behaviorism—and of history in depth; and he calls the division of the world into a number of civilizations "an optical illusion." In this he is manifestly at odds with Henri-Irénée Marrou, who rejects "the myth—for it is a myth—of the structural unity of civilizations,"[37] but who defines a civilization as a partially coherent whole, with fluid spatial and chronological limits, organized around a central principle, but also characterized by the persistence of archaic traits and the embryonic manifestation of new directions of future development.[38]

Veyne does not seek, however, to restore the importance of

34. Alain Dufour, "Comment on écrit l'histoire et comment on la pense," *Cahiers Vilfredo Pareto*, X, 27 (1972), 171–77.
35. Michel de Certeau, "Une épistémologie de transition: Paul Veyne," *Annales ESC*, XXVII (November–December 1972), 1317–27.
36. Aron, "Comment l'historien écrit l'épistémologie," p. 1324.
37. Marrou, *De la connaissance historique*, p. 174.
38. Henri-Irénée Marrou, "Histoire de la civilisation: Antiquité," in Comité International des Sciences Historiques, *IXe Congrès International des Sciences Historiques*, I, 323–40.

the event. There is, he affirms, no such thing as an "eventmental" (*événementiel*) atom. Nor is there any such thing as an "elementary social fact," but not because a fact is a construct, sign, or symbol; rather because events occur in an "intrigue"—never in isolation—and intrigues are never duplicated or repeated. Lacking stability, events are enriched retroactively as "the passage of time brings to light new *items*, in relation to which an event of the past takes on a new significance," so that after the student revolts of 1968 "the study of medieval heresies takes on greater relief," and "after 1917 we see more clearly certain aspects of 1789. We see them, to be sure, but did they already exist before we took notice? Or is time the creator that has incorporated them in the event?"[39]

The answer depends in part on how one interprets "time." It is certain, however, that events acquire a new significance as they are placed in different historical perspectives just as they may take on different meanings in different spatial perspectives. One wonders, therefore, why Veyne is so hostile to longue durée and to the concept of culture areas.

Serial history, he continues, has value not as an instrument of functional analysis (which he does not discuss) but as a means of distinguishing events from *historical* events: "An historical event only takes on all its intellectual zest if one places it in a descriptive inventory of the events of the same series that have occurred up to our own day; its essence does not change with the times, but its interest increases indefinitely. In brief, historians study two objects in one: an event, of which the description is finished, and history, which is infinite."

Veyne similarly accepts comparative history, understood as a

39. Paul Veyne, "A Contestation of Sociology," trans. Brenda Porster Amato, *Diogenes*, No. 75 (Fall 1971), p. 20 (1–23). One critic (a second Genevan) suggests that a succession of constantly revised intrigues may promote a history of the triumphant, that is, of the last to triumph or live in expectation of triumph. See Ruth Silberman, "Comment, paraît-il, on écrit l'histoire," *Cahiers Vilfredo Pareto*, X, 27 (1972), 179–86.

comparison of "intrigues"—that is, of events situated in similar series but referring to different temporal durations, spatial extensions, or role-players, and connected by a narrative with a purposive explanation. While also assenting to Max Weber's notion of an ideal type as "an instrument of interpretation," he categorically refuses typological history or the transformation of ideal into real types. For there are no real types, there are only topics or problems and *items* (a term that seems to refer to the factors that give meaning to events and topics).

In the final analysis, history is not a science "but a *particular case of general sociology*," which itself is not a science but "really history sliced up by *items*" and thus a deformation and mutilation of history.[40] It lacks a special method, and historical theories and models are useless except as hermeneutical instruments. It is primarily a work of erudition and a work of art, a demonstration of the historian's ability to define a topic and analyze it in terms of intrigue. The *"Annales* School" itself has no unity other than the sense of community born of the pursuit of the topical approach.[41]

In a section entitled "Structure of the Eventmental Field"—which is curious, because he generally denies the existence of structure—Veyne portrays an intrigue as "an itinerary" that can be traced by historians, each one in his own manner, "across the

40. Veyne, "A Contestation of Sociology," pp. 17, 23.
41. Most of the foregoing analysis is based on Veyne, *Comment on écrit l'histoire,* pp. 38–39, 46–47, 56–57, 62, 132, 144, 152, 156–57, 167, 173–75, 232–34, 266, 271–72, 339–40. Some of the views that Veyne develops here were present in his article, "*Panem et circenses:* L'Evergétisme devant les sciences humaines," *Annales ESC,* XXIV (May–June 1969), 785–825. In a book review for *Annales ESC,* XXVII (May–June 1972), 668–69, he appears to adopt a more moderate stand according to which history becomes "analysis, conceptualization," and "if one wants, science." The term "science" is ambiguous in French but Veyne's use of it suggests that he may have had some second thoughts. In a later article, "L'Histoire conceptualisante," in Le Goff and Nora, eds., *Faire de l'histoire,* II, *Nouvelles approches,* 62–92, he explicitly states that there cannot be a science *of* history. He rather envisions history as a conceptualizing discipline.

very objective eventmental field (which is infinitely divisible and not comprised of eventmental atoms); no historian describes the totality of this field, for an itinerary involves a choice." An event, moreover, is not a specific thing with a "natural unity" but "a crossing of possible itineraries" or interactions between people and things.[42]

These are useful definitions of "event" and "intrigue." The rejection of the notion of an event as an *out-come* or *ob-ject*,[43] as something out there, in favor of the concepts field and itinerary may be especially attractive to historians who think of their discipline in terms of communications analysis. Inquiry along such lines might have borne fruit but for Veyne's loss of interest in the event as a subject of investigation once he subordinated it to intrigue (narrative) and series.

Furthermore, even after citing the philosopher Gilles Granger, Veyne neglects to note Granger's conception of the opposition between event and structure as "the chief source of the epistemological problems raised by the sciences of man."[44] In effect, he could not take this step without embracing the notion of structure.

A scholar presumably without *Annales* connection, Paul Gaudemar, projects a threefold system of relationships—between structures and events, between events and history, and between structures and history—to which every discipline must give attention, but in terms of its own disciplinary objectives. The models of the social sciences thus cannot satisfy fully the needs of the historian just as the overall approach of historians cannot

42. Veyne, *Comment on écrit l'histoire*, pp. 51–52. Philosopher Arthur C. Danto writes that events are "stowed in the order of their happening, they overlap (for they are of varying sizes) and interpenetrate." They are also of varying duration. See Danto, *Analytical Philosophy of History* (Cambridge: Cambridge University Press, 1965), pp. 147–48. I find Veyne's ambition to situate events in a field of force theoretically more satisfying.

43. On the conception of an object, see Henri Van Lier, "Objet et esthétique," *Communications*, No. 13 (1969), pp. 93–96; Abraham A. Moles, "Objet et communication," *ibid.*, p. 5 (1–21).

44. Granger, "Evénement et structure," pp. 149–86.

serve as a model for the (other) social sciences. Historians, however, should not forget that they not only deal with events and structures but also incorporate them in a temporally, spatially, and socially based history.[45]

The event benefits from a long interest in Western societies to explore its very instability in order to obtain somewhat greater control, however fragile, over events in general. At least several generations, and perhaps a full century or more, before Machiavelli became the advocate of a political state organized to cope with the needs of the present rather than simply to suit the tastes of the past, Florentine adventurers (undertakers of ventures) and merchants began to imagine *fortuna* not as a storm or ill wind, or as an unknown force to be feared and avoided, but as a short future that could be brought partially under men's control. By being ready to take advantage of events, weigh risks, give more careful attention to bookkeeping, improve their calculations of distances (from their market outlets and sources of supply) and their knowledge of geography, and observe a precise mechanical time for opening and closing shop and performing the acts of municipal government in their cities, the business leaders of Renaissance Italy got into the habit of basing their future actions on their knowledge of the events of the past. They thus sometimes were able to transform *fortuna* from a storm into a way of making a fortune.[46]

45. Paul Gaudemar, in a comment on this, entitled "Evénement, structure, histoire: Limites du rôle de la pensée formelle dans les sciences de l'homme," in J. Lacroix, ed., *Recherches et dialogues philosophiques et économiques,* "Cahiers de l'Institut de Science Économique Appliquée," No. 96 (Series M, No. 6) (Paris: I.S.E.A., December 1959), pp. 187–207. Gaudemar was then a teacher at the Faculté des Lettres et Sciences Humaines, University of Toulouse.

46. Christian Bec, "Au début du XVe siècle: Mentalité et vocabulaire des marchands florentins," *Annales ESC,* XXII (November–December 1967), 1206–26; Josef Macek, *"La Fortuna* chez Machiavel," *Le Moyen âge,* No. 2 (1971), 305–28, and No. 3–4 (1971), 493–523; Josef Macek, "Pour une sémantique historique," in *Mélanges en l'honneur de Fernand Braudel,* II, 343–52. For suggestions of a similar situation in Venice, see Alberto

The trend since the Renaissance toward a determination of the cost of action and—in a limited sense—toward the rationalization of action, founded on the principle that identical events are the products of identical causes and produce in turn identical effects, began to be channeled in the latter part of the nineteenth century toward the goal of a science of action. With his perception that chance, or the accidental (*le hasard*), is not necessarily that which cannot be foreseen but may be that which has not been foreseen, Lucien Febvre joined Henri Berr in embracing the aims of a science of action. In 1968, sociologist Roger Bastide called for the formulation of "a science of events," a discipline that would seek to ascertain how a given event is likely to act upon and orient future events, and compel them to follow a predetermined course. Bastide noted, moreover, that some events—*les événements types* or event types—conform closely to certain models of myth.[47] Again during the 1960s, a further spurt of interest in the event was initiated through the attempt to elaborate a more satisfactory science of action on the basis of the recently developed principles of game theory.[48]

As we have seen, individual scholars have played an important

---

Tenenti, "Temps et 'ventura' à la Renaissance: Le Cas de Venise," in *Mélanges en l'honneur de Fernand Braudel*, I, *Histoire économique du monde méditerranéen 1450–1650* (Toulouse: Edouard Privat, 1973), 599–610; Alberto Tenenti, "The Sense of Space and Time in the Venetian World of the Fifteenth and Sixteenth Centuries," trans. J. R. and Sheila Hale, in John Rigby Hale, ed., *Renaissance Venice* (London: Faber, 1973), pp. 17–46.

47. Lucien Febvre's comments in Victor Chapot, "Le Hasard en histoire," in *Science et loi*, Ve Semaine Internationale de Synthèse (Paris:, 1934), pp. 201–20; Roger Bastide, "La Connaissance de l'événement," in Georges Balandier, Roger Bastide, Jacques Berque, and Pierre George, eds., *Perspectives de la sociologie contemporaine: Hommage à Georges Gurvitch* (Paris: Presses Universitaires de France, 1968), pp. 159–68.

48. G.-H. Bousquet, "Le Hasard: Son rôle dans l'histoire des sociétés," *Annales ESC*, XXII (March–April 1967), 419–28; Marc Barbut, "En marge d'une lecture de Machiavel: 'L'Art de la Guerre' et la praxéologie mathématique," *Annales ESC*, XXV (May–June 1970), 567–73; Ernest Coumet, "La Théorie du hasard est-elle née par hasard?" *ibid.*, pp. 574–98.

role in rehabilitating the event. In 1964, under the impact of current examples of tyrannicide, Roland Mousnier published his *L'Assassinat de Henri IV, 14 mai 1610*. A study of an event, *L'Assassinat* was written in apparent defiance of current *Annales* conceptions (but, in effect, in agreement with Lucien Febvre's view that there is such a thing as a *gros événement*), for Mousnier was eager to show that some special events are creators of new events. The effect of such special events is neither local in character nor of short duration. It may flout, indeed, the stated intentions of their authors. Almost simultaneously, in February 1964, at a colloquium sponsored by the Catholic Center of French Intellectuals, and especially in 1965, at a colloquium on social history held at the Ecole Normale Supérieure of Saint-Cloud, Maurice Crubellier made an intelligent defense of the need for an autonomous social history or for a more sociocultural and less socioeconomic history and for one that would stress the importance of traditional mind sets (*mentalités*) but seek out no less fervently the "voluntary creative act that introduces something new in the life of a society even if its author lacks a perfectly clear awareness of his aim or of the infinite chain of consequences of his act of initiation."

Crubellier's definition of the event, as stated above, excludes the purely accidental, natural calamities, and cyclical crises. It might debar even the invention that does not result in innovation. For the event with which he is concerned is the "pure and full event," the event that is not only a sign or symbol but also a motive force (*événement moteur*). His focus is fixed not on the event that can be inserted in a series, but on the event that can claim autonomy because it can be delimited spatially and temporally with ease (a battle, a treaty, the advent or fall of a government) and because it exerts a momentary impact; he focuses even more on the event that initiates a new structure.[49]

49. Roland Mousnier, *L'Assassinat de Henri IV, 14 mai 1610* (Paris: Gallimard, 1964), translated by Joan Spencer as *The Assassination of Henry IV: The Tyrannicide Problem and the Consolidation of the French*

An event of this kind is the major event in Michelet's *Le Peuple*
(1846): the decline in the price of cotton cloth, in 1842, to six
sous and the subsequent availability of cotton prints not only to
the wife of the artisan but also to the wife of the factory worker.
The "combined efforts of science and art to force ungrateful
cotton fabrics to undergo every day so many brilliant transformations and to spread them everywhere within the reach of the
poor" produced a further group of events with revolutionary
(structural or structuring) consequences: "a revolution in clean-
liness and embellishment of the homes of the poor; underwear,
bedding, table linen, and window curtains were now used by
whole classes who had not used them since the beginning of the
world." It was a complex of events creating a new system of
popular structures: a rising capacity to consume, "democratic
progress," and "an initiation into art."[50]

Perceived by Michelet, Lacombe, and Crubellier, and by the
proponents of genetic structuralism (often Marxists), the close
relationship between structures and events was noted also by the
sociologist Jean Baechler. In a seminal article published in 1968,
Baechler attributes the development of the structures of commercial capitalism and economic growth in Western Europe to
the comparatively low valuation of political and religious authority since the eleventh century and to the high valuation of
efficiency. Through this persistent valuation, change itself—that

---

Absolute Monarchy in the Early Seventeenth Century (London: Faber;
New York: Scribner's, 1973). For a review of the latter, see Alfred Soman,
"Good Mousnier in Bad Translation," *Reviews in European History*,
I (June 1974), 14–20; Roland Mousnier and René Pillorget, "Contemporary
History and Historians of the Sixteenth and Seventeenth Centuries,"
Journal of Contemporary History, III, 2 (1968), 97 (93–108). For Maurice
Crubellier's views, see his "Enseignement de l'histoire et formation humaine,"
Recherches et débats du Centre Catholique des Intellectuels Français,
No. 47, pp. 73–74, and especially his "L'Evénement en histoire sociale," in
L'Histoire sociale, pp. 35–43, with comments by Pierre Vilar, Ernest
Labrousse, and Jésus Ibarrola, pp. 44–47, for the quotations from Crubellier
and for a more extensive development of his conception of the event.
    50. Michelet, *The People*, pp. 44–45.

is, the appearance of new events—became an essential part of Europe's system of structures. All this could not have happened, however, without some precocious protostructural events by means of which efficiency and change first became acceptable in some small but important European circles.[51]

One might conjecture, too, that the conception of history as a narrative history of events was itself the product of the penchant of the Western European group of societies to give direction to each particular action. For some groups at least, change acquired a visible directed structure. "Mutation," for example, was one of the favorite terms of the sixteenth-century magistrate and historian Estienne Pasquier to indicate that society and its needs will change constantly. Pasquier convincingly argued, nevertheless, that change need present no insuperable obstacle to the maintenance of a nation's or a whole society's identity and continuity.[52]

A final path by means of which scholars associated with the *Annales* and the Sixième Section rehabilitated the event was through their attention to mass culture, exemplified by the creation in 1960 of a new Sixième Section research unit, the Centre d'Etudes des Communications de Masse (SECMAS). Interested

51. Jean Baechler, "Essai sur les origines du système capitaliste," *Archives européennes de sociologie*, IX, 2 (1968), 205–63.

52. George Huppert, "Naissance de l'histoire en France: Les 'Recherches' d'Estienne Pasquier," *Annales ESC*, XXIII (January–February 1968), 84, 99 (69–105); Huppert, *The Idea of Perfect History: Historical Erudition and Historical Philosophy in Renaissance France* (Urbana, Ill.: University of Illinois Press, 1970), translated by Françoise and Paulette Braudel as *L'Idée de l'histoire parfaite*, in series "Nouvelle Bibliothèque Scientifique" (Paris: Flammarion, 1973). For a review of the latter, see Roger Chartier, "Comment on écrivait l'histoire au temps des guerres de religion," *Annales ESC*, XXIX (July–August 1974), 883–87. The idea of the need for "mutations" or the belief that men will be able to cope more effectively with the vicissitudes of *fortuna* if they alter their habits and modify their institutions pervades also Niccolò Machiavelli's *Prince* and *Discourses*. See Allan H. Gilbert, *Machiavelli's Prince and Its Forerunners: "The Prince" as a Typical Book "de Regimene Principum"* (Durham, N.C.: Duke University Press, 1938), pp. 206, 217–18.

in the relationship between mass culture and the event, several SECMAS members proposed as early as 1961 the concept of "informative unit" as the proper elementary unit of mass communications analysis.[53] In 1972, under the cumulative impact of the growing concern with the problems of the event and, perhaps, of Foucault's recent conception of the event as a sign to be inserted in a series, the SECMAS review *Communications* published a special number entitled "The Event."

One of the two historians who contributed to this *Communications* issue, Emmanuel Le Roy Ladurie, devoted his attention to the relationship between events and systems—how, in particular, an innovation with no deep roots like the antibourgeois peasant resistance of 1790–1799 in France's west (*la chouannerie*) became the "matrix-event" of a new political-mental structure of long duration; how, more generally, an event may reinforce an existing structure and how it may undermine it, collide with other events, or initiate a new structure. His interpretation buttresses, and in turn is reinforced by, that of other contributors who sought to explain how order (structure) is created from noise (events): that is, how some events disrupt an old function or modify or transform a system or structure, and in this manner become inseparable from the structure itself.[54] Le Roy Ladurie's explanation is also very similar to Charles Péguy's vision of the critical event—the event that through some circumstance, especially in a time of crisis, becomes "a fragment of the future

53. Roland Barthes, "Le Centre d'Etudes des Communications de Masse —le C.E.C.MAS," *Annales ESC*, XVI (September–October 1961), 991–92. The authors of the concept "unité informative" were Violette Morin, Claude Frère, and Marie-Claude Gardelle. See also Jules Gritti, "Le Centre d'Etudes des Communications de Masse: Bilan triennal, perspectives," *Annales ESC*, XXII (September–October 1967), 1121–25.

54. Emmanuel Le Roy Ladurie, "Evénement et longue durée dans l'histoire sociale: L'Exemple chouan," *Communications*, No. 18 (1972), pp. 72–84. See also Edgar Morin, "Le Retour de l'événement," *ibid.*, pp. 6–20, and "L'Evénement-sphinx," *ibid.*, pp. 173–92.

event" or "the event of the event": the formative element of a new structure.[55]

The response of the *Annales* editors to the *Communications* issue devoted to "the event" was to comment in their unnumbered blue pages—where brief summaries are made of important books and articles—that they considered this "return of the event" not a return to narrative history or an annulment of their combat against a narrative history of events, but an effort to rethink the problem of the event and thus to continue the combat of the founders.[56]

While the effort to rethink the event has been legitimated by *Annales* scholars, the event's resurgence has also been used to contest the rights of histoire globale, as in an article by the Marxist politicologist Blandine Barret-Kriegel printed in the *Annales* under the old rubric "Débats et combats." She prophetically opens with the words: "Everywhere one greets the return of the event." Then she launches into an attack on Braudel's conception of the multiple times of history before proceeding to salute the event's return as a vindication of the political history (preferably Marxist) toward which the *Annales* once, seemingly, had turned its back.[57]

Such criticisms may suggest an inevitable irreconcilability be-

55. Charles Péguy, "Clio: Dialogue de l'histoire et de l'âme païenne," *Oeuvres en prose 1909–1914*, avant-propos and notes by Marcel Péguy (Paris: Gallimard, copyright 1957), pp. 293–301, available in English translation in *Temporal and Eternal* (London: Collins, 1958). See also Robert Marichal, "La Critique des textes," in Samaran, ed., *L'Histoire et ses méthodes*, p. 1339 (1247–1366). For a non-*Annales* view of the proto-structural event similar to that of the foregoing, see the study by American economic historian Herman Freudenberger and German economist G. Mensch, "Innovation and Regional Industrialization," MS made available to me in 1973 by Freudenberger.

56. Under the rubric "Le Choix des *Annales*," *Annales ESC*, XXVII (May–June 1972).

57. Blandine Barret-Kriegel, "Histoire et politique ou l'histoire science des effets," *Annales ESC*, XXVIII (November–December 1973), 1437–62.

event and histoire globale. Braudel has added two
...tory pages to Part Three of the second edition of *La
...erranée*, however, to show that events and total history
...e not inconsistent:

I decided to publish this third part under the sign of events only
after much hesitation. It derives frankly from a traditional history.
. . . It must be included, however, since it would be wrong to reduce
histoire globale simply to a study of stable structures or of slow
evolution. The permanent frameworks, the conservative societies, the
economies that are prisoners of so many impossibilities, the civilizations that have stood the test of centuries, all these legitimate ways
of investing history with depth give access to the essence of man's
past, at least to what, as men of 1966, we choose to regard as that
essence. But essence is not totality. . . .
Events are dust. They are brief glimmers, hardly alight before they
return to night and often to oblivion. Each event, nevertheless, however brief, bears testimony, lights up a corner of the landscape and
sometimes even deep layers of history. And not only political history,
for every sector of history—political, economic, social, cultural, and
even geographic—is illumined by the intermittent flare of such
eventmental signs.

Events are signs. But how does one determine what signs to
use (or to choose)? How does one determine their relative
significance? In terms of the problem at hand, of course, but the
question of criteria remains, and Braudel has suggested five basic
principles. Those events are significant that signify, that is, (1)
that have an explanatory function; (2) that have spatial or/and
temporal consequences; (3) that served as signs (were significant)
for contemporaries; (4) that serve as signs for the historian's
craft (or for other disciplines); and (5) that contribute to the
formation of a series, whether economic or political (and, let us
add, social or cultural).[58] In language less poetic than Braudel's
but basically similar, Jean-Paul Aron holds that an event is

58. Braudel, *La Méditerranée*, II, 223–24. The version of this passage in
the authorized translation by Siân Reynolds (*The Mediterranean*, II, 901–
3) is not quite as faithful to the original as I need for my analytical
purposes.

fundamentally a sign—almost an *item* in the cybernetic sense—of varying value depending upon its immediate and long-term audio-graphic, or acoustical, and other reverberations.[59]

Let us bear in mind, however, that this new conception of the event may be itself the product of the transformation of events in contemporary societies into standardized *ob-jects* of rapid mass consumption. Without this standardization it may have been more difficult to conceive of them as signs. History as a study of eventmental signs or functions may be thus a product of the contemporary mass society of standardized events in which centers have been set up for the study of mass communications. In the final analysis, however, "*une histoire autre*" must seek to recover the eventmental field—uncover the hidden behind the revelations and reverberations of the standardized events. This means not the abandonment but the strengthening of general and mass communications analysis. It requires the creation of a discipline more Hermaean and Hestian than ever, a history of many temporal dimensions, a serial history, a history of eventmental signs and of other signs and functions, a history of people as well as of signs and things. It requires histoire globale.

59. Jean-Paul Aron, "L'Audiographie de l'événement," *Communications*, No. 18 (1972), pp. 156–61. See also Stafford Beer, *Decision and Control: The Meaning of Operational Research and Management Cybernetics* (London: Wiley, 1966).

9 The *Annales* Paradigm

Michel Foucault has observed that no group engaged in the production of discourse is without "its procedures of *exclusion*"; in no society is everyone (who) free to say everything (what) under any circumstance (when).[1] For Fernand Braudel and many other *Annales* scholars, however, history is "pluridimensional."[2] Being a school of *débats et combats*, they generally do not shut their doors on controversy. Indeed, under "the ecumenical care of Lucien Febvre's successors," it seems as if they have chosen "to ignore no point of view, whether revolutionary or simply innovative," and to absorb almost every novelty instantaneously into the dominant current that they have comprised in France for a quarter of a century.[3]

The Hispanicist Richard Herr suggests that they constitute in some respects a quasi-religious sect: "The words *structures sociales* and *conjoncture* have become their Open, Sesame! If conjuncture ever stood for a precisely defined idea, the coincidence of certain economic factors to bring about specific facts, it has risen above it to the symbol of a faith."[4] Addressing herself

1. Foucault, *L'Ordre du discours*, p. 11.
2. Braudel, "Sur une conception de l'histoire sociale," pp. 318–19.
3. Glénisson, "L'Historiographie française contemporaine," p. lxiii. Glénisson himself deplores the virtual elimination of competitive methodologies by *Annales* dominance over the community of French professional historians. He holds that Marxist historiography has been left as the only serious rival of the *Annales* School.
4. Richard Herr, "Conclusion," in Herr and Parker, eds., *Ideas in History*, pp. 366–67 (349–75).

at least in part to the consequence of *Annales* domin
with that of the Labrousse orientation), the Brit
Betty Behrens complained in 1965 about another
related matter: a decline in intelligibility. There were ~
new monographs on various aspects of French eighteenth-century
history, she observed, with such diverse frames of reference, so
much jargon, so many fuzzy concepts, and such authorial zeal to
tell everything and display new techniques in each and every
particular that it was impossible to glean much meaning from
them, especially since the unity formerly attained by using
politics as a general frame of reference had been broken.[5] Another British historian, Richard Cobb, has been critical of the
quantifying and "thinking by numbers" characteristic of so
much *Annales* scholarship, which he rightly considers a poor sub-
stitute for overall interpretation. J. H. Plumb appreciates the
warmth and excitement of Braudel's *Méditerranée*—and consequently regrets the loss in the English translation of Braudel's
crackling, sparkling style—but deplores his and especially the rest
of the *Annales* School's "penchant for the decorative statistic,"
for "pages and pages" of statistics "displayed to little purpose"
(a generalization from which he excludes only Pierre Goubert
and Emmanuel Le Roy Ladurie). An American critic dares to
hope, therefore, that American historians may be able to serve the
function of leading French historiography out of the "arid
wastes" into which "some of the later *Annalistes* have recently
taken so much of it."[6]

5. Betty Behrens, " 'Straight History' and 'History in Depth,' the Ex-
perience of Writers on Eighteenth-Century France," *Historical Journal*,
VIII (1965), 117–26.
6. Richard Cobb, "Thinking by Numbers—1, 2: Historians in White
Coats," *Times Literary Supplement*, Dec. 3, 1971, pp. 1527–28; J. H.
Plumb, "History as Geography, Economics, Folklore—as Everything That
Touches the Lives of Men," *New York Times Book Review*, Dec. 31,
1972; David H. Pinkney, "The Dilemma of the American Historian of
Modern France Reconsidered," *French Historical Studies*, IX (Spring
1975), 181 (170–81). Soboul, *La Civilisation et la Révolution française*, I,
23–33, has expressed a similar distrust of quantification.

An *Annales* empiricist no less suspicious of "methodology" than these critics, Pierre Goubert, contests this gloomy picture of French historiography, affirming that French scholarship has produced local and provincial histories that proceed from a concern for whole societies and that the interest in parish registers and local history has given a tremendous boost to historical demography, a field in which French historians were the first to excel. Goubert concedes, nevertheless, that with success has come excess, an overproduction of monographs devoid of synthesis.[7]

One of the basic arguments of the present study, however, has been that Braudel has not been alone among French historians in producing works of exceptional merit and brilliance. The third generation of *Annales* scholars has been by and large equal to the challenge, having published since the mid-1950s, or since 1960, one major synthesis, or *essai de synthèse*, after another. Following an initial endeavor to decide which authors and titles to identify with the achievement of synthesis or *essai de synthèse*, and which to weed out, I abandoned the task as hopeless, convinced that I would select too few or too many. I shall assume instead that the point has been proved and that there is no need to belabor the questions of intellectual fecundity and theoretical insight. This is not to say that one should accept the work of *Annales* scholars uncritically, nor that it is without shortcomings.

As an example of this critical outlook, let us consider the second volume (covering the years 1660–1789) of a projected four-volume collective *Histoire économique et sociale de la France* under the joint editorship of France's two prince historians, Fernand Braudel and Ernest Labrousse. Despite very able individual contributions by Labrousse, Pierre Léon, Pierre Goubert, Jean Bouvier, Charles Carrière, and Paul Harsin, the volume suffers from two serious defects. As Isser Woloch has observed, it fails to give adequate "theoretical understanding to institutional factors"—family, state power, and religious institutions—and it fails

7. Pierre Goubert, "Local History," *Daedalus*, C (Winter 1971), 113–27.

—"a failure of nerve," a basic reluctance to visualize in new ways a problem and period linked so intimately to existing mythical models—to project or to consider projecting the conclusions beyond 1789, into the early decades of the nineteenth century, during which much the same structures and patterns of conjuncture persisted perhaps "largely unchanged, even if momentarily interrupted by the Revolution."[8] It is none the less one of the best works of economic history in any language and based, to boot, on the most recent findings of historical research.

If French historical scholarship were incapable of synthesis and if the criticisms directed at *Annales* syncretism, eclecticism, and mania for the new were wholly justified, the future of French historiography would be deservingly dreary. For as Braudel himself has shown so brilliantly, a civilization or culture—let us say also a group engaged in the production of discourse—that aspires to preserve its vitality must, to be sure, be able to borrow and create new traits. But to conserve its autonomy it must be able and ready to refuse. It must choose from among the many offers of various contributors, being vigilant not to incorporate what is incompatible with its own structures if it desires to retain its independence and identity.[9] Cultural resistance, refusal, or interdiction (taboo) is one of the important means of preserving the basic character of a culture.[10]

On closer analysis, however, it is clear that no other group of twentieth-century scholars in any country has made a more valuable contribution to historiography and historical method than the *Annales* School. As a result of *Annales* research, for example, we are able today to explain a whole society and its message systems and to define structure, conjuncture, function, and event far better than historians of the era before 1946.

8. Isser Woloch, "French Economic and Social History," *Journal of Interdisciplinary History*, IV (Winter 1974), 435–57.
9. Braudel, "L'Apport de l'histoire des civilisations," pp. 20.10–11 to 20.12–14; *La Méditerranée*, II, 101.
10. Meyerson, *Les Fonctions psychologiques*, p. 148.

C. Vann Woodward holds that history, unlike the sciences, "has not been periodically endowed with 'a common paradigm'" or set of first principles and that it probably never will be.[11] I would argue, on the contrary, that the total effect of *Annales* inquiry since 1929, but especially between 1946 and 1972, has been to create an historical paradigm or "disciplinary matrix" for the world community of historical scholarship.[12]

A basic thesis of this book is indeed that the *Annales* paradigm is the third in the history of the discipline. The first paradigm was the exemplar conception of history as a study *and* instrument of contemporary politics. It began with Thucydides and culminated in Francesco Guicciardini's vision of the presence of historical truth—to quote a twentieth-century interpreter—"in the specific instance, in the *particolare*, in the clash of egotisms as these work themselves out in great events."[13] The second paradigm was a more strictly linear model of general progress and development. The *Annales* paradigm constitutes an inquiry into how one of the systems of a society functions or how a whole collectivity functions in terms of its multiple temporal, spatial, human, social, economic, cultural, and eventmental dimensions. But as Maurice Mandelbaum explains, without specific reference to the *Annales*, a historiography that seeks to initiate an *inquiry* is less concerned with the "relationship of antecedent to consequent" than with

11. C. Vann Woodward, "The Future of the Past," *American Historical Review*, LXXV (February 1970), 726 (711–26), presidential address to the meeting of the American Historical Association, Washington, D.C., Dec. 29, 1969.

12. On paradigmatic change, see Thomas S. Kuhn, "Postscript" to *The Structure of Scientific Révolutions*, 2d enlarged ed. (Chicago: University of Chicago Press, 1970), pp. 175, 182, 187. See also David A. Hollinger, "T. S. Kuhn's Theory of Science and Its Implications for History," *American Historical Review*, LXXVIII (April 1973), 370–93.

13. Sidney Alexander, "Introduction" to Francesco Guicciardini, *The History of Italy*, trans., edited, with notes and an introduction, by Sidney Alexander (New York: Macmillan, 1969), p. xviii.

the determination of the relationship between part and whole.[14] More than this, the *Annales* paradigm demands a general inquiry into the various communications functions, including the concealed or symbolic functions of communication. Marxist historiography presents a special case. It is both a rival and a precursor of the *Annales* paradigm. Indeed, it is not one method but some version of any one of the three paradigms depending on the practitioner.

Within the *Annales* School there is some conflict between the advocates of a whole-society historical analysis (histoire globale) and the proponents of functionalism. But functionalism is implicit in the whole-society approach. There is no necessary logical disagreement between the two.

The openness of the *Annales* to innovation (inquiry) and the absence of a logical conflict between a whole-society approach to history and functionalism have, nevertheless, not spared the *Annales* from the "revolt against the father" or "*meurtre du père*"[15] (manifest in the Events of 1968 but present earlier and later in a lower key or at a hidden level), whether that father and authority is de Gaulle, Braudel, or the old dominant culture, and from a subsequent search for new fathers, such as Max Weber, *notre père à tous*. Edgar Morin has shrewdly observed, however, that the marginality of the young—their existence as an unstable category—may inspire them to a wide variety of expression.[16]

In changing societies—that is, societies in which generations are agents of change and not simply age categories or biological arrays—each generation will differ from its predecessor and suc-

14. Maurice Mandelbaum, "A Note on History as Narrative History," *History and Theory*, VI, 3 (1967), 413–19.

15. Mendel, *La Révolte contre le père*, pp. 104–5, 110–11, 310, depicts the Marquis de Sade as Foucault's "maître-ès-modernité." See also Raymond Boudon, "La Crise universitaire française: Essai de diagnostic sociologique," *Annales ESC*, XXIV (May–June 1969), 738–64.

16. Edgar Morin, "Culture adolescente et révolte étudiante," *ibid.*, pp. 765–76.

cessor. According to the philosopher Julián Marías, the members of a creative first generation will take off along new lines without realizing the full implications of their gesture. Those of the second generation "know what they are and cling to this awareness," while the third generation "has little need to create" but produces the "most 'representative' figures." The representative, however, "is seldom what is most authentic. This is a generation of 'heirs' who have begun to live within a tradition." For that very reason "the basic beliefs on which the society has by now become firmly founded begin to weaken gradually and to rupture in certain individuals." The fourth generation may continue to acknowledge the tradition but they will reinterpret it, for they are unable to reconcile themselves to the old "style" and "life form in question."[17]

This valuable interpretation overlooks two points. One is that in changing times every generation is potentially a first generation. The other is that certain generations play a key role in effecting a paradigm shift that future generations will preserve and reinforce despite momentary rebellions and dissensions. In the case of the *Annales*, the first three generations have a accomplished a paradigm shift. The third and fourth (scholars born after 1935 or 1940), moreover, are playing an "authentic" role in clarifying the paradigm despite their partial reaction against it.

Built into this third historical paradigm is the tradition of history as *inquiry*, which should give the paradigm the flexibility that a set of first principles sometimes lacks. The alternative to the acceptance of this paradigm shift may be what Marc Bloch feared[18] and what Michel Foucault once hoped for—a turning away from all historical modes of thought as the old history ceases to be able to answer the needs of the present and of the *prospective* future. But the acceptance of this paradigm shift by professional historians will not suffice. Advocates must turn their

17. Marías, *Generations*, pp. 170–80.
18. Bloch, *Apologie pour l'histoire*, p. x.

energies also to persuading their governments, the business community, and the public at large of the utility of history, of the practices and vocabulary of the third paradigm, and of the methods by means of which the discipline of history can be made to serve the needs of the twentieth and twenty-first centuries.[19]

19. Paul Leuilliot, "Histoire locale et politique de l'histoire," preface to Guy Thuillier, *Economie et société nivernaise au début du XIXe siècle* (Paris, The Hague: Mouton, 1974), published simultaneously in *Annales ESC*, XXIX (January–February 1974), 139–50.

⍭ Subject and Reference Index

Abdel-Malek, Anouar, 48, 51; "L'Avenir de la théorie sociale," 150; "Marxism and the Sociology of Civilizations," 150-51

Abel, Wilhelm, *Agrarkrisen,* trans. as *Crises agraires,* 46; *Massenarmut,* 46

Action, cost and science of, 38, 66, 85, 92, 103, 109, 126, 132, 141, 157-58, 198, 201, 217, 223-24, 227

Afanassev, Georges, *Le Commerce des céréales,* 199

Africa, 148, 152

Age categories, 47, 181, 237; *see also* Generation(s)

Agrégation d'histoire, 15, 43

Agriculture, 68, 70, 76, 84, 140, 148, 167, 178

Agulhon, Maurice, "Esquisse pour une archéologie de la République," 159; *La République au village,* 182; *La Sociabilité méridionale,* 181

Alexander, Sidney, "Introduction" to Guicciardini, *The History of Italy,* 236

Althusser, Louis, 49; "Esquisse du concept d'histoire," 112-13; *Montesquieu,* 113

American Jewish Committee, *Aspects of French Jewry,* 54

Amiot, Michel, "Le Relativisme culturaliste," 208

Ancien régime, 60, 167, 170

Anderson, Robert T., *Traditional Europe,* 99

Andrews, Richard Mowery, review of Braudel, *The Mediterranean,* 65, 114, 140

Annales d'histoire économique et sociale, Annales d'histoire sociale, Mélanges d'histoire sociale, and *Annales: Economies, Sociétés, Civilisations,* 9-13, 25, 41, 43, 59, 99, 113-14, 148-49, 169, 176, 186, 219, 227, 229

Annales de Géographie, 11, 41

Annales School, 11, 22, 37-39, 42-43, 45, 50, 56, 58, 79, 92-93, 104, 110, 113, 116, 118, 122, 158, 165-67, 172, 180-81, 185-86, 218-19, 221, 225, 232-33, 235, 237; school of *débats et combats,* 22, 229, 232

L'Année Sociologique, 11, 41

Anthropocentrism, 81, 206-8

Anthropology, 37, 55, 88, 119-20, 126, 130, 134, 148, 163, 166, 170-71, 186-87, 189, 201, 204, 206, 212, 215

Aragon, Louis, *La Culture,* 137-38

Arbellot, Guy, "La Grande mutation des routes," 141

Ariès, Philippe, 163, 173; *L'Enfant,* trans. as *Centuries of Childhood,* 172; *Histoire des populations françaises,* 160-61; "La Mort inversée," 160-61; *Le Temps de l'histoire,* 103, 215; *Western Attitudes toward Death,* 160-61

Aristocracy, 99, 166-67, 173-74, 202

Arnould, Maurice, et al., *Vingt années d'histoire économique et sociale,* 71

Aron, Jean-Paul, "L'Audiographie de l'événement," 230-31

Aron, Raymond, 93; "Comment l'historien écrit l'épistémologie," 218-19; *De Gaulle, Israel, and the Jews*, 53; *Paix et guerre*, trans. as *A Theory of International Relations*, 92; "Relativism in History," 35; "Thucydide," 212

Art, 85, 90, 168, 191-92, 226; nonart, 156

Asia, 136, 144-49

Atlantic, 74, 199

Attitudes, *see* Tradition

Authority, 145-46, 212, 226, 237

Auzias, Jean-Marie, *Clefs pour le structuralisme*, 205

Aymard, Maurice, "The *Annales*," 40, 61; "The [*sic*] Geohistory," 63

Bacon, Francis, 28

Baechler, "Essai sur les origines du système capitaliste," 227

Baehrel, René, *Une croissance*, 68

Baille, Suzanne, Fernand Braudel, and Robert Philippe, *Le Monde actuel*, 150

Bailyn, Bernard, "Braudel's Geohistory," 114

Bakhtin, Mikhail, *Rabelais and His World*, 163-64

Balandier, Georges, *Anthropologie politique*, 95

Balandier, Georges, Roger Bastide, Jacques Berque, and Pierre George, *Perspectives de la sociologie*, 224

Balkans, 177, 180

Baltic, 74, 176

Banu, Ion, 145; "La Formation sociale 'asiatique,' " 147

Barbut, Marc, "En marge d'une lecture de Machiavel," 224; "Sur le mot et le concept de 'modèle,' " 61

Barraclough, Geoffrey, *An Introduction to Contemporary History*, 64

Barret-Kriegel, Blandine, "Histoire et politique," 229

Barthes, Roland, "Le Centre d'Etudes des Communications de Masse," 228; "Le Discours de l'histoire," trans. as "Historical Discourse," 208; "Histoire et sociologie du vêtement," 133; "Pour une psycho-sociologie," 99; *Système de la mode*, 133

Bastide, Roger, "Colloque sur le mot 'structure,' " 61; "La Connaissance de l'événement," 224; ed., *Sens et usages du terme structure*, 61; "Y a-t-il une crise de la psychologie des peuples?" 142-43

Batany, John, "Des 'Trois Fonctions' aux 'Trois Etats'?" 94

Bautier, Robert-Henri, "Feux, population et structure sociale," 176

Bec, Christian, "Au début du XVe siècle," 223

Becker, Carl, "What Are Historical Facts?" 104

Beer, Stafford, *Decision and Control*, 231

Behrens, Betty, " 'Straight History,' " 233

Bell, Rudolph M., 21, 100

Benveniste, Emile, 205

Berger, Gaston, Director General of Higher Education, 16, 43

Berkelbach Van der Sprenkel, Otto, "Max Weber on China," 144

Berkhofer, Robert F., "Clio and the Culture Concept," 143

Berlin, Isaiah, "Foreword" to Meinecke, *Historism*, 33

Berr, Henri, 11, 14, 41, 50, 113, 224; *La Synthèse en histoire*, 194

Berthet, Bernard, "De la forêt inutile," 87

Bertin, Jacques, "Principe de l'Atlas," 85; *La Sémiologie graphique*, 91

Bertin, Jacques, Jean-Jacques Hémardinquer, Michael Keul, and W. G. L. Randles, *Atlas des cultures vivrières*, 85

Besançon, Alain, "Psychoanalysis" and "Vers une histoire psychanalytique," 160

Bloch, Marc, 11, 13-14, 19, 41, 50, 59, 77, 79, 106, 114, 125, 162, 169; *Apologie pour l'histoire*, trans. as *The Historian's Craft*, 37, 162,

Bloch, Marc (*cont.*)
238; "Pour une histoire comparée," trans. as "Toward a Comparative History," 125; *La Société féodale*, 91
Blot, Jacques, "Le Révisionnisme," 67, 135
Bodin, Jean, *Method for the Easy Comprehension of History*, 28-29
Bois, Paul, *Paysans de l'Ouest*, 166
Bollème, Geneviève, 49, 170, 190-91; *Les Almanachs populaires* and *La Bibliothèque Bleue*, 163
Book(s), 189-90, 213; titles, 191-93
Born, Karl Erich, "Neue Wege," 42
Boudon, Raymond, "La Crise universitaire," 237
Bourdieu, Pierre, "The Thinkable and the Unthinkable," 132
Bourgeois(ie), 67, 99, 124-25, 128, 136-37, 144, 147, 166
Bousquet, G.-H., "Le Hasard," 224
Bouvier, Jean, 49, 234; "L'Appareil conceptuel," 131; "Feu François Simiand?" 200
Braudel, Fernand, 13, 19, 22, 41-47, 50-52, 54, 58, 64-67, 92-93, 97, 99-100, 111-14, 117-18, 123, 125-26, 133, 135, 138-39, 141, 143, 148, 159, 167, 169, 185-86, 197, 211, 217-19, 229, 234-35, 237; "L'Apport de l'histoire des civilisations," 150, 235; *Capitalism and Material Life*, 71, 73; "La Catalogne, plus l'Espagne, de Pierre Vilar," 117; *Civilisation matérielle*, 68, 70-71, 73-75, 82, 96, 103, 109-10, 150; *Ecrits sur l'histoire*, 46, 68, 110, 114, 116-17, 121, 128, 150, 159; "Gaston Berger," 44; "Histoire et sciences humaines," 115; "Histoire et sciences sociales: La Longue durée," trans. as "History and the Social Sciences," 91, 98, 109, 116, 125, 127-28, 153, 158; "Histoire et sociologie," 110, 114, 116, 121-22; "Lucien Febvre," 59, 114; *La Méditerranée* (1949 ed.), 66, 77, 93, 106, 108, 114, 150; *La Méditerranée* (1966 ed.), trans. as *The Mediterranean*, 52-53, 68-70, 74, 76-78, 82, 93, 110, 115, 135, 150,
167-68, 230, 233; *Il Mondo Attuale*, 150; "Les 'Nouvelles' *Annales*," 60; "Personal Testimony," 44, 50, 68; "Pour une économie historique," 159; "Pour une histoire sérielle," 68, 117, 121; "Préface" to Kula, *Théorie économique*, 127; "Retour aux enquêtes," 215; "Sur une conception de l'histoire sociale," 46, 96, 232
Braudel, Fernand, and Ernest Labrousse, eds., *Histoire économique et sociale*, 234
Braudel, Fernand, and Frank Spooner, "Prices in Europe," 199
Brunner, Otto, *Neue Wege der Sozialgeschichte*, 45-46
Bryson, Gladys, *Man and Society*, 30
Bunge, Mario Augusto, ed., *The Critical Approach*, 26
Bureaucracy, 145, 212
Burguière, André, 21; "De Malthus à Max Weber," 177; "Famille et société," 176; "Société et culture à Reims," 213
Burke, Peter, ed., *Economy and Society*, 91

Čajkanović, Veselin, *O srpskom vrhovnom bogu*, 63
Cameron, Rondo, "Europe's Second Logistic," 70-72, 83
Cammett, John M., *Antonio Gramsci*, 138
Capitalism, 67, 144, 147, 188, 226
Carnival, 163-64
Carpentras, 176
Cassirer, Ernst, *The Problem of Knowledge*, 118, 183
Castillo, Alvaro, "Population et richesse," 180
Caude, Roland, and Abraham A. Moles, *Méthodologie*, 216
Causality, 207, 224; *see also* Action and Chance
Cedronio, Marina, "Profilo Storico," 40
Centre de Recherches Historiques, 43, 93; "Pour un Atlas d'histoire," 85
Centre de Synthèse, 41

Centre d'Etudes des Communications de Masse, 227-28

Centre d'Etudes et de Recherches Marxistes, *Sur le "mode de production asiatique*," 147-48

Centre International de Synthèse, *Civilisation*, 135

Centre National des Hautes Etudes Juives (Brussels) and Institute of Contemporary Jewry of the Hebrew University of Jerusalem, *La Vie juive*, 54

Certeau, Michel de, "Une épistémologie de transition," 219

Chabert, Alexandre, 106; *Structure économique*, 108

Chambaz, Jacques, 67

Chance, 79, 210, 224

Change, 29-30, 32, 35, 38, 58, 65, 80, 83-84, 106-7, 110-11, 127, 131, 133, 135-36, 138-39, 149-50, 157, 159-60, 167, 181, 186-87, 189, 194, 197-98, 200-2, 211, 226-27, 236-38; lexical, 161-62

Chapot, Victor, "Le Hasard en histoire," 224

Chartier, Roger, "Comment on écrivait l'histoire," 227

Chaunu, Huguette and Pierre, *Séville et l'Atlantique*, 68, 195

Chaunu, Pierre, 116, 122, 177, 180, 196; "Le Climat et l'histoire," 84; "Dynamique conjoncturelle," 195; "L'Economie," 47; "Les Entraves au changement," 97, 158, 179, 203; *L'Espagne et Charles Quint*, 164, 179; "Histoire et prospective," 158; *Histoire, science sociale*, 77, 88-89, 179-80; "La Pesée globale," 69, 75, 103; "Une histoire religieuse sérielle," 202; "Un nouveau champ pour l'histoire sérielle," 203

Chérif, M.-H., "Expansion européenne," 84

Chesneaux, Jean, "Le Mode de production asiatique," 146-48

Children, childhood, 159, 170-71, 173, 179

Chill, Emmanuel, *Power, Property, and History*, 213

China, 26, 74-75, 138

Chombart de Lauwe, Paul-Henry,

Pour une sociologie des aspirations, 214

Cinema, film, TV, 60, 90-91, 159, 213, 216

Cities, 50, 55, 60, 68-69, 78-79, 86, 165-68, 174, 176, 181, 223

Citron, Suzanne, "Dans l'enseignement secondaire," 149

Civilization(s), 51-52, 54, 67, 69, 103, 109, 111, 126, 134-39, 144, 148-52, 156, 158, 167-68, 183, 219, 230, 235; commercial, 52, 177; Jewish, 52-56, 99

Classes, 33, 135, 169-70

Classical age, 206-7; *see also* Ancien régime

Claval, Paul, *Essai sur l'évolution de la géographie humaine*, 141; *Géographie générale des marchés*, 88-89

Clémens, René, "Prolégomènes," 106-7

Climate, 80-84, 107, 140, 168

Cobb, Richard, "Thinking by Numbers," 233

Cochran, Thomas C., "History and Cultural Crisis," 212

Cohen, Marcel, "La Linguistique et l'histoire," 157

Collège de France, 14-15, 41, 103, 120, 209

Collomp, Alain, "Famille nucléaire," 175

Colloque International de Sociologie de la Littérature, *Littérature et société*, 131

Colportage, 170, 190-91

Comité Français des Sciences Historiques, *Actes du Congrès historique du centenaire de la Révolution française*, 128

Comité International des Sciences Historiques, *IXe Congrès International des Sciences Historiques*, 90, 219

Commerce, 67, 79-80, 87, 128, 148, 177-78, 195, 210

Committee for the History of World War II, 43

Communication, 38, 43, 59, 62, 64, 66-67, 76, 78, 85, 87, 95, 97-100, 103, 115, 128, 133, 137, 140, 142,

Communication (cont.)
149-50, 167, 174-75, 182, 187, 189, 191, 207, 212-14, 222, 228, 231, 237; circles of, 88-89
Communications, 63, 228-29
Communism, 138, 143-44
Community, 145-46, 168; see also Cities and Villages
Comparative method, 37, 60, 125, 185, 193, 197-99, 215, 220-21
Conjoncture économique, structures sociales: Hommage à Ernest Labrousse, 200
Conjuncture, 16, 46-47, 93-99, 107, 109, 121, 124, 127, 161, 181, 203, 232, 235
Conscious and unconscious, 97, 99, 103, 119-20, 148, 154-55, 158-60, 181, 185-86, 188, 204-5, 219; consciousness, 29-30, 40, 142, 154, 157, 201, 215
Consensus and nonconsensual, 25, 51, 115, 143, 159, 171, 182
Construct(s), 36, 58, 85, 103-6, 109, 113, 123, 125, 129, 149, 154, 194, 201, 216, 219; see also Fact(s)
Consumption, 69, 72, 75, 98, 189, 195, 200, 211, 214-16, 226, 231
Contemporary history, 36, 51, 59-60, 64-65, 91, 134, 138-40, 142, 147-49, 157-59, 166, 202, 207, 214-16, 230-31, 236
Continental vs. maritime, 64, 68, 80, 87, 103, 115, 168, 199
Continuity, discontinuity, 34, 38, 77, 122-24, 127, 129, 141, 158, 206, 208-10, 227; see also Mutation
Coquery-Vidrovitch, Catherine, "Anthropologie politique," 95, 152; "Recherches sur un mode de production africain," 148
Coumet, Ernest, "La Théorie du hasard," 224
Cournot, Antoine-Augustin, Considérations, 122-23, 194
Couturier, Marcel, Recherches sur les structures sociales de Chateaudun, 174
Credit, 78, 161
Crisis, 20, 40, 47, 95, 107, 127-28, 175, 189, 228; see also Depression
Crouzet, François, 49; "The Economic History of Modern Europe," 169
Crouzet, Maurice, ed., Histoire générale des civilisations, 137
Crubellier, Maurice, "Enseignement de l'histoire," 27, 225-26; "L'Evénement," 225-26; Histoire culturelle, 211-12, 215
Cuddihy, John Murray, The Ordeal of Civility, 55
Culture(s), 29-31, 33, 37, 85-87, 99, 103, 109-10, 134, 136, 138-39, 141-42, 144, 149-51, 170, 191, 199, 202, 212, 216-17, 227, 235, 237; areas, 51, 134, 136, 138-39, 142, 166, 198-99, 220; cultural diffusion, 62, 157, 209; cultural levels (high culture, popular culture), 142, 163-65, 168-70, 181
Curtius, Ernst Robert, The Civilization of France, 40
Cycles, 33, 68, 104, 106, 109, 127-28, 194, 200

Danto, Arthur C., Analytical Philosophy, 222
Darmon, Jean-Jacques, Le Colportage de librairie, 163
Darmon, Jean-Pierre, "Problèmes de la guerre," 162; "Un cours nouveau," 162
Darnton, Robert, "The High Enlightenment," 170; "In Search of the Enlightenment," 170, 191; "Le Livre français," 191; "Reading, Writing and Publishing," 189-91
Da Silva, José-Gentil, 21, 48; Banque et crédit en Italie, 161-62; "L'Histoire: Une biologie de l'événement politique," 162
Daumard, Adeline, 123; La Bourgeoisie parisienne, 124; "Données économiques et histoire sociale," 97, 122-23; "Une référence pour l'étude des sociétés urbaines," 123
Daumard, Adeline, and François Furet, "Méthodes de l'histoire sociale" and "Problèmes de méthode," 125
Davies, James C., "The J-Curve of Rising and Declining Satisfactions," 167

Davis, Lance E., "'And It Will Never Be Literature,'" 105
Davis, Natalie Zemon, 20; "The Reasons of Misrule," 164
De Gaulle, Charles, 53, 237
Delevoy, Robert L., *Dimensions du XXe siècle*, 64
Delorme, Marie-Raymonde, "Une Maison des Sciences de l'Homme," 44
Demography, 60, 67, 72, 75, 82, 85-86, 96, 107, 140, 159, 167, 171-73, 176, 179-81, 194, 202-3, 210, 217, 234
Denzer, Horst, ed., *Jean Bodin*, 29
Depression, 47, 128
Despotism, Oriental, 144-45; *see also* Economy *and* Production
Determinism, 77, 82, 139-41
Detienne, Marcel, 162; "En Grèce archaïque," 88
Deutsch, Karl W., John Platt, and Dieter Senghaas, "Conditions Favoring Major Advances," 50
Deuxième Conférence Internationale d'Histoire Economique, 151
Development (evolution), 32-33, 38, 131, 134, 149-51, 160, 204, 207, 219, 230, 236; economic, 67, 200; *see also* Economic growth
Devèze, Michel, *L'Europe et le monde*, 87; *Histoire des forêts*, 86; "Superficie et propriété des forêts," 86
Dialectic, 38, 60, 77, 112, 127, 130-31, 140, 148-50, 187, 204-5, 207
Diamond, Stanley, *In Search of the Primitive*, 55
Dilthey, Wilhelm, *Pattern and Meaning in History*, 27, 34
Discourse, 43, 62, 191-92, 206, 209-10, 232, 235; *see also* Language
Disease, 80, 82, 99, 178
Distribution, redistribution, 69, 105, 149, 187-89
Divitçioglu, Sencer, "Modèle économique de la société ottomane," 147
Doctorate, *de troisième cycle* and *d'Etat* or *ès lettres*, 41, 116-17
Donation, give and take, 62, 187-88
Draft animals, 70-72, 177
Dreyfus affair, 58

Duby, Georges, 49, 63, 132, 167; "Dans la France du Nord-Ouest," trans. as "Northwest France," 174; *Guerriers et paysans*, trans. as *The Early Growth of the European Economy*, 188; "Histoire des mentalités," 161, 173; "L'Histoire des systèmes de valeurs," trans. as "History of Systems of Values," 111; "Histoire sociale," 133; "Lignage, noblesse et chevalerie," 174; "Les Sociétés médiévales," trans. as "History of Medieval Societies," 181; "Structures familiales," 174
Dufour, Alain, "Comment on écrit l'histoire," 219
Du Fresnoy, Nicolas Lenglet, 31-32
Dumézil, Georges, 49, 94; *Heur et malheur du guerrier*, trans. as *The Destiny of the Warrior*, 94; *L'Idéologie tripartie*, 94; *Jupiter, Mars, Quirinus*, 94; *Naissance d'archanges*, 94
Dumont, Fernand, "La Fonction sociale de l'histoire," 35
Dumoulin, Jérôme, and Dominique Moïsi, eds., *The Historian Between the Ethnologist and the Futurologist*, published in French by Ecole Pratique des Hautes Etudes as *L'Historien entre l'ethnologue et le futurologue*, 95, 111, 159
Dupront, Alphonse, 191; "L'Histoire après Freud," 155; "Présent, passé, histoire," 158; "Problèmes et méthodes d'une histoire de la psychologie collective," 155, 194; "Sémantique historique," 192-93
Duration, 65, 89, 103, 106-12, 115, 121-25, 127-30, 134, 139-41, 143, 149, 152, 157-58, 181, 186, 198, 209-10, 219-21, 225, 228; *see also* Time
Durkheim, Emile, 11

Earle, Peter, ed., *Essays*, 70, 80
Ecole des Hautes Etudes en Sciences Sociales, 16, 41-42
Ecole Normale Supérieure, 11, 56-58, 192, 225
Ecole Pratique des Hautes Etudes, 9-10, 14-15, 20, 43

Ecology and environment, 22, 60, 76-77, 79, 81, 83-84, 86, 96, 141-42, 156, 177-79, 181
Economic growth, 105, 107, 157, 200, 226; see also Development
Economies-societies, 96-97, 170, 230
Economy, 12, 14, 31, 35, 44, 69-70, 96, 110-11, 124, 126, 151, 157, 167, 173, 181, 183, 187-88, 196-98, 202, 207; backward, 141; command, customary, revenue, tribute, 144-49
Education, 55-56, 138-39, 148-50, 178, 202
Efficiency, 105, 226-27
Egemonia, hegemony, 137, 150
Ehrard, Jean, 49, 190
Eisenstadt, S. N., review of Wittfogel, Oriental Despotism, 144-45
Elliott, J. H., "Mediterranean Mysteries," 69
Empire(s), imperial(ism), post-imperial(ism), 64-65, 69, 78, 93, 167
Empiricism, 105, 154, 191, 211, 234
Encyclopédie Française, 41, 48
Energy and power devices, 33, 70-75, 141-42, 144, 177
England, 29, 74, 176-78
Enlightenment, 128, 170, 191
Episteme, ordering code, 205-8; see also Function(s)
Epochs, critical, of contrasts, of melody, organic, and psychic, 34, 47, 65; see also Crisis
Escarpit, Robert, 49; "Le Littéraire et le social," 189; Sociologie de la littérature, 45
Establishment, 14, 16, 41, 46, 218
"Etat de recherches sur l'histoire économique quantitative de la Belgique," 123
Ethnoculture, ethnohistory, ethnosociology, 51, 55, 59, 64-65, 178
Europe, 30, 34, 60, 70-75, 86-87, 96, 99, 135-36, 144, 152, 155, 167, 175-77, 199, 211, 220, 227; extra-European orientations, 56, 60
Europocentrism, Europophobia, 134, 149, 151-52, 155, 201
Evantail de l'histoire vivante: Hommage à Lucien Febvre, 140, 159

Event(s), eventism, eventfulness, 19-20, 27, 30, 43, 46, 65-66, 93, 95, 98-99, 103-4, 109, 114, 121, 127-28, 130, 171, 194, 201, 204, 209-11, 214-31, 235-36; audiography of the event, 230-31; critical event, 228-29; current event, 55-56, 148, 214-16; événement moteur, "pure and full" event, 225; event types, 224; gros événement, paradigmatic event, 53, 59, 210, 225; matrix-event, 228; science of events, 224; see also Action, Contemporary history, History, and Noise factor
Events of May-June 1968, student rebellion, 16, 41, 59, 220, 237
Exchange, 62, 67-68, 86, 97, 99, 161, 185, 187, 189, 191; see also Commerce, Communication, and Donation
Expectations, rising, 167

Fact(s), historical and social, 36, 84, 103-4, 106, 118, 124, 190, 194, 196-97, 201, 204, 220; literary, 189; of repetition and of succession, 217; total social and whole mental, 36, 103-4, 106, 109, 119-20, 124-25, 154; "fact-fetishism," 214; see also Construct(s)
Family, household, kinship, 29, 46, 67, 88, 97, 119, 145, 162, 169-81, 234
Fashion, 90, 99, 133, 219
Faucher, Daniel, 63
Faye, Jean-Pierre, Langages totalitaires and Théorie du récit, 206
Febvre, Lucien, 11-15, 19, 41-44, 47, 50, 53, 58-59, 77, 103, 105-6, 112-14, 135, 164, 169-70, 181, 194, 201, 224-25, 232; "Avant-propos" to "Education et instruction," 48; "Avant-propos" to Morazé, Trois essais, 104; "Ce que peuvent nous apprendre les monographies familiales," 171; Combats pour l'histoire, 56-58, 79, 104; "De la création en histoire," 106; "De 1892 à 1933," 104; "L'Effort scientifique de la Renaissance," 156-57; "Folklore et folkloristes," 135; "Générations," 48; "L'Individualité," 106; "Lit-

Febvre, Lucien (*cont.*)
térature et vie sociale," 190;
Philippe II et la Franche-Comté,
64, 171; *Pour une histoire à part
entière*, 78, 115, 135, 157; *Le
Problème de l'incroyance*, 162-63;
"Le Progrès," 157; "Les Recherches collectives," 104; "La Sensibilité," 79, 160; "Souvenirs d'une
grande histoire," 57; "Une gigantesque fausse nouvelle," 78-79; "Un
Livre qui grandit: *La Méditerranée*," 115; "Vers une autre histoire," 58, 104; "Vingt ans après,"
43; "Vivre l'histoire," 56, 95-96,
123
Febvre, Lucien, in collaboration with
Lionel Bataillon, *La Terre*, trans.
as *A Geographical Introduction
to History*, 64, 139
Febvre, Lucien, and François
Crouzet, "Der internationale
Ursprung einer Kultur," 62
Ferguson, Adam, 30
Ferro, Marc, 48, 213; "The Aspira-
tions of Russian Society," 188-89;
"Le Film," 159; *La Grande Guerre*,
trans. as *The Great War*, 211-14;
"1917: History and Cinema," 90;
La Révolution de 1917, trans. as
*The Russian Revolution of Febru-
ary 1917*, 188; "Société du XXe
siècle," 159
Fête, 163-65; *see also* Play *and*
Theater
Feudalism, 91, 126-27, 136, 144, 147-
49, 186-87, 193
Fields: epistemic, 206-7; of force,
60, 78, 80, 118, 140, 198, 205-6, 210,
214, 221-22, 231; semantic, 192
Fischer, David Hackett, *Historians'
Fallacies*, 38, 54
Fishlow, Albert, and Robert W.
Fogel, "Quantitative History," 105
Flandrin, Jean-Louis, 49, 192; "En-
fance et société," 172; "Sentiments
et civilisation," 193
Fleury, Michel, and Louis Henry,
*Des registres paroissiaux à l'his-
toire de la population*, 172;
Nouveau manuel, 172; "Pour con-

naître la population de la France,"
172
Folklore, 88, 135, 159, 162-63, 184,
212
Food-gathering and hunting, 179
Forests, firewood, and timber, 70-
72, 86-87
Formalism, 184-85; *see also* Func-
tion(s)
Fortuna, 223, 227
Foucault, Michel, 34-35, 113, 207, 210,
228, 238; *L'Archéologie du savoir*,
trans. as *The Archaeology of
Knowledge*, 206-9; *Les Mots et les
choses*, trans. as *The Order of
Things*, 35, 206, 208; *L'Ordre du
discours*, trans. as "Orders of Dis-
course," 209-11, 232
Fox, Edward Whiting, 99; *History
in Geographic Perspective*, trans.
as *L'Autre France*, 87
Francastel, Pierre, "L'Esthétique des
Lumières," 165; "Histoire de la
civilisation," 90
France, 13, 29, 40, 50-52, 74, 136,
141, 149, 165, 169, 174, 176, 178,
199, 212, 216, 228
François, Michel, "Organisation col-
lective," 101
Freedom, 32-33, 62, 193
Freud, 55, 154-55
Freudenberger, Herman, and G.
Mensch, "Innovation and Regional
Industrialization," 229
Freund, Julien, "Quelques aperçus
sur la formation de l'histoire de
Jean Bodin," 29
Friedmann, Georges, 14, 44; *La
Crise du progrès*, 157
Friedmann, Georges, with the aid
of F.-I. Isambert, "Sciences so-
ciales," 186
Frontiers, boundaries, *envelopes*, 62,
108, 147
Fruit, René, *La Croissance écono-
mique*, 157
Function(s), functionalism, 30, 32,
35, 38, 58, 79, 90, 92-94, 97, 104,
109-11, 117, 119, 126, 130-32, 135,
143, 145, 155-56, 159, 171, 176, 179,

Function(s) (*cont.*)
181-91, 193-96, 199-200, 203-11, 220, 228, 230-31, 235-37
Furet, François, 49, 124, 128-29, 191; "Le Catéchisme révolutionnaire," 128-29; "Histoire et ethnologie," trans. as "History and Primitive Man," 182; "L'Histoire quantitative," 202; "Les Intellectuels français," 155-56; ed., *Livre et société*, 190, 192; "Pour une définition des classes inférieures," 129; "Quantitative History," 202; "Sur quelques problèmes posés par le développement de l'histoire quantitative," 156, 195, 201
Future, 35-36, 132, 158, 223, 238; *see also Prospective* demography, geography, history

Gaignebet, Claude, "Le Combat de Carnaval et de Carême," 164
Game theory, 224; *see also* Action
Gaudemar, Paul, "Evénement," 222-23
Gautier, Etienne, and Louis Henry, *La Population de Crulai*, 172
Geffroy, Annie, Pierre Lafon, and Maurice Tournier, "Lexicometrical Analysis," 192
Geistesgeschichte and *Geisteswissenschaften*, 33-35
Generation(s), 47, 122-24, 181, 212, 237-38; *Annales*, 14, 46-47, 51, 57, 59-61, 64, 123, 161, 218, 234, 238; of '98, 64
Genovese, Eugene D., "On Antonio Gramsci," 138
Genres de vie, 86, 134, 167, 170
Geography, 11-12, 15, 44, 69, 77-78, 86-87, 107-10, 115, 136, 139-43, 149, 162-63, 165, 167, 218, 223, 230; "volontaire" or "prospective," 141
Geohistory, 47, 77, 79, 85, 125, 134, 140, 142-43, 199
Gershoy, Leo, "Some Problems," 104
Gilbert, Allan H., *Machiavelli's Prince*, 227
Gindin, Claude, "La Pensée historique de Jean Meuvret," 172
Glass, D. V., and D. E. C. Eversley,

eds., *Population in History*, 172-73, 177
Glénisson, Jean, "L'Historiographie française," 42, 93, 232
Goblot, Jean-Jacques, "L'Histoire des 'civilisations,'" 150
Godelier, Maurice, 146; "Modes de production," 179; "La Notion de 'mode de production asiatique,'" 147
Goldmann, Lucien, "Genèse et structure," 131; "La Pensée des 'Lumières,'" 75; "Pour une approche marxiste," 131; *Sciences humaines*, trans. as *The Human Sciences*, 76, 131; "Le Structuralisme génétique," 131; Le Sujet de la création culturelle," 131
Goubert, Pierre, 48, 167, 172, 233-34; *Beauvais et le Beauvaisis*, 173; *Cent mille provinciaux*, 173; "En Beauvaisis," 173; "Historical Demography," 173; "In memoriam: Jean Meuvret," 199; "Local History," 234; "Recent Theories," 173; "Une richesse historique en cours d'exploitation," 173
Goy, Joseph, 42; "A propos du discours historique 'militant,'" 153
Graham, Hugh Davis, and Ted Robert Gurr, eds., *Violence in America*, 167
Gramsci, Antonio, 137-38, 150
Granger, Gilles, "Evénement et structure," 132, 222; *Méthodologie économique*, 61
Grappin, Charles, "La Logique de l'histoire," 155
Great Fear, 78-79
Great man, hero, 130-31, 166
Greece, 31, 63, 87-88, 162
Gritti, Jules, "Le Centre d'Etudes des Communications de Masse," 228
Groh, Dieter, "Strukturgeschichte," trans. as "L'Histoire structurale," 211
Guenée, Bernard, "Espace et Etat," 93; "Histoire, annales, chroniques," 28; "L'Histoire de l'Etat en France," 93; "Y a-t-il un Etat des XIVe et XVe siècles?" 93

Guicciardini, Francesco, 28, 31, 36; *The History of Italy*, 236
Guitton, Henri, 106; "Théorie des cycles," 108
Guizot, François, 137; *Histoire de la civilisation*, 130-31, 136
Gurevich, Aron Iakovlevich, *Problemy genezisa feodalizma*, 186-87; "Représentations et attitudes à l'egard de la propriété," 187
Gurvitch, Georges, 120-21, 132; "Les Sociétés globales," 121; "La Sociologie du jeune Marx," 119; ed., *Traité de sociologie*, 110, 121; *La Vocation actuelle de la sociologie*, 119, 121

Hajnal, John, "European Marriage Patterns," 177
Hale, John Rigby, *Renaissance Venice*, 224
Hall, Edward T., *The Silent Language*, 98-99
Halperin Donghi, Tulio, "Histoire et longue durée," 132
Hauser, Henri, 14, 198
Heers, Jacques, *Le Clan familial*, 174
Helleiner, Karl, "The Population of Europe," 81-82
Hémardinquer, Jean-Jacques, 21, 85, 143; ed., *Pour une histoire de l'alimentation*, 99
Henry, Louis, 171; *Anciennes familles genevoises*, 172; "Une richesse démographique en friche," 172-73
Heresy, 12, 16, 51, 60, 220
Hermes, 21, 62-64, 66-67, 77, 80, 87, 90-91, 100, 109, 133, 141, 188, 231
Herodotus, *The Histories*, 27
Herr, Richard, and Harold T. Parker, eds., *Ideas in History*, 45, 232
Hestia, 21, 63, 67, 77, 87, 89-90, 100, 109, 154, 160, 231
Hexter, Jack, "Fernand Braudel," 44, 70, 110, 116, 118, 168
Hicks, John, *A Theory of Economic History*, 145-46
Hierarchy, 34, 59, 98, 113, 120, 136, 148, 156, 163, 168, 212
Higham, John, "Beyond Consensus" and "The Cult of the 'American Consensus,'" 143

L'Histoire sociale, 111-12, 123, 226
Historical School, 32-33, 45
Historiography, German, 11, 20, 33, 38, 40-41, 45, 47, 50, 211
History: chronicle, 27-28; comprehensive, general, 201-2, 205, 207, 217-18; conjectural, natural, "raisonnée," theoretical, 30-33; counterfactual, 104-5; critical-explanatory, 27-28; cultural, 225, 230; demasculinization of, 158-59; developmental, evolutionary, 11, 29, 32, 38, 40; economic, 167-68, 194, 200, 218, 230, 235-36; "eventmental," idiographic, narrative, 11, 20, 27-28, 32, 91, 93-94, 127, 204, 210-11, 218, 221-22, 227, 229; exemplar, 25-28, 30, 35, 38, 236; functional-structural, 25, 29, 38-39, 46, 93, 204; historyless, 158, 163; immobile, 47, 60, 77, 95-96, 109; inquiry, 83-85, 118, 236-38; institutional, scientific, 217-18, 234; local, 89-90, 234; new economic, 104-6; nonhistory, transhistory, 35, 155-56, 204, 209; oral, 60, 103, 155, 159, 163, 191; pluridimensional, 232; political, 11, 19, 30, 46, 92-95, 103, 168, 229-30; *prospective*, 101; psychosocial, 142, 191; quantitative, 48, 55, 61, 70-76, 89, 97-101, 123-24, 158, 166, 170, 180, 183, 190-91, 194-97, 201, 212, 233; retrogressive method, 162, 166; rural, 13; serial, "ponctuelle," 20, 38, 66, 80, 183, 194-205, 210-11, 220, 231; social, 46, 58, 95-97, 122, 125, 143, 163, 167-70, 180-82, 191, 200, 203, 218, 223, 225, 230; social and economic, 43-44, 83-84, 90, 93, 96-97, 111, 168, 182, 225; total, "globale," 97, 103, 108-12, 115-18, 120-22, 124, 126-27, 129, 132-33, 168-69, 181-82, 183, 196, 201-5, 207, 210-11, 218-19, 229-31, 237; universal, 103, 151, 197; use of term, 192
Hobsbawm, Eric J., *The Age of Revolution*, 74; "From Social History to the History of Society," 188-89; "Karl Marx's Contribution," 111, 156

Holborn, Hajo, "Greek and Modern Conceptions of History," 32
Hollinger, David A., "T. S. Kuhn's Theory," 236
Homans, George Caspar, *Social Behavior*, 126
Hook, Sidney, ed., *Philosophy and History*, 27, 104
Hughes, H. Stuart, *The Obstructed Path*, 42
Humanism, 59, 110, 113, 115
Hume, David, 30
Huppert, George, 21; *The Idea of Perfect History*, trans. as *L'Idée de l'histoire parfaite*, 227; "Naissance de l'histoire," 227

Ideal types, 104, 119, 121, 125, 144, 149, 151, 221
Ideas, *mentalités*, mind sets, 109-10, 119-20, 136, 140, 154, 157, 159, 170, 181-82, 190-91, 193-94, 198, 203, 219, 225, 228
Ideology, 55, 80, 113, 132-33, 156, 181, 202
Iggers, Georg G., "The Dissolution of German Historism," 45; *The German Conception of History*, 34, 45; *New Directions in European Historiography*, 46
Individual(ism), 34, 181, 217-18; *see also* Particularism
Innovation, 40, 56, 135, 157, 190, 217, 225, 228, 232, 237
Intrigue, 220-22
Islam, 86
Israel, 53
Italy, 176-78, 223

Jeannin, Pierre, "Une histoire planétaire," 69, 158
Jews, 51-56, 58, 176
Journalism, 213-16
Juillard, Etienne, "La Géographie volontaire," 141

Kelley, Donald, R., "The Development and Context of Bodin's Method," 29; *Foundations of Modern Historical Scholarship*, 29
Keylor, William R., "A New Academic Discipline," 42

Kinser, Samuel, "Braudel and Vilar," 42; "Structural History," 42
Klineberg, Otto, "Toward a Sociology of the Jews," 54
Knight, Melvin M., "The Geohistory of Fernand Braudel," 67
Knowledge, 206-8, 223
Koenigsberger, H. G., "Fernand Braudel," 53-54, 168
Košuta, Leo, "Il Mondo Vero," 164
Kriegel, Annie, Marc Ferro, and Alain Besançon, "L'Expérience de 'La Grande Guerre,' " 90
Krleža, Miroslav, 198
Kuhn, Thomas S., 10; "Reflections on My Critics," 38; *The Structure of Scientific Revolutions*, with "Postscript," 236
Kula, Witold, "Histoire et économie," 198; "On the Typology of Economic Systems," 126; "La Seigneurie et la famille paysanne," 179; *Théorie économique du système féodal*, 123, 126-27, 179
Kulturgeschichte, 33, 35
Kuznets, Simon, 76, 195; "Statistical Trends," 197

Labasse, Jean, "L'Organisation de l'espace," 141
Labrousse, C.-E. (Ernest), 13, 22, 112-13, 123-24, 127-28, 132, 169, 203, 226, 233-34; *La Crise de l'économie française*, 128; *Esquisse du mouvement des prix*, 128, 195; "Introduction" to *L'Histoire sociale*, 111; "1848-1830-1789," 128; "Prix et structure régionale," 199; "Voies nouvelles," 125
Lacombe, Paul, 226; *De l'histoire considérée comme science*, 217-18; *La Famille*, 171; *La Psychologie*, 154
Lacroix, J., ed., *Recherches et dialogues*, 132, 223
Lajusan, Alfred, "La Carte des opinions françaises," 213
Lakatos, Imre, and Alan Musgrave, eds., *Criticism*, 38
Lamprecht, Karl, *What Is History?* 33-34
Lane, Frederic C., and J. C. Rie-

Lane, Frederic C. (*cont.*)
mersma, eds., *Enterprise and Secular Change*, 125
Lane, Michael, ed., *Introduction to Structuralism*, 208
Language, linguistics, 60, 90, 98, 154, 158-63, 185, 189, 191-92, 206-7; *see also* Discourse
"The Language-Field of Nazism," 206
Languedoc, 80, 166-69
Laqueur, Walter, and George L. Mosse, eds., *The New History*, 92
Laslett, Peter, 180; ed., *Household and Family*, 177; "Our Mediterranean," 69; *The World We Have Lost*, 177
Lavoisier, Antoine-Laurent de, 72
Le Bon, Sylvie, "Un positiviste désespéré," 208
Lebrun, François, *Les Hommes et la mort en Anjou*, 160-61
Lecourt, Dominique, *Pour une critique de l'épistémologie*, 208; "Sur l'archéologie et le savoir," 209
Lefebvre, Georges, 22, 169; *La Grande Peur*, trans. as *The Great Fear*, 78-80; "Quelques réflexions sur l'histoire des civilisations," 137
Lefebvre, Henri, *La Fin de l'histoire*, 156; "Réflexions sur le structuralisme," 195
Lefort, Claude, "Histoire et sociologie," 114
Léger, Fernand, *Fonctions de la peinture*, trans. as *Functions of Painting*, 65
Le Goff, Jacques, 51, 93, 167; *La Civilisation de l'Occident médiéval*, 51; "Histoire et ethnologie," trans. as "The Historian and the Common Man," 95, 158; "Is Politics Still the Backbone of History?" 94; "Les Mentalités," 181
Le Goff, Jacques, and Pierre Nora, eds., *Faire de l'histoire*, 47, 133, 165, 181, 202, 213, 215
Le Goff, Jacques, and Ruggiero Romano, "Paysages et peuplement rural," 86

Lehmann, William Christian, *Adam Ferguson*, 30
Lemarchand, Guy, "Le Féodalisme," 193-94
Léon, Pierre, 97, 234; "Histoire économique et histoire sociale," 96
Leontief, Wassily W., "The Problem of Quantity and Quality," 195; "Theoretical Assumptions," 105
Lerner, Daniel, ed., *Quantity and Quality*, 195
Le Roy Ladurie, Emmanuel, 51, 84, 122, 167, 176, 233; "Apologie pour les damnés de la thèse," 117; "La Civilisation rurale" and "Rurale (Civilisation)," 169, 175; "Les Comptes fantastiques de Gregory King," trans. as "The Fantastical Accounts of Gregory King," 196; "Du Quantitatif en histoire," 173, 203; "Evénement et longue durée," 228; *Histoire du climat*, trans. as *Times of Feast, Times of Famine*, 81, 83-84; "Histoire économique et histoire sociale," 169; "Histoire et climat," 81; "L'Histoire immobile," 96; *Les Paysans de Languedoc*, trans. as *The Peasants of Languedoc*, 80, 84, 140, 168; "Pour une histoire de l'environnement," 81; "Révoltes et contestations rurales," 166-67; "La Révolution quantitative," 200; "Systèmes de la coutume," 175; *Le Territoire de l'historien*, 81, 84, 117, 169, 173, 175, 196, 200; "Un concept: L'Unification microbienne du monde," 82; "Voies nouvelles," 68
Leuilliot, Paul, "Histoire locale," 239; "Lucien Febvre," 50; "Préface: Défense et illustration de l'histoire locale," in Thuillier, *Aspects de l'économie nivernaise*, 89-90
Lévêque, Pierre, and Pierre Vidal-Naquet, *Clisthène l'Athénien*, 88
Lévi-Strauss, Claude, 55, 119-30, 25-26, 130, 155, 189, 198; "L'Anthropologie sociale devant l'histoire," 158, 205; *Anthropologie structurale*, 97, 99; *Anthropologie structurale deux*, 37, 120, 159, 185, 204; "Le Champ de l'anthropologie," 37; "Les Dis-

Lévi-Strauss, Claude (*cont.*) continuités culturelles," 159; "Introduction à l'oeuvre de Marcel Mauss," 154, 204; *La Pensée sauvage*, 205; "La Structure et la forme," 184-85

Lévy-Bruhl, Henri, "Une notion confuse," 103

Lévy-Bruhl, Lucien, 120

Lévy-Leboyer, Maurice, "L'Héritage de Simiand," 200; "La 'New Economic History,'" 105

Lhomme, Jean, 106; "Essai de comparaison," 108; "Matériaux pour une théorie de la structure," 108

Literacy, 128, 150, 167, 178, 190

Littleton, S. Scott, *The New Comparative Mythology*, 94

Logic, 33-34, 55, 119, 139-40, 154-55, 162, 204-5; *see also* Rational(ism)

Lombard, Maurice, "La Chasse," 88; *Espaces*, 87; *L'Islam*, 87; "Un problème cartographié," 87

Longchambon, Henri, "Les Sciences sociales en France," 138-39

Lorwin, Val R., and Jacob M. Price, eds., *The Dimensions of the Past*, 78, 166, 195

Lutfalla, Michel, "Modernité du *Tableau économique*," 76

McCormick, Richard L., "Ethno-Cultural Interpretations," 51

Macdonald, Dwight, *Against the American Grain*, 214

Macek, Josef, "La *Fortuna* chez Machiavel," 223; "Pour une sémantique historique," 223

Machiavelli, Niccolò, 28, 223, 227

Machine, 207

McKinney, John C., and Edward A. Tiryakian, eds., *Theoretical Sociology*, 36

Macroeconomy, microeconomy, 76, 126

Magic, miracle, 170, 187

Maison des Sciences de l'Homme, 15, 44, 101, 138

Mandelbaum, Maurice, "A Note on History," 235

Mandrou, Robert, 48, 163; "Les *Annales* en Pologne," 45; "Avant-propos" to Porchnev, *Les Soulèvements populaires*, 136; "Cultures ou niveaux culturels," 170; *De la culture populaire*, 163; "Histoire et cinéma," 91; interviewed by Antoine Casanova and François Hincker, "Histoire sociale," 112; *Introduction à la France moderne*, 160; "Littérature de colportage," 170; "Pour une histoire de la sensibilité," 160

Mann, Hans-Dieter, *Lucien Febvre*, 42, 48, 65, 106

Manuel, Frank E., "The Use and Abuse of Psychology in History," 42

Manufactures, 70, 76, 86

Marchal, André, 106; "De la dynamique des structures," 108; "Prise de conscience," 107

Marczewski, Jean, "Buts et méthodes," 195; *Introduction à l'histoire quantitative*, 195, 197; "Quantitative History," 76; "Les Variables historiques," 197

Marías, Julián, *Generations*, 47, 238

Marichal, Robert, "La Critique des textes," 26, 229

Market(s), 167, 199, 223; national, 135-36; world, 88

Marranos, 54

Marriage patterns, 174-80; *see also* Family

Marrou, Henri-Irénée, 49; *De la connaissance historique*, 34, 92, 103, 219; "Histoire de la civilisation," 219

Martini, Giuseppe, "Una 'geohistoria' del Mediterraneo," 114

Marx, Karl, 12, 75, 111, 118-19, 134, 136, 149, 152; *Pre-capitalist Economic Formations*, 137

Marxism, Marxist method, 38-39, 45, 67-68, 86, 111-13, 121, 126-28, 130-32, 134-35, 137-38, 143-45, 147-53, 166, 170, 186, 191, 198, 208-9, 226, 229, 232, 237

"Le Marxisme et l'histoire de France," 67

Mass phenomena, 45, 108, 158-59, 189, 211-12, 214-17, 227-28, 231

Masterman, Margaret, "The Nature of a Paradigm," 38, 59
Material life, 85, 90, 124, 158, 167-68, 181-82, 198, 209
Mauro, Frédéric, 49; *Le XVIe siècle européen*, 93, 96; "Théorie économique," 125-26
Mauss, Marcel, 121, 185, 188; "Civilisation," 135; "Essai sur le don," trans. as *The Gift*, 119; *Sociologie et anthropologie*, 119, 154
Mazauric, Claude, 49; "Note sur l'emploi de 'régime féodal,'" 193; *Sur la Révolution française*, 127, 193
Media, 142, 207, 213-16
Mediterranean, 50, 52, 69-70, 74, 88, 136, 140, 147, 150, 176, 199
Meinecke, Friedrich, *Historism*, 33
Mélanges en l'honneur de Fernand Braudel, 95-96, 169, 203, 215, 223
Mendel, Gérard, *La Révolte contre le père*, 208, 237
Message systems, 94-99, 161, 235; see also Communication
Metz, Christian, "Réflexions sur la 'Sémiologie graphique,'" 91
Meuvret, Jean, "Les Crises de subsistances," 172; "Demographic Crisis in France," 172; *Etudes d'histoire économique*, 172, 199; "La Géographie des prix," 199; ed., *Production et productivité agricoles*, 69
Meyerhoff, Hans, "History and Philosophy," in *The Philosophy of History*, 33-34
Meyerson, Ignace, 63, 121, 186; "Discontinuités," 66; *Les Fonctions psychologiques*, 66, 120, 122, 185, 235
Mezzogiorno, 150
Michelet, Jules, 165-66, 171; *The People*, 171, 226
Migrations, animal, plant, and viral, 80, 82, 85
Millenarianism, 146, 155, 163, 167, 181
Miller, David B., review of Gurevich, *Problemy genezisa feodalizma*, 187
Miller, Dean A., "Royauté et ambiguïté sexuelle," 94

Mobility, mobilization, movement, 63, 107, 131, 135-36, 140, 211-14, 223, 237; immobility, 135, 140, 190, 204, 213-14; see also Stability
Model, 61, 69, 105, 113, 117, 125-26, 129, 134, 136, 151-52, 159, 206-7, 209, 219, 221-24, 235-36; *Annales*, 9, 11, 13-14, 110-11, 168; total, 75
Modern(s), modernists, modernity, modernization, 30, 55, 64-65, 128, 137, 147, 150, 157, 166-67, 177, 179, 201, 206-7, 237
Moles, Abraham A., "Objet et communication," 222; "Philosophie et esthétique," 216; "Sur l'aspect théorique du décompte de populations mal définies," 54; "Sur le contenu d'une sociologie juive," 54
Money, 67-68, 104, 107, 161, 207
Monod, Gustave, Director General of Secondary Education, 15
Montesquieu, Charles-Louis de Secondat, Baron de, 113, 115
Morazé, Charles, 14-15, 43-44, 48; "The Application of the Social Sciences to History," 154; "Essai sur la méthode de François Simiand," 200; "L'Histoire et l'unité des sciences de l'homme," 154; *La Logique de l'histoire*, 155, 157; *Trois essais*, 104, 155
Morin, Edgar, *Le Cinéma*, 91; "Le Cinéma," 159; "Culture adolescente," 237; "Le Retour de l'événement," 228
Mornet, Daniel, *Histoire de la littérature classique*, 190
Mousnier, Roland, 174-75; *L'Assassinat de Henri IV*, trans. as *The Assassination of Henry IV*, 225; "Notes sur la thèse principale," 116-17; "Préface" to Couturier, *Recherches*, 174; "Problèmes de méthode," 124
Mousnier, Roland, and Ernest (C.-E.) Labrousse, with the collaboration of Marc Bouloiseau, *Le XVIIIe siècle*, 137
Mousnier, Roland, and Pillorget, René, "Contemporary History," 226

Murphey, Murray G., *Our Knowledge of the Historical Past*, 36
Mutation, 38, 106-7, 141, 161, 207, 227
Myth, 29-30, 35, 60, 79, 120, 135, 162, 189, 219, 224, 235

Nadel, George H., 45-46, "Philosophy of History," 26, 31; ed., *Studies in the Philosophy of History*, 144
Nation, national autonomy, nationalism, nationality, nation state, 29, 32-33, 135, 171
Nature, 33, 35, 85, 107, 139-40, 156; human, 31
Navies, 70, 74
Nef, John U., *Western Civilization*, 74
Neomania, 16, 56, 133, 219, 232, 235
Noise factor, 210, 228, 231
Nora, Pierre, 84; "L'Evénement monstre," 215; "Pour une histoire contemporaine," 215-16; "Le Retour de l'événement," 215

Ortega y Gasset, José, 47
Ozouf, Jacques, "Mesure et démesure," 213; "L'Opinion publique," 213
Ozouf, Mona, "Le Cortège et la ville," 165; "La Fête sous la Révolution française," 165; "Space and Time," 165

Pagliaro, Harold E., ed., *Studies in Eighteenth-Century Culture*, 30
Panic, 78-80
Papaioannou, Kostas, "The Consecration of History," 30-31; "Nature and History," 27, 30-31
Paradigm, 9, 13, 26, 28-29, 32, 38, 100, 236, 238; *Annales*, 9, 11, 17, 20, 25, 37-40, 42, 56, 58-59, 236-38
Parain, Charles, "Une falsification: L'Archéo-civilisation," 135; "Un nouveau mythe," 135
Paris, 50, 74, 79, 90, 124, 165-66, 219
Parsons, Talcott, "Theory," 191
Particularism, 29, 32, 38, 217-18, 236; *see also* Individual(ism)
Pasquier, Estienne, 227

Past, 35-36, 60, 132, 135, 139, 156, 162, 190, 206, 215-16, 220, 223
Path analysis, 78-80
Peasants, 68, 89, 99, 135, 141, 146, 166-68, 179, 228
Péguy, Charles, "A nos amis," 212; *Le Choix de Péguy*, 100; "Clio," English trans. in *Temporal and Eternal*, 100, 229; *Oeuvres en prose*, 100, 212, 229
Pelletier, Antoine, "La Notion de civilisation," 148-49
Pelletier, Antoine, and Jean-Jacques Goblot, *Matérialisme historique*, 149
Pelorson, Jean-Marc, "Michel Foucault et l'Espagne," 209
Peltant, Sarah, "Conversation avec Braudel," 44, 50
People, 65, 76-77, 115, 164, 166, 171, 182, 198, 206, 208, 226, 231
Perroux, François, 76, 88, 106, 195; *Les Comptes de la nation*, 107-8; *Cours d'économie politique*, 107; "The Gift," 188; "Théorie générale du progrès économique," 157
Peyrefitte, Alain, *Rue d'Ulm*, 58
Piaget, Jean, *Le Structuralisme*, 132
Philosophy, 11, 16, 30-31, 113, 139, 163, 205, 209, 219
Physiocracy, 75-76
Pinkney, David H., "The Dilemma of the American Historian," 233
Pipes, Richard, ed., *Revolutionary Russia*, 188-89
Pirenne, Henri, 93
Plakans, Andrejs, "Peasant Farmsteads," 177
Play, 173, 187; *see also* Carnival *and* Fête
Pleshkova, S. L., "Ob uchebnom posobii 'Problemy genezisa feodalizma,' " 187
Plumb, J. H., "History as Geography, Economics, Folklore," 233
Poland, 45, 72, 179
Poliakov, Léon, "Capitalisme et marchands marranes," 54
Political science, politics, 31, 110, 113, 139, 162, 167-68, 170-71, 202, 226, 233, 237

Polybius, 27, 36
Porchnev, Boris, *Les Soulèvements populaires*, 136
Ports, 68, 79, 86
Positivism, 10, 219
Post, John D., 84; "The Economic Crisis of 1816-1817," 83; "Meteorological Historiography," 83; "A Study in Meteorological and Trade Cycle History," 83
"Pour ou contre une politicologie scientifique," 92-93
Poverty, 181, 188, 226
Power, 94-95, 99, 124, 128, 161, 170-71, 174, 179, 207, 234
Precapitalism, 146-47
Preindustrial world, 70-75, 96, 128
Present events, 35-36, 132, 158, 162, 215-16, 223; *see also* Contemporary history
Price(s), 88, 107, 127, 194, 198-200, 203, 210, 226
Primitive man, 155-56
Printing press, 128, 190
Problem-solving, 38, 48, 114, 116-18, 155-56, 201
Production, modes of, productivity, 67-68, 70, 76, 84-86, 89, 94, 109, 134, 137, 144-49, 153, 167, 178-79, 189, 195, 200, 203, 209, 216, 218, 232, 235
Professionalization in history and critical method, 31-35
Progrès neutre, 133
Progress, 30-33, 38, 135-36, 155-59, 201, 207, 226, 236; economic, 157
Property, 62, 95, 128, 145, 166-67, 174, 187, 193, 212
Propp, Vladimir I., *Morphologie du conte*, and English and Italian translations of the Russian: *Mythology of the Folktale* and *Morfologia della fiaba*, 184-85
Prosopography, 60
Prospective demography, geography, history, 149, 151, 158, 238
Prost, A., "Vocabulaire," 193
Protection, 178-79
Provence, 68, 88, 166, 175, 218-19
Psychology, psychoanalysis, 42, 44, 48, 63, 79, 97, 107, 109, 111, 118,

124, 154-55, 159-60, 162-63, 181, 185, 191, 204, 208-9, 215, 218
Public opinion, 95, 188-89, 191, 203, 206, 212-13, 216
Public works, 145, 148

Quesnay, François, 75-76

Rabelais, Rabelaisian, 12, 66, 164
Ranke, Leopold von, 32, 36
Rational(ism), rationalization, reason, 35, 60, 113, 115, 124, 131, 137, 143, 155, 224
Rebellion, 146, 166-67, 181, 220, 228, 237
Redlich, Fritz, "Potentialities and Pitfalls," 105
Relativism, 34-35, 104
Religion, 31, 51, 60, 80, 107, 110, 158, 176, 181, 187-88, 202, 207, 212, 226, 234
Rémond, René, "France: Work in Progress," 92; "L'Histoire, science du présent," 92
Renaissance, 206-7, 223-24
Renouvin, Pierre, 22, 93; "Histoire des faits politiques," 92; "Préface" to Ferro, *La Grande Guerre*, 214
Repetition, routine, 127, 135, 160, 165, 168, 217
Repgen, Konrad, and Stephan Skalweit, eds., *Spiegel der Geschichte*, 124
Reproduction, fertility, 67, 94, 145
Revault d'Allonnes, Olivier, "Michel Foucault," 208
Revolution, 76, 114, 127-28, 136, 201, 226, 232; French, 60, 72, 79, 123, 127-29, 165-66, 192-93, 220, 235; Russian, 188, 220
Revue de Synthèse, 11, 41, 113
Reynolds, Beatrice, "Shifting Currents in Historical Criticism," 28
Riasanovsky, Nicholas V., comment on Wittfogel, "Russia and the East," 145
Rich, E. E., and C. H. Wilson, eds., *The Cambridge Economic History*, 71, 82, 199
Richet, Denis, "Autour des origines

Richet, Denis (*cont.*)
idéologiques" and "Croissance et blocages," 128-29
Richet, Denis, and Albert Soboul, "Correspondance," in *Annales ESC,* 129
Rites of passage, 129, 165
Roche, Daniel, 49, 192; "Les Primitifs du Rousseauisme," 191
Roland-Lowenthal, Charlotte, "Sociologie juive," 54
Rosen, Lawrence, "Language, History, and the Logic of Inquiry," 205
Rotenstreich, Nathan, *Between Past and Present,* 34
Roubin, Lucienne A., "Espace masculin, espace féminin," 88
Rouge, Maurice-François, "L'Organisation de l'espace," 140
Roupnel, Gaston, 57
Rousseau, Jean-Jacques, 191
Routes and transport, 62, 64, 70, 77-80, 141, 145, 167-68
Rude, Fernand, ed., *Barnave,* 213
Rural sector, 68, 78, 86, 88, 145, 165-66, 168, 172

Sachs, Ignacy, "Du Moyen-âge à nos jours," 151; "Overall and Prospective History," 151
Saint-Simonians, 47, 135
Salmon, J. H. M., review of Braudel, *Ecrits sur l'histoire,* 114
Samaran, Charles, ed., *L'Histoire et ses méthodes,* 26, 92, 101, 173, 229
Schaff, Adam, *Histoire et vérité,* 129-30; "Why History Is Constantly Rewritten," 130
Science(s), cultural, 33-34, 189; historical, human, social, 11-12, 16, 19, 36, 40, 43-44, 50, 55, 59, 92, 103, 138, 142, 150-52, 154-55, 196, 207, 215, 221-23, 230; biological, natural, physical, 33-34, 60, 85-86, 109, 118, 139, 168, 204, 206-7, 218; socio-psychological, 33
Science et loi, Ve Semaine Internationale de Synthèse, 224
Sebag, Lucien, *Marxisme et structuralisme,* 120

Secret or hidden elements, 48, 57, 120, 146, 158, 160, 185-86, 205, 216, 231, 237
Secularization, 55-56; desacralization, 207, 212
Sédov, Léonid, "La Société angkorienne," 147
Segal, Lester A., "Nicolas Lenglet Du Fresnoy," 32
Semiotics, 60, 95, 204-5; *see also* Sign(s)
Sensitivity, 79, 160
Series, 106, 122, 183, 193-94, 196, 198, 201, 210-16, 220-22, 225, 228, 230; *see also* History
Sewell, William H., Jr., "Marc Bloch," 125
Siegel, Martin, "Henri Berr's Revue de Synthèse Historique," 42; "Toward a Prehistory of the *Annales,*" 42
Siegfried, André, *Itinéraires de contagions,* 80
Sign(s), signification, symbol, 34, 57, 60, 66, 90, 93, 95, 98, 103-4, 106, 118-20, 124, 132, 155, 160-61, 173, 183, 185, 191-94, 198, 203, 205, 207, 216, 219, 225, 228, 230-31, 237
Silberman, Ruth, "Comment, paraît-il, on écrit l'histoire," 220
Simiand, François, 67-68, 200; "Méthode historique," 196
Sixième Section, 9, 14-16, 20, 22, 41-43, 48-50, 52, 56-58, 101, 116, 139, 151, 154-55, 190, 193, 227; *Programme d'enseignement,* 57
Slavery, 86, 144-45, 147, 174
Slicher van Bath, B. H., 81
Smith, Jay Harvey, "Village Revolution," 90
Smith, Robert J., "L'Atmosphère politique," 58
Smith, Pierre, and Dan Sperber, "Mythologiques de Georges Dumézil," 94
Soboul, Albert, 49, 123, 129; "Avant-propos" to Mazauric, *Sur la Révolution française,* 127, 129; *La Civilisation et la Révolution française,* 112, 127, 166, 233; "Description et mesure," 112; "Le Héros

Soboul, Albert (*cont.*)
et l'histoire," 130; "L'Historio-graphie classique de la Révolution française," 129; "Survivances 'féo-dales,' " 194
The Social Sciences, Problems and Orientations, 126
Social, society, societies, 30-32, 35-37, 66-67, 69, 76, 80, 82, 86-88, 90-91, 95-97, 108, 110-11, 113, 115, 118-21, 126, 128, 130-32, 134, 136-42, 144-49, 152, 156-57, 159, 162-63, 166-67, 169-70, 173-74, 176, 178, 181-83, 186-88, 190, 193, 197-98, 205, 209, 211, 213-15, 218, 227, 236-37; cold societies, 159; whole societies, 98, 103, 107, 112-13, 118, 120-26, 169-70, 183, 185, 194, 202-3, 208, 227, 234-37
Sociology, 11-12, 44, 51, 54, 58, 60, 109, 121, 142-43, 163, 170, 189, 191, 202, 214-15, 218, 221, 226
Soman, Alfred, "Good Mousnier," 226
Sombart, Werner, 54
Sopher, David E., "Place and Loca-tion," 142
Sorbonne, 14-16, 22, 169, 175
Soriano, Marc, 57; *Les Contes de Perrault,* 163; "Quelques travaux récents," 164
Soriano, Marc, Jacques Le Goff, Emmanuel Le Roy Ladurie, and André Burguière, "Débats et com-bats: Les Contes de Perrault," 163
Space, 36, 63, 66, 77, 87-88, 91, 94, 98-99, 103, 105-7, 109, 115, 118, 122, 126, 135, 140-42, 154, 157, 165, 175, 178-79, 197-98, 214, 217, 219-21, 223, 225, 230, 236; feminine and mas-culine, 63, 88; *see also* Territoriality
Spain, 64, 78, 156, 164, 177, 180
Spitzer, Allan B., "The Historical Problem of Generations," 48
Spuler, Bertold, comment on Witt-fogel, "Russia and the East," 145
Stability, 110, 129, 133, 149, 186, 211, 220, 230; *see also* Mobility
Standardization, 214-16, 231
Starn, Randolph, "Historians and 'Crisis,' " 47

State(s), 29, 46, 77-79, 91, 93, 113, 140, 171, 196, 212, 223, 234; *see also* Nation *and* Political science
Stern, Alfred, "The Irreversibility of History," 27, 33
Stern, Fritz, ed., *The Varieties of History,* 91
Stoianovich, Traian, 9-11, 13-14, 16-17; "The Balkan *Domestic* Family," 180; *A Study in Balkan Civiliza-tion,* 117; "Theoretical Implica-tions," 75, 82; "With and Without the Accidents," 140
Strasbourg, 10, 12, 50
Structuralism, 131-32, 183, 219, 226
Structuralisme et marxisme, 111, 132, 208
Structure(s), 30-32, 46, 48, 61, 67, 83, 91, 93, 95-99, 106-9, 112, 114-15, 117, 119-22, 127-33, 140, 145-46, 149, 152, 154, 163, 168, 181, 189, 203-5, 208-9, 212, 217-18, 222-23, 225-30, 232, 235; economic, 106-8, 112; mental, 111-12, 130; social, 16-17, 111-12, 121, 124, 167, 174, 176
Strukturgeschichte, 45-46
System, system of systems, 106-7, 113, 119, 130, 132, 142-43, 152, 184, 199, 202, 204-5, 208, 228, 236

Taboo, exclusion, interdiction, 120, 163-64, 206, 209, 232, 235
Tannenbaum, Edward R., "French Scholarship," 125
Teams, research, 13, 49, 85, 100, 191
Technique(s), 158, 162, 167, 186
Technology, 113, 140-42, 177-79, 186, 200, 206, 213-16, 226
Tenenti, Alberto, "Ars moriendi," 160; "The Sense of Space and Time," 224; *Il Senso della Morte e l'Amore della Vita,* 160; "Temps et 'ventura,' " 224; *La Vie et la mort,* 160
Tenèze, Marie-Louise, "Introduction à l'étude de la littérature orale," 163
Tenth International Congress of His-tory (Rome), *Relazioni,* 125
Territoriality, linearity, 52-53, 55, 76, 98-99, 148

Theater, drama, 90, 115-16, 118, 127, 165, 200, 218; spectacle, 163-64; theater of the absurd, 156
Thematic analysis, 188
Things, 206-7, 231
Thomas, Hilah F., "Innovation and Continuity in the *Annales*," 42; "Theory and Practice," 42
Thompson, E. P., " 'Rough Music,' " 164
Thorner, Daniel, "Marx on India," 137; "Peasant Economy," 151
Thucydides, 36, 237; *The Peloponnesian Wars*, 26
Thünen, Johann Heinrich von, 88, 178
Thuillier, Guy, *Aspects de l'économie nivernaise*, 90; *Economie et société nivernaise*, 239
Tilly, Charles, 79-80; "Quantification," 78, 166
Tilly, Louise A., "Materials of the Quantitative History of France," 195
Time, 27, 36, 61, 65-66, 77, 83-84, 91, 93-94, 97-99, 103, 105, 107-13, 115, 118, 122, 124, 126-28, 130, 135, 154-55, 163, 165, 175, 181, 197-98, 203, 214-15, 217-20, 223, 225, 229-31, 236; *see also* Duration
Times Literary Supplement, "Why Didn't the Masses Revolt?" 211
Tirat, Jean-Yves, "Problèmes de méthode," 124
Tiryakian, Edward A., "Structural Sociology," 36
Tocqueville, Alexis de, 213
Topics, *topoi*, 61, 221
Totality, globality, 100, 103-5, 113, 118-21, 125, 129, 131, 133, 137, 142, 151-52, 169-70, 182-83, 196, 211, 216, 219, 222, 230, 236
Tournier, Maurice, R. Arnault, L. Cavaciuti, Annie Geffroy, and F. Theuriot, "Le Vocabulaire de la Révolution," 192
Toutain, Jules, "Hermès," 62-63, 67
Toynbee, Arnold J., 52
Tradition, 127-28, 134, 145, 149, 160, 166, 212-14, 230, 238
Trénard, Louis, "Histoire et séman-
tique," 192; *Histoire sociale des idées*, 160
Trevor-Roper, Hugh R., "Capitalism and Material Life," 69
Tripartite society, ternary rules, trinitarianism, 94, 110, 167, 181, 207, 211
Truth, 27, 29, 236
Tyranny, tyrannicide, 193, 225

Unamuno, Miguel de, 64
Universals, generality, 29, 32, 38, 217-18
University, 14-16, 219
Usher, Abbott Payson, "Analysis and Evaluation," 73; "The Significance of Modern Empiricism," 154
Utterström, Gustaf, "Climatic Fluctuations," 81-82

Valensi, Lucette, "Calamités démographiques," 83-84
Valéry, Paul, *Regards sur le monde actuel*, 65
Van Lier, Henri, "Objet et esthétique," 222
Varagnac, André, 49, 134-35
Variables, 105, 107, 117, 120, 130, 140, 142, 183, 197, 203
Veblen, Thorstein, "The Intellectual Pre-eminence of Jews," 55-56
Venice, 176, 223
Venturi, Franco, "Oriental Despotism," 145
Vernant, Jean-Pierre, "Du Mythe à la raison," 162; "Espace et organisation politique," 88; *Mythe et pensée*, 63
Veyne, Paul, 218-20; *Comment on écrit l'histoire*, 143, 221-22; "A Contestation of Sociology," 220-21; "L'Histoire conceptualisante," 221; "Panem et circenses," 221
Viallaneix, Paul, *La Voie royale*, 166
Vico, Giambattista, 29; *The New Science*, 63
Vidal de la Blache, Paul, 11, 77, 86
Vidal-Naquet, Pierre, 143, 162; "Histoire et idéologie," 145
Viet, Jean, *Les Méthodes structuralistes*, 120, 152

Vilar, Pierre, 117, 226; "General History," typescript translation by David R. Ringrose of "Historia general," 111-12; "Histoire marxiste," 112, 131; "Histoire sociale," 131; "Pour une meilleure compréhension entre économistes et historiens," 196
Villages, 145, 165, 172; see also Community and Rural sector
Villages désertés et histoire économique, 86
Voinovitch, Louis, Histoire de Dalmatie, 77
Voltaire, 29, 36, 115
Vovelle, Gaby and Michel, Vision de la mort, 160-61
Vovelle, Michel, Mourir autrefois, 161; Piété baroque, 161
Vries, Jan de, "The Classics in Translation," 70

Wachtel, Nathan, 51; "La Vision des vaincus," trans. as "The Vision of the Vanquished," 162; La Vision des vaincus: Les Indiens du Pérou, 162
Wagner, Fritz, Moderne Geschichtsschreibung, 45
Wallerstein, Immanuel, The Modern World-System, 82
War, 69, 93, 148, 162, 167, 179, 200, 212-13
Waterwheel, windmill, 70, 72-74, 177
Weber, Max, 104, 143-44, 221, 237

Wheeler, Morton, "Present Tendencies in Biological Theory," 118
White, Hayden, "The Irrational," 29-30
White, Morton, "The Logic of Historical Narration," 27
Williams, Gwyn A., "The Concept of 'Egemonia,'" 138
Wittfogel, Karl August, Oriental Despotism, 144; "Russia and the East," 145
Woodward, C. Vann, "The Future of the Past," 236
Wolff, Philippe, "L'Etude des économies et des sociétés," 92, 97, 173
Woloch, Isser, "French Economic and Social History," 234-35
Women, 63, 71, 88, 97, 158-59, 174, 176-78, 180
Work, workers, 70-73, 126, 161-62, 164, 173, 178-79, 186, 191, 200, 226

Xenopol, A. D., "Les Faits de répétition," 217; "Natur und Geschichte," 217; "Zur Logik der Geschichte," 217

Youth, 159, 173, 179, 237
Yver, Jean, "Les Caractères originaux du groupe de coutumes de l'Ouest de la France," 175; "Les Deux groupes de coutumes du Nord," 175; Egalité entre héritiers, 175

Zionism, 151

French Historical Method

Designed by R. E. Rosenbaum.
Composed by York Composition Company, Inc.,
in 10 point Linotype Janson, 3 points leaded,
with display lines in ATF Garamond.
Printed letterpress from type by York Composition Company
on Warren's Number 66 text, 50 pound basis.
Bound by Vail-Ballou Press, Inc.
in Holliston book cloth
and stamped in All Purpose foil.

Library of Congress Cataloging in Publication Data
(For library cataloging purposes only)

Stoianovich, Traian.
    French historical method.

    Includes bibliographical references and index.
    1. France—Historiography.   I. Title.
DC36.9.S76   944'.007'2   75-36996
ISBN 0-8014-0861-X